Brothers & Sisters

It's All Relative

A Peanuts® Book

Charles M. Schulz

TOPPER BOOKS

AN IMPRINT OF PHAROS BOOKS • A SCRIPPS HOWARD COMPANY

NEW YORK

First published in 1989

PEANUTS Comic Strips: © 1967, 1971, 1972, 1973, 1974, 1975, 1976, 1977,
1978, 1979, 1980, 1981, 1982, 1983, 1984, 1985, 1986, 1987, 1988
United Feature Syndicate, Inc.

Library of Congress Catalog Card Number: 88-043040
Pharos ISBN: 0-88687-414-9

Printed in United States of America

TOPPER BOOKS
An Imprint of Pharos Books
A Scripps Howard Company
200 Park Avenue
New York, NY 10016

10   9   8   7   6   5   4   3   2   1

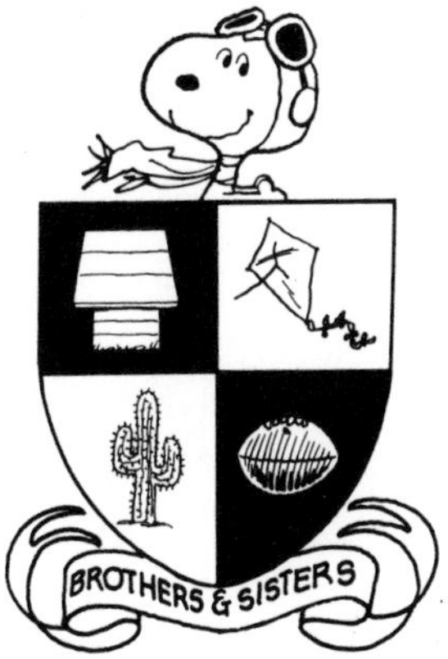
BROTHERS & SISTERS

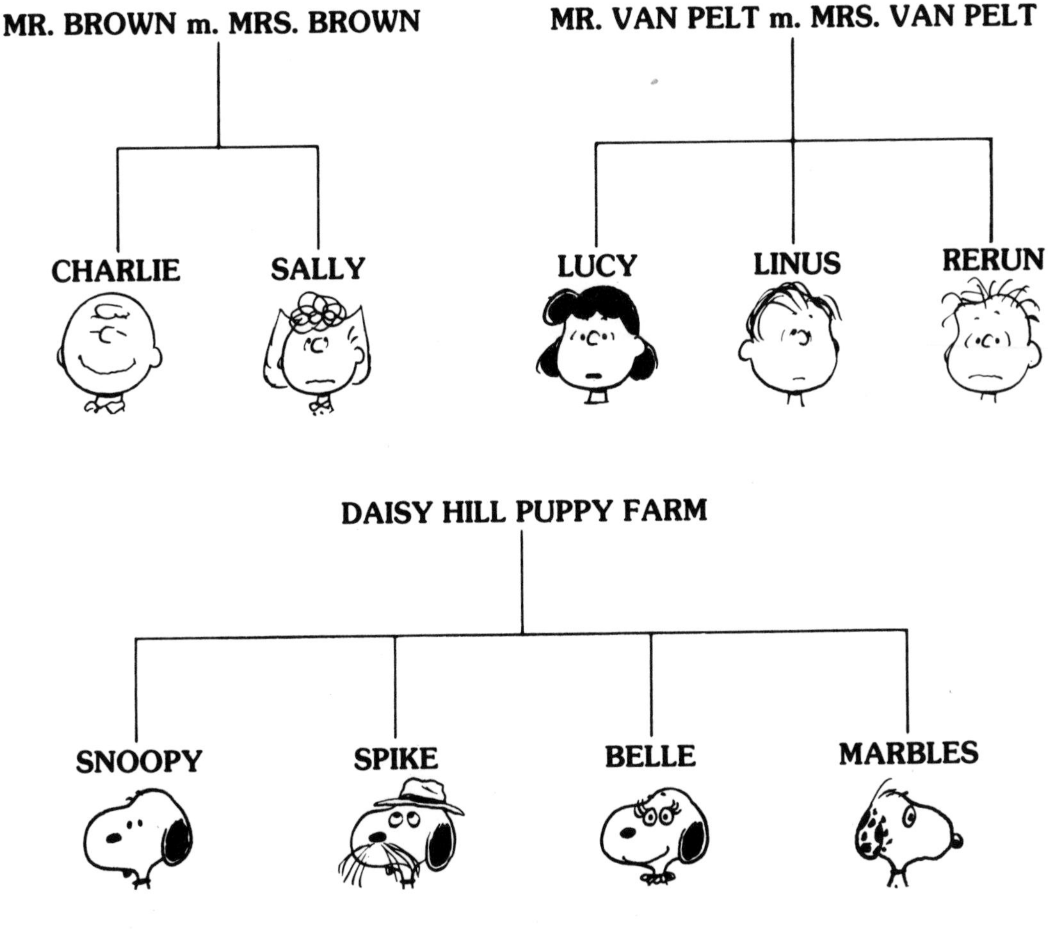
MR. BROWN m. MRS. BROWN
CHARLIE
SALLY
MR. VAN PELT m. MRS. VAN PELT
LUCY
LINUS
RERUN
DAISY HILL PUPPY FARM
SNOOPY
SPIKE
BELLE
MARBLES

IT'S ALL RELATIVE

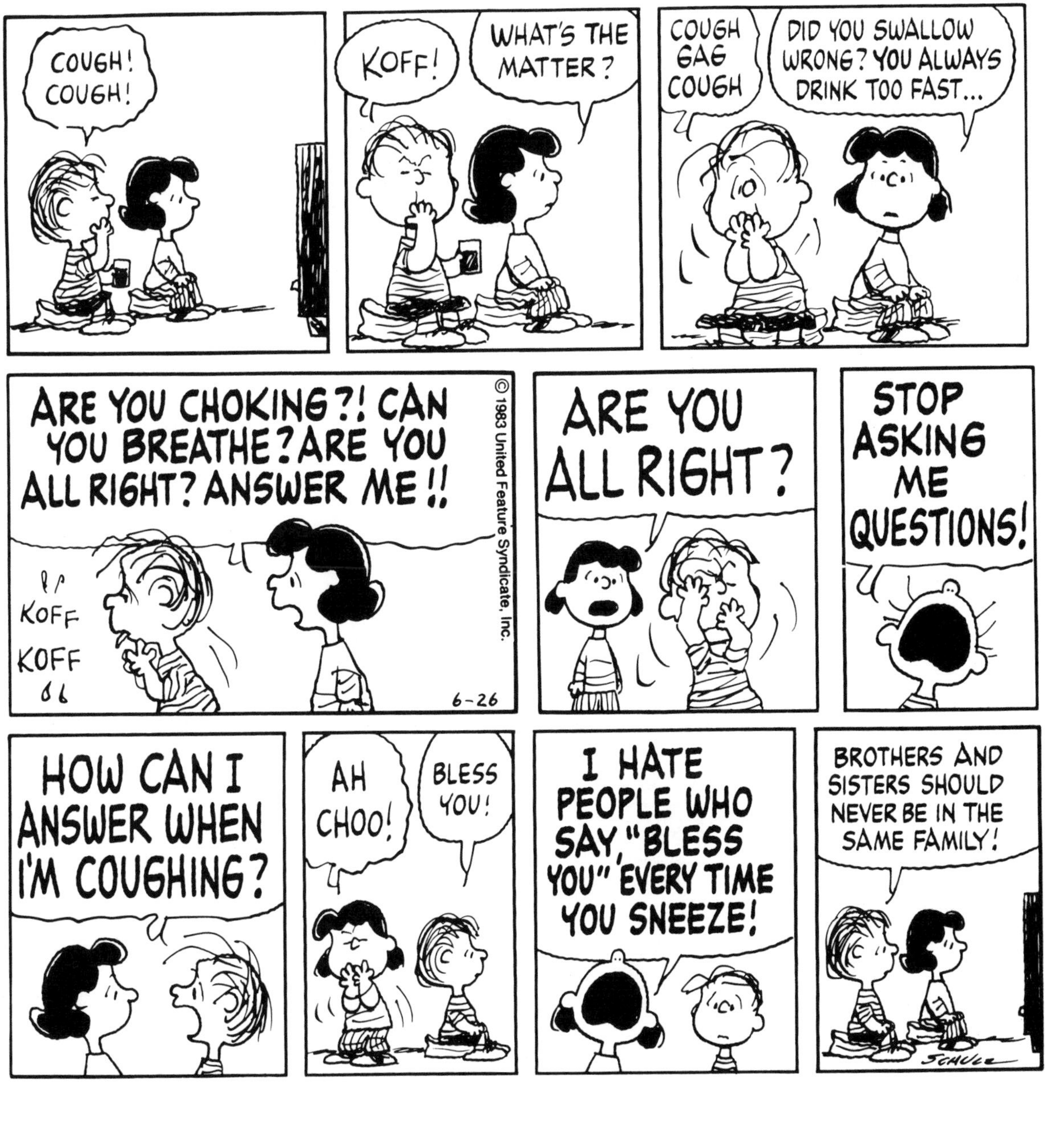
COUGH! COUGH!
KOFF!
WHAT'S THE MATTER?
COUGH GAG COUGH
DID YOU SWALLOW WRONG? YOU ALWAYS DRINK TOO FAST...
ARE YOU CHOKING?! CAN YOU BREATHE? ARE YOU ALL RIGHT? ANSWER ME!!
KOFF KOFF
© 1983 United Feature Syndicate, Inc.
6-26
ARE YOU ALL RIGHT?
STOP ASKING ME QUESTIONS!
HOW CAN I ANSWER WHEN I'M COUGHING?
AH CHOO!
BLESS YOU!
I HATE PEOPLE WHO SAY, "BLESS YOU" EVERY TIME YOU SNEEZE!
BROTHERS AND SISTERS SHOULD NEVER BE IN THE SAME FAMILY!

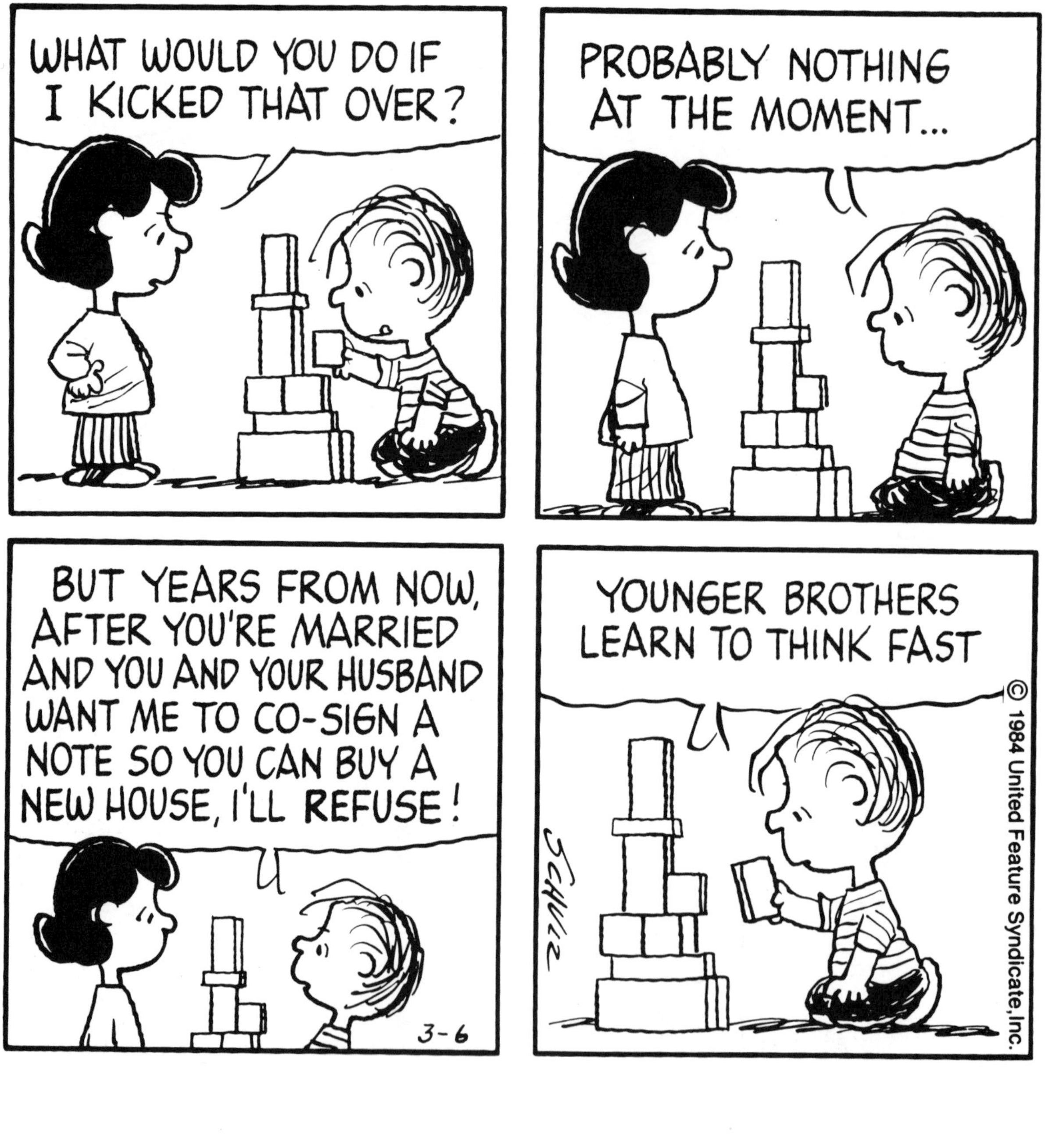
WHAT WOULD YOU DO IF I KICKED THAT OVER?
PROBABLY NOTHING AT THE MOMENT...
BUT YEARS FROM NOW, AFTER YOU'RE MARRIED AND YOU AND YOUR HUSBAND WANT ME TO CO-SIGN A NOTE SO YOU CAN BUY A NEW HOUSE, I'LL REFUSE!
3-6
SCHULZ
YOUNGER BROTHERS LEARN TO THINK FAST
© 1984 United Feature Syndicate, Inc.

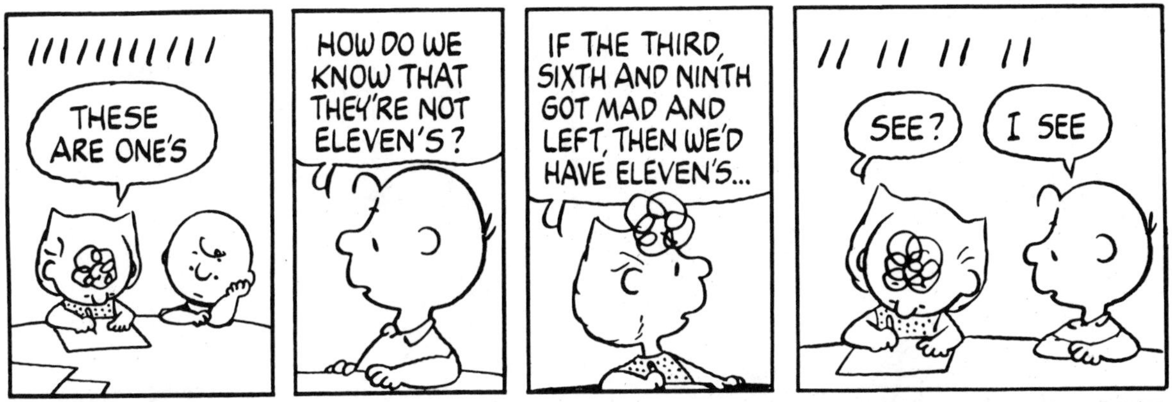
//////////
THESE ARE ONE'S
HOW DO WE KNOW THAT THEY'RE NOT ELEVEN'S?
IF THE THIRD, SIXTH AND NINTH GOT MAD AND LEFT, THEN WE'D HAVE ELEVEN'S...
// // // //
SEE?
I SEE

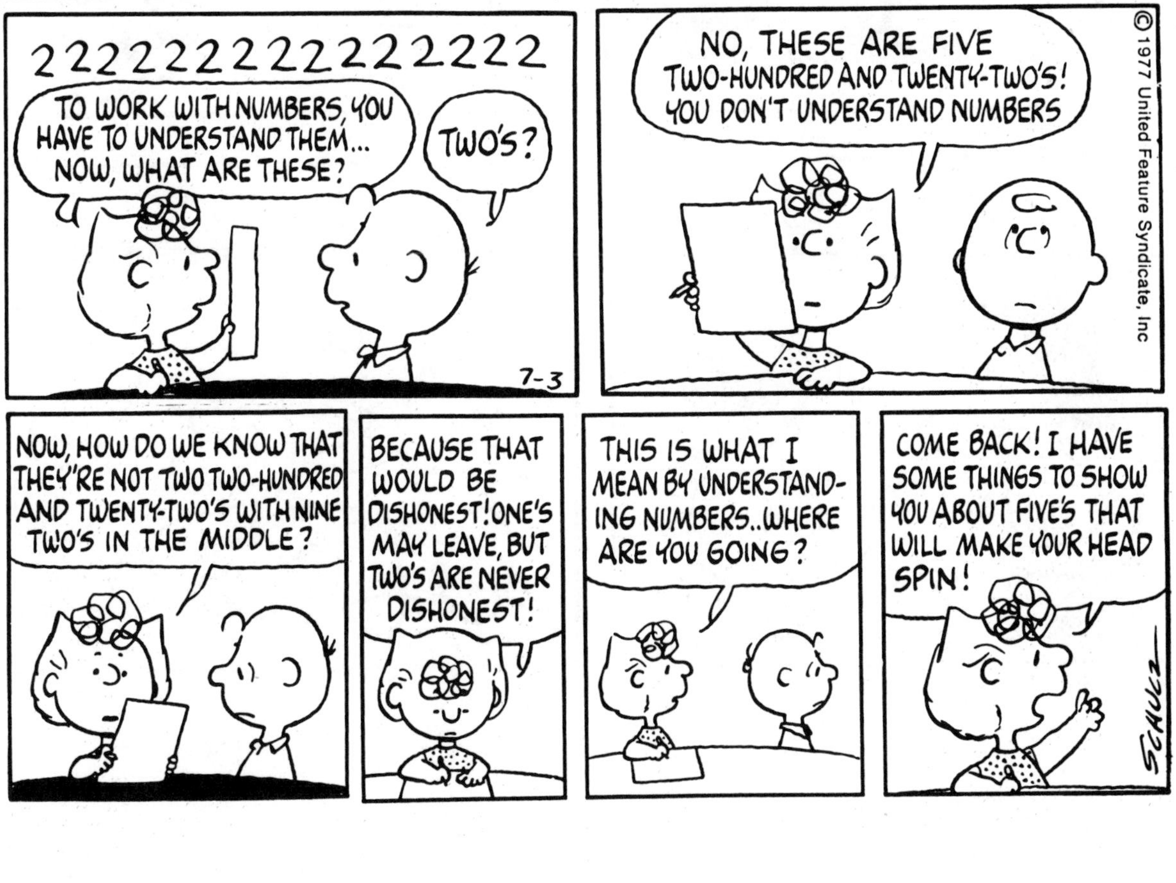
222222222222222
TO WORK WITH NUMBERS, YOU HAVE TO UNDERSTAND THEM... NOW, WHAT ARE THESE?
TWO'S?
7-3
NO, THESE ARE FIVE TWO-HUNDRED AND TWENTY-TWO'S! YOU DON'T UNDERSTAND NUMBERS
© 1977 United Feature Syndicate, Inc
NOW, HOW DO WE KNOW THAT THEY'RE NOT TWO TWO-HUNDRED AND TWENTY-TWO'S WITH NINE TWO'S IN THE MIDDLE?
BECAUSE THAT WOULD BE DISHONEST! ONE'S MAY LEAVE, BUT TWO'S ARE NEVER DISHONEST!
THIS IS WHAT I MEAN BY UNDERSTANDING NUMBERS..WHERE ARE YOU GOING?
COME BACK! I HAVE SOME THINGS TO SHOW YOU ABOUT FIVE'S THAT WILL MAKE YOUR HEAD SPIN!
SCHULZ

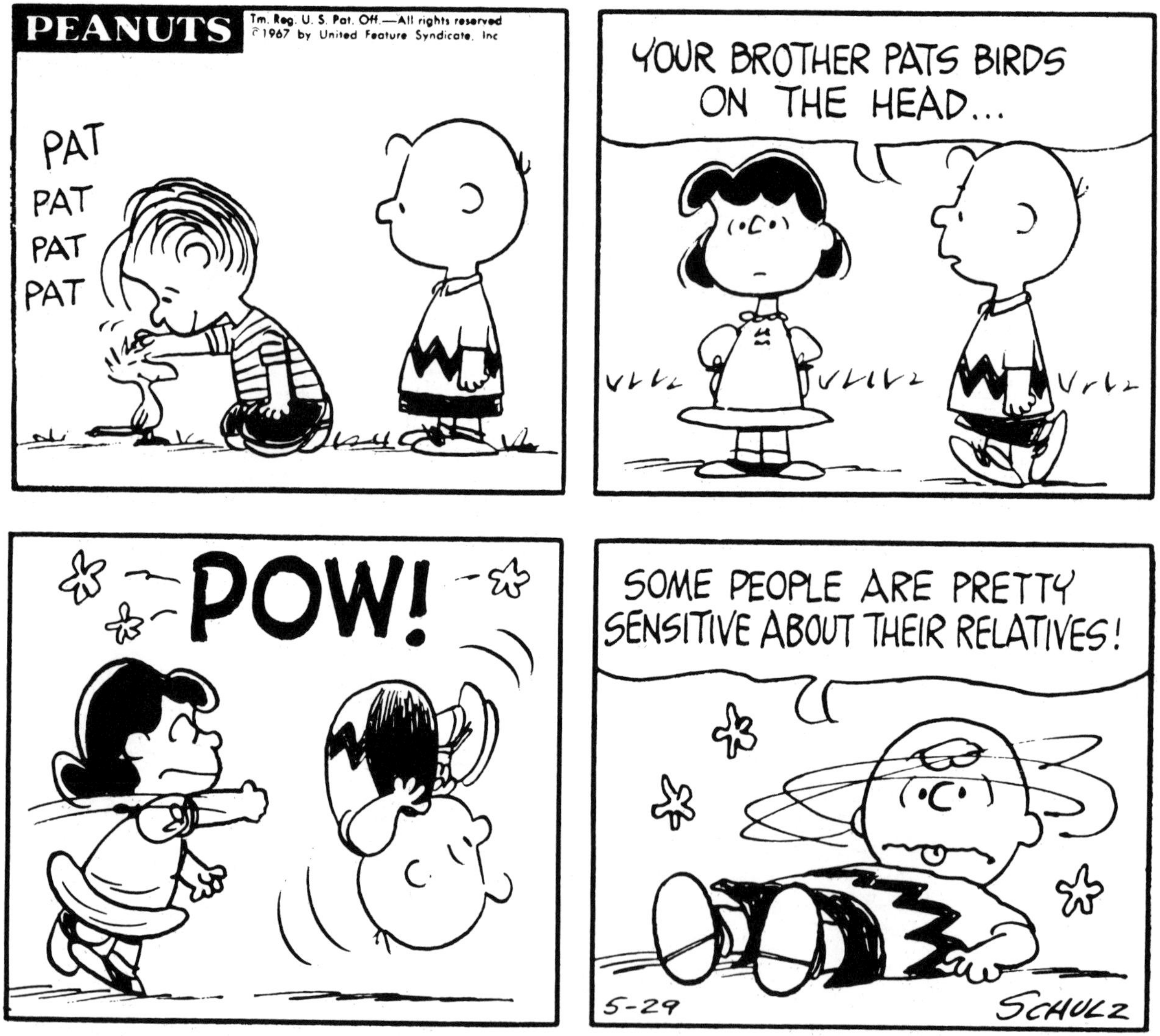
PEANUTS
Tm. Reg. U. S. Pat. Off.—All rights reserved
© 1967 by United Feature Syndicate, Inc
PAT
PAT
PAT
PAT
YOUR BROTHER PATS BIRDS ON THE HEAD...
POW!
SOME PEOPLE ARE PRETTY SENSITIVE ABOUT THEIR RELATIVES!
5-29
SCHULZ

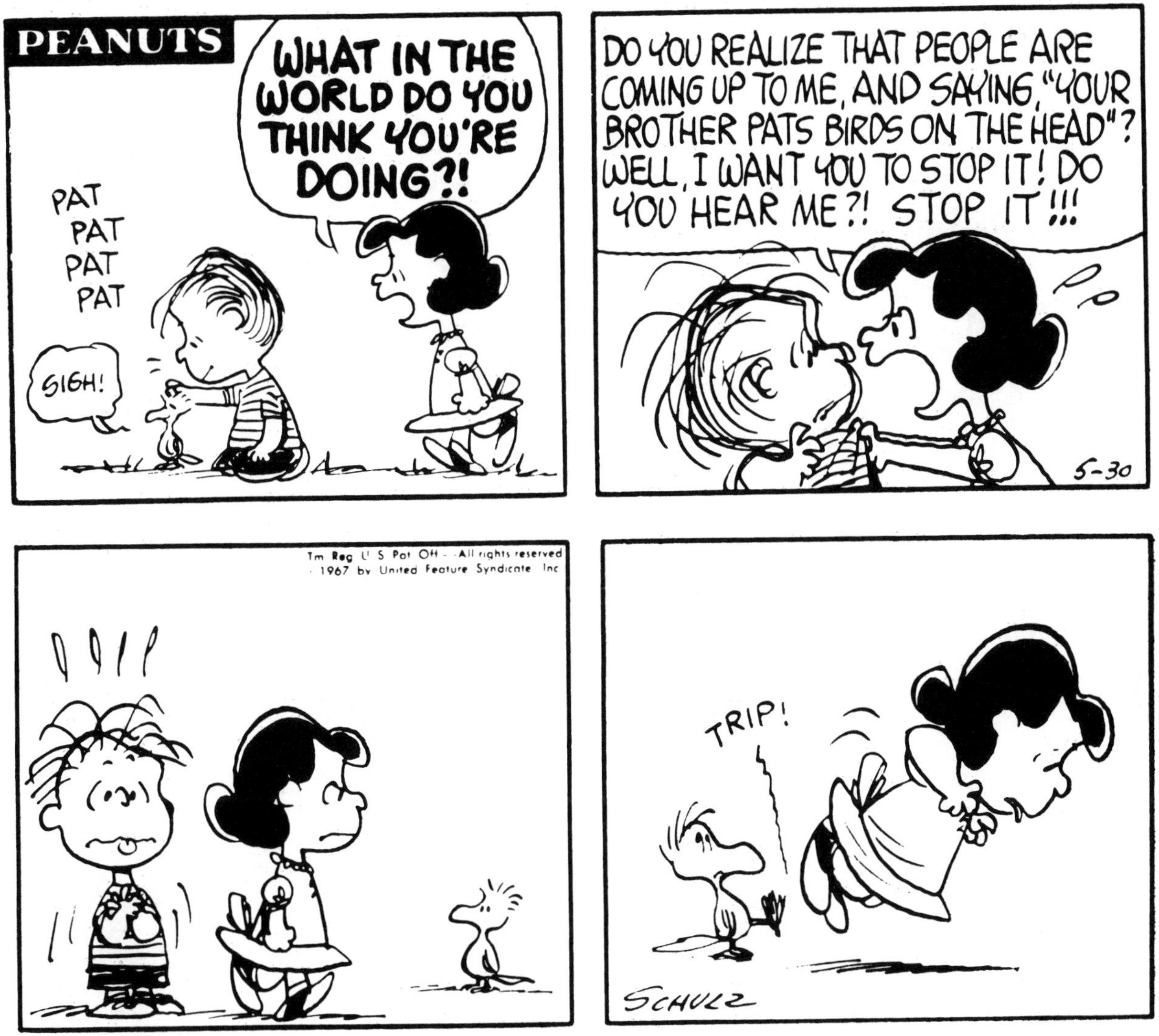
PEANUTS
WHAT IN THE WORLD DO YOU THINK YOU'RE DOING?!
PAT PAT PAT PAT
SIGH!
DO YOU REALIZE THAT PEOPLE ARE COMING UP TO ME, AND SAYING, "YOUR BROTHER PATS BIRDS ON THE HEAD"? WELL, I WANT YOU TO STOP IT! DO YOU HEAR ME?! STOP IT!!!
5-30
Tm Reg U S Pat Off - All rights reserved
1967 by United Feature Syndicate Inc
TRIP!
SCHULZ

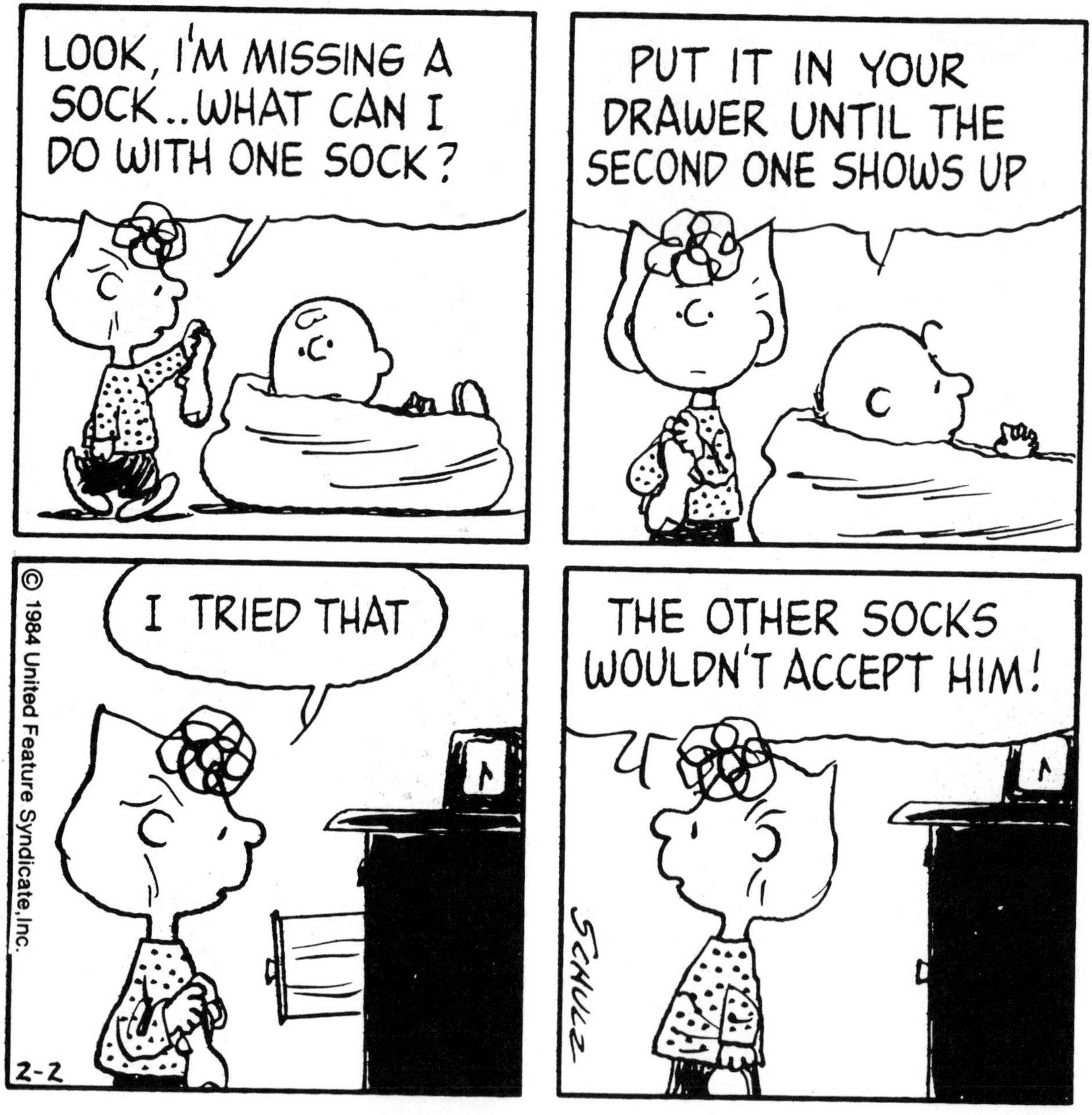
LOOK, I'M MISSING A SOCK..WHAT CAN I DO WITH ONE SOCK?
PUT IT IN YOUR DRAWER UNTIL THE SECOND ONE SHOWS UP
I TRIED THAT
THE OTHER SOCKS WOULDN'T ACCEPT HIM!
© 1984 United Feature Syndicate, Inc.
2-2
SCHULZ

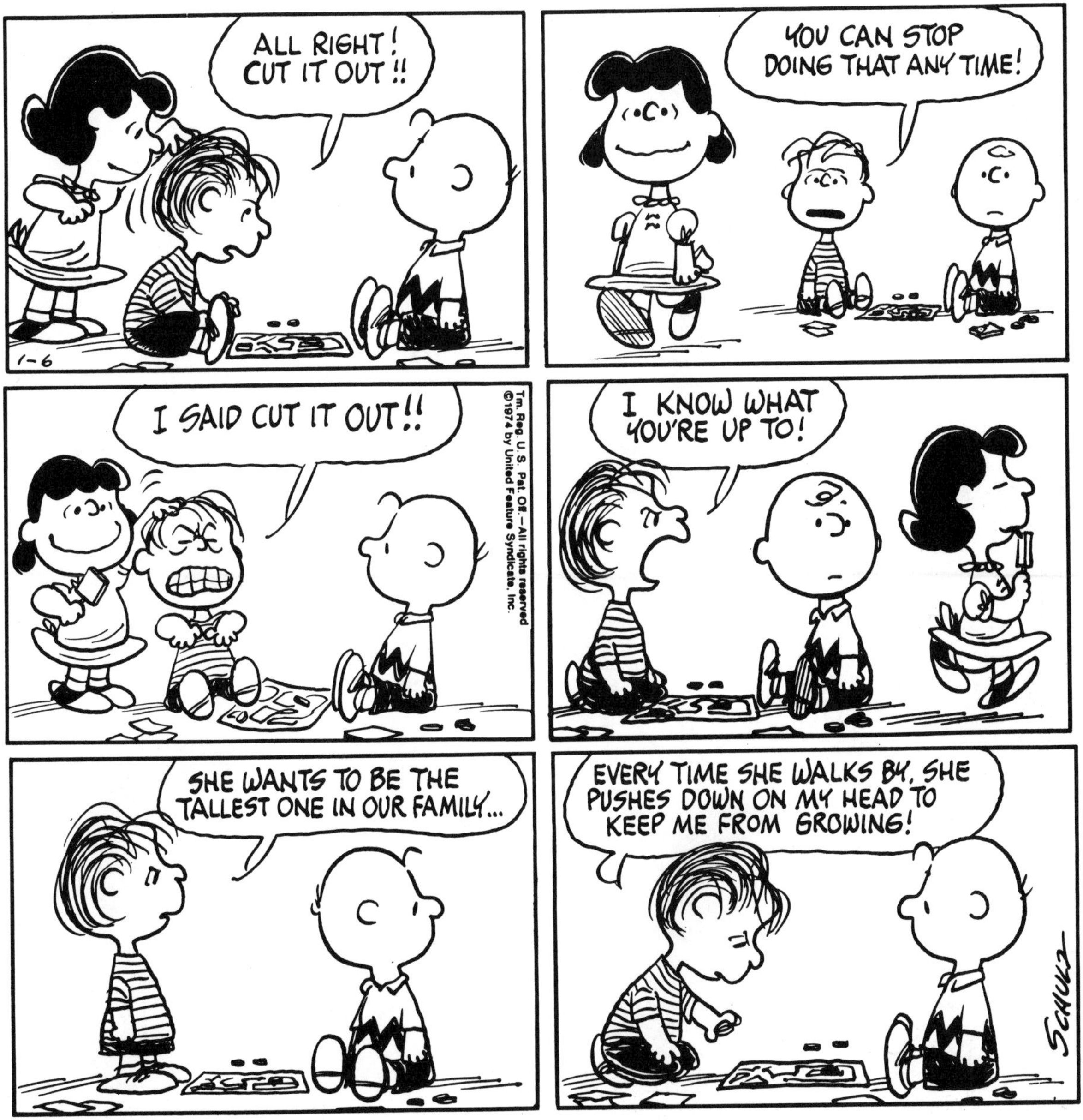
ALL RIGHT! CUT IT OUT!!
1-6
YOU CAN STOP DOING THAT ANY TIME!
I SAID CUT IT OUT!!
Tm. Reg. U.S. Pat. Off.—All rights reserved ©1974 by United Feature Syndicate, Inc.
I KNOW WHAT YOU'RE UP TO!
SHE WANTS TO BE THE TALLEST ONE IN OUR FAMILY...
EVERY TIME SHE WALKS BY, SHE PUSHES DOWN ON MY HEAD TO KEEP ME FROM GROWING!
SCHULZ

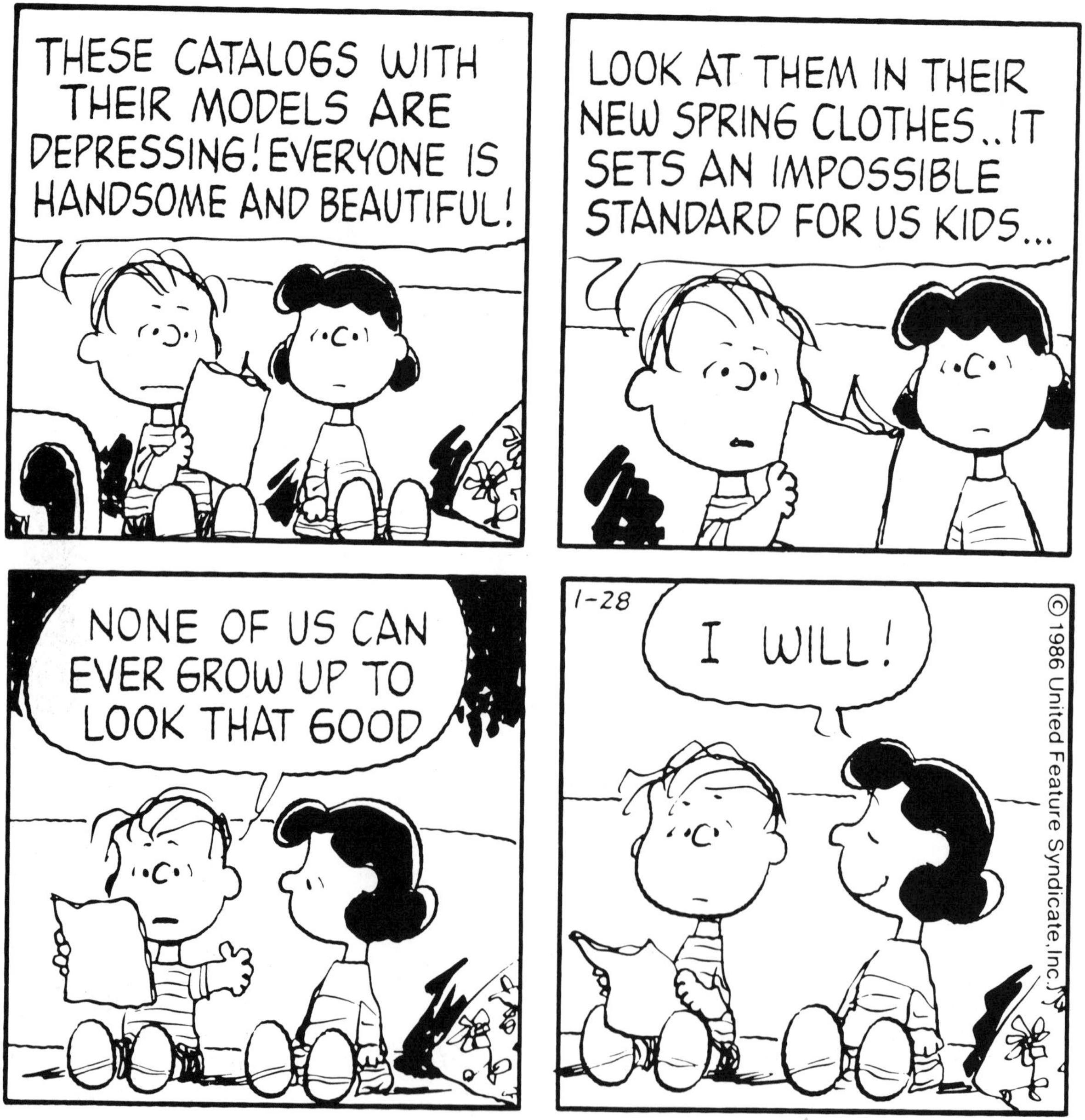
THESE CATALOGS WITH THEIR MODELS ARE DEPRESSING! EVERYONE IS HANDSOME AND BEAUTIFUL!
LOOK AT THEM IN THEIR NEW SPRING CLOTHES..IT SETS AN IMPOSSIBLE STANDARD FOR US KIDS...
NONE OF US CAN EVER GROW UP TO LOOK THAT GOOD
1-28
I WILL!
© 1986 United Feature Syndicate, Inc.

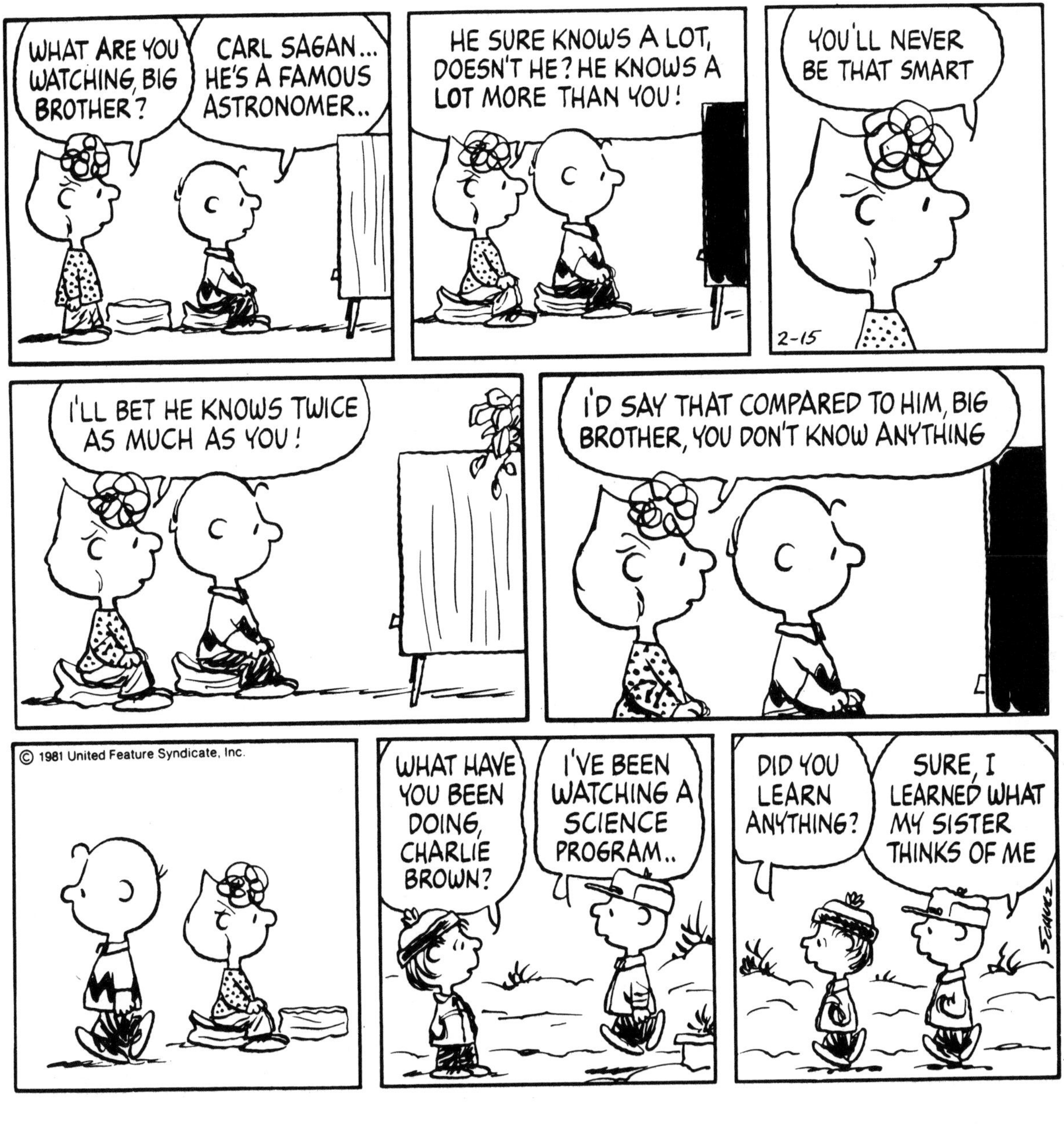
WHAT ARE YOU WATCHING, BIG BROTHER?
CARL SAGAN... HE'S A FAMOUS ASTRONOMER..
HE SURE KNOWS A LOT, DOESN'T HE? HE KNOWS A LOT MORE THAN YOU!
YOU'LL NEVER BE THAT SMART
2-15
I'LL BET HE KNOWS TWICE AS MUCH AS YOU!
I'D SAY THAT COMPARED TO HIM, BIG BROTHER, YOU DON'T KNOW ANYTHING
WHAT HAVE YOU BEEN DOING, CHARLIE BROWN?
I'VE BEEN WATCHING A SCIENCE PROGRAM..
DID YOU LEARN ANYTHING?
SURE, I LEARNED WHAT MY SISTER THINKS OF ME
SCHULZ

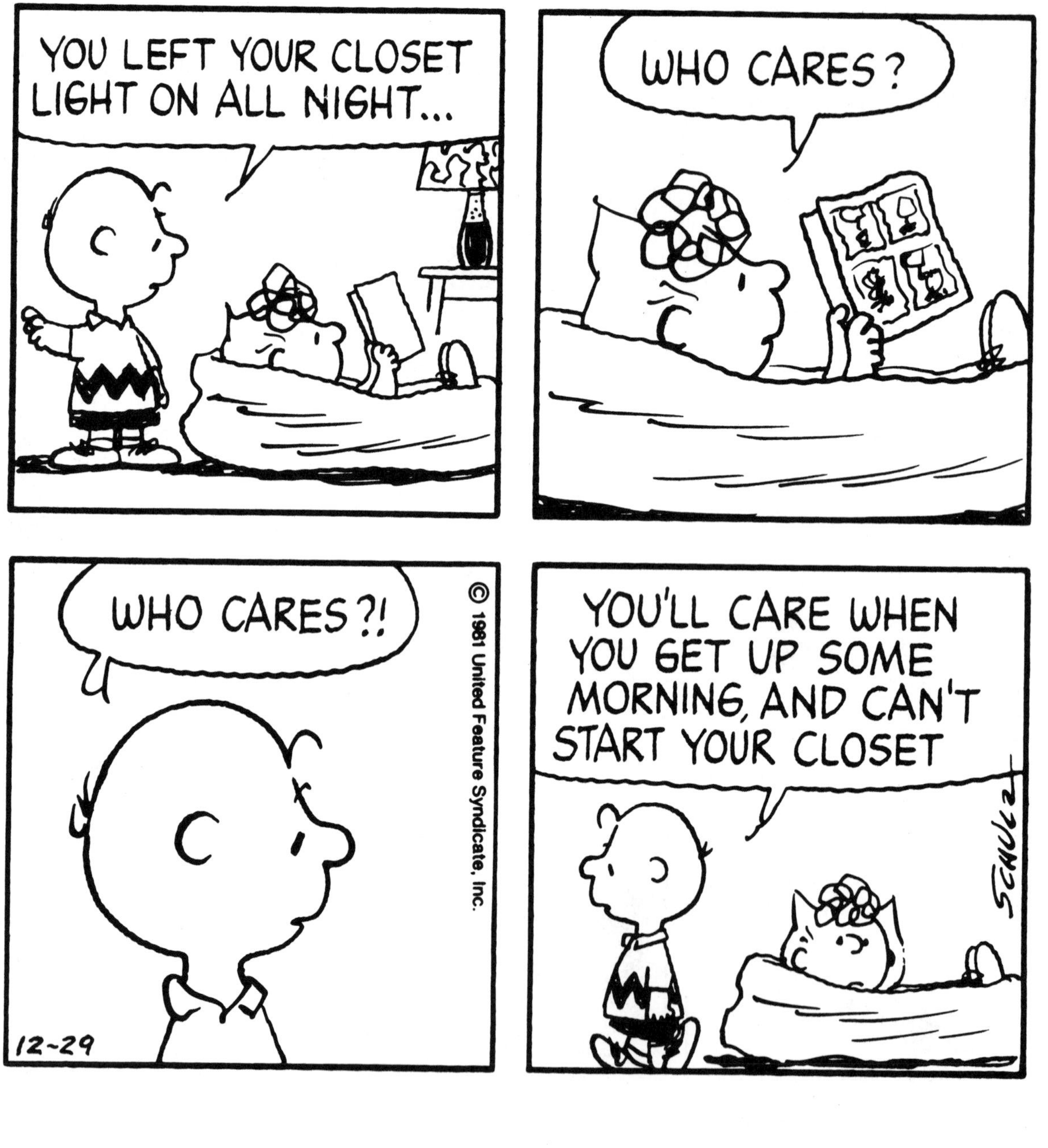
YOU LEFT YOUR CLOSET LIGHT ON ALL NIGHT...
WHO CARES?
WHO CARES?!
© 1981 United Feature Syndicate, Inc.
12-29
YOU'LL CARE WHEN YOU GET UP SOME MORNING, AND CAN'T START YOUR CLOSET
SCHULZ

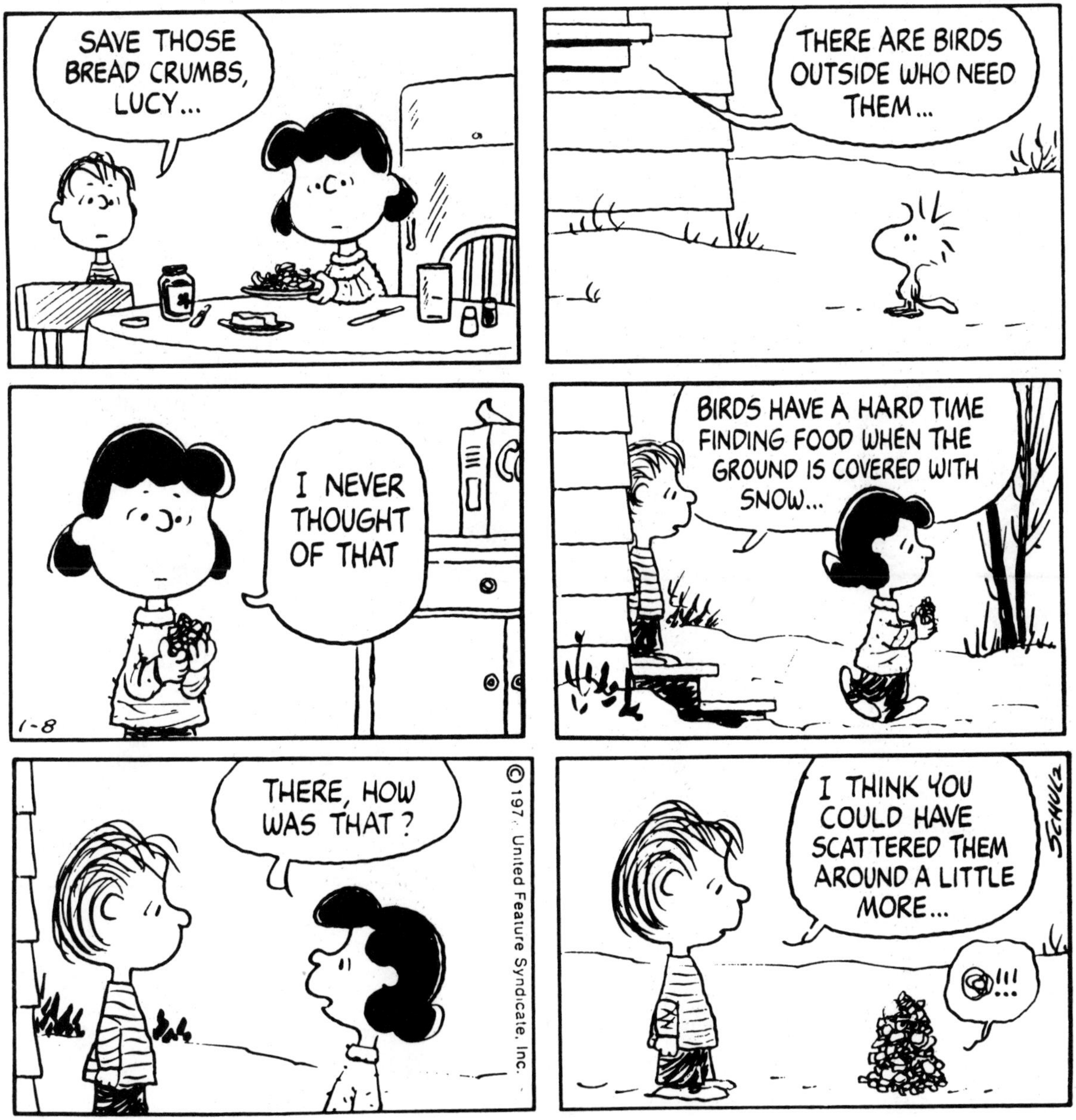
SAVE THOSE BREAD CRUMBS, LUCY...
THERE ARE BIRDS OUTSIDE WHO NEED THEM...
I NEVER THOUGHT OF THAT
1-8
BIRDS HAVE A HARD TIME FINDING FOOD WHEN THE GROUND IS COVERED WITH SNOW...
THERE, HOW WAS THAT?
© 197 United Feature Syndicate, Inc.
I THINK YOU COULD HAVE SCATTERED THEM AROUND A LITTLE MORE...
SCHULZ
!!!...

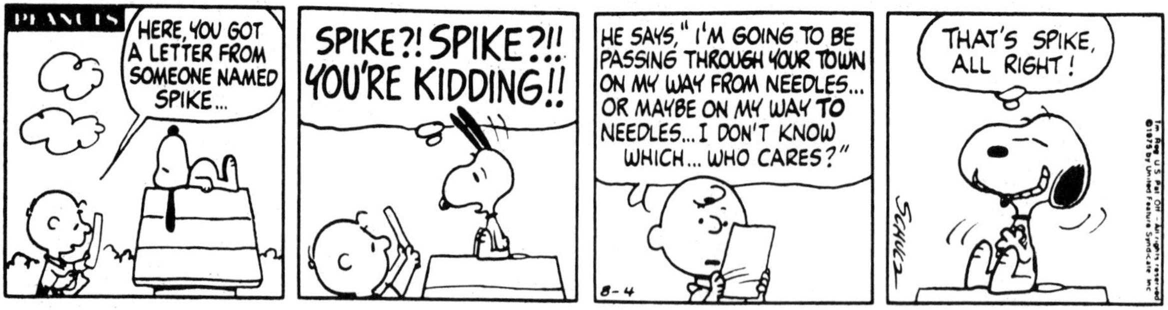
PEANUTS
HERE, YOU GOT A LETTER FROM SOMEONE NAMED SPIKE...
SPIKE?! SPIKE?!! YOU'RE KIDDING!!
HE SAYS, "I'M GOING TO BE PASSING THROUGH YOUR TOWN ON MY WAY FROM NEEDLES... OR MAYBE ON MY WAY TO NEEDLES... I DON'T KNOW WHICH... WHO CARES?"
8-4
THAT'S SPIKE, ALL RIGHT!
Tm. Reg. U.S. Pat. Off.—All rights reserved © 1975 by United Feature Syndicate, Inc
SCHULZ

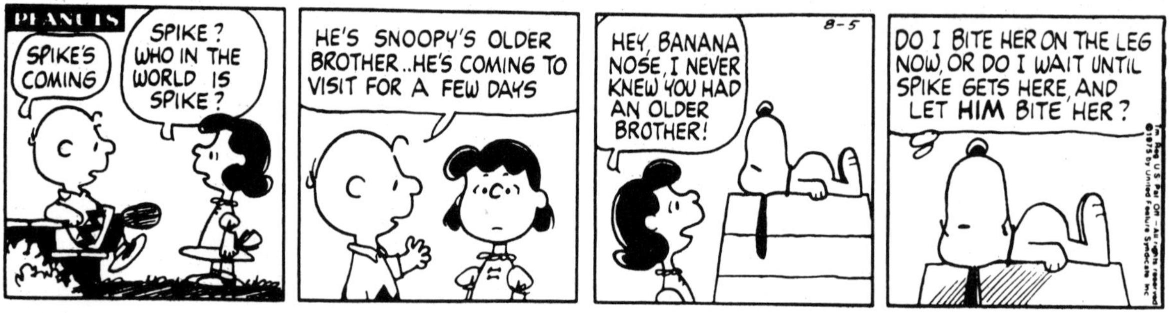
PEANUTS
SPIKE'S COMING
SPIKE? WHO IN THE WORLD IS SPIKE?
HE'S SNOOPY'S OLDER BROTHER..HE'S COMING TO VISIT FOR A FEW DAYS
8-5
HEY, BANANA NOSE, I NEVER KNEW YOU HAD AN OLDER BROTHER!
DO I BITE HER ON THE LEG NOW, OR DO I WAIT UNTIL SPIKE GETS HERE, AND LET HIM BITE HER?
Tm. Reg. U.S. Pat. Off.—All rights reserved © 1975 by United Feature Syndicate, Inc

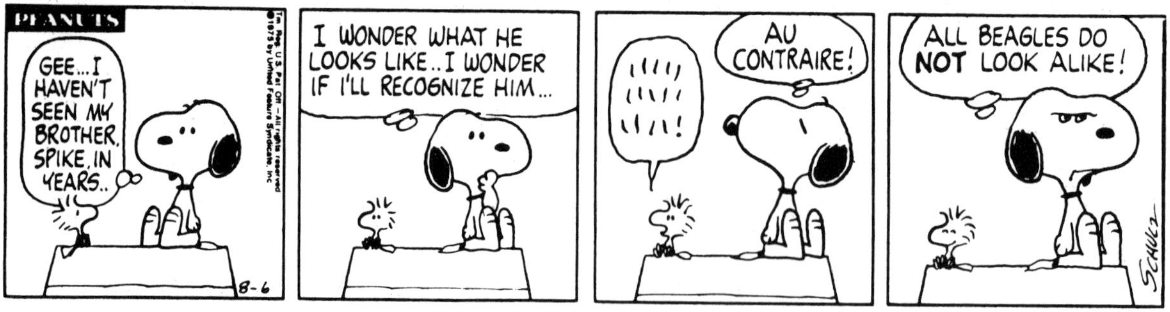
PEANUTS
GEE...I HAVEN'T SEEN MY BROTHER, SPIKE, IN YEARS..
Tm. Reg. U.S. Pat. Off.—All rights reserved © 1975 by United Feature Syndicate, Inc
8-6
I WONDER WHAT HE LOOKS LIKE..I WONDER IF I'LL RECOGNIZE HIM...
AU CONTRAIRE!
ALL BEAGLES DO NOT LOOK ALIKE!
SCHULZ

IT'S ALL RELATIVE

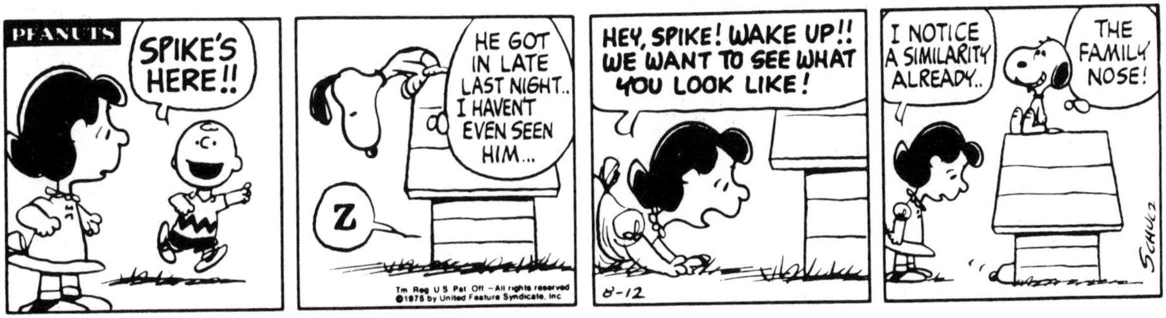

PEANUTS
SPIKE'S HERE!!
HE GOT IN LATE LAST NIGHT.. I HAVEN'T EVEN SEEN HIM...
Z
Tm Reg U S Pat Off – All rights reserved ©1975 by United Feature Syndicate, Inc
HEY, SPIKE! WAKE UP!! WE WANT TO SEE WHAT YOU LOOK LIKE!
8-12
I NOTICE A SIMILARITY ALREADY..
THE FAMILY NOSE!
SCHULZ

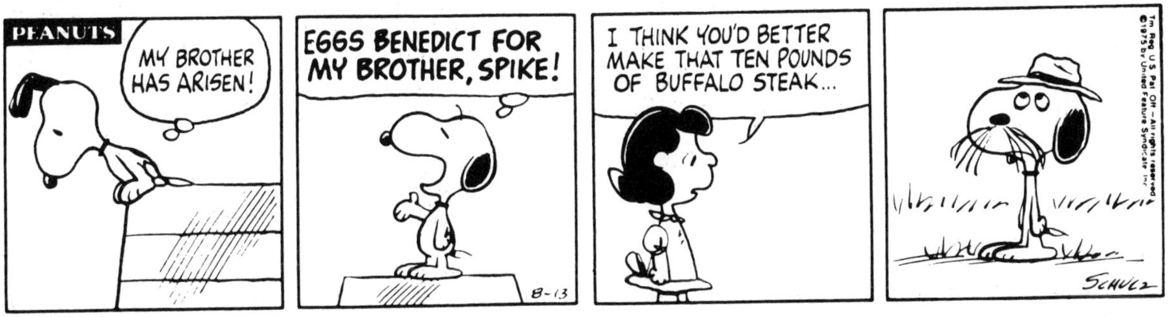

PEANUTS
MY BROTHER HAS ARISEN!
EGGS BENEDICT FOR MY BROTHER, SPIKE!
8-13
I THINK YOU'D BETTER MAKE THAT TEN POUNDS OF BUFFALO STEAK...
Tm Reg U S Pat Off – All rights reserved ©1975 by United Feature Syndicate, Inc
SCHULZ

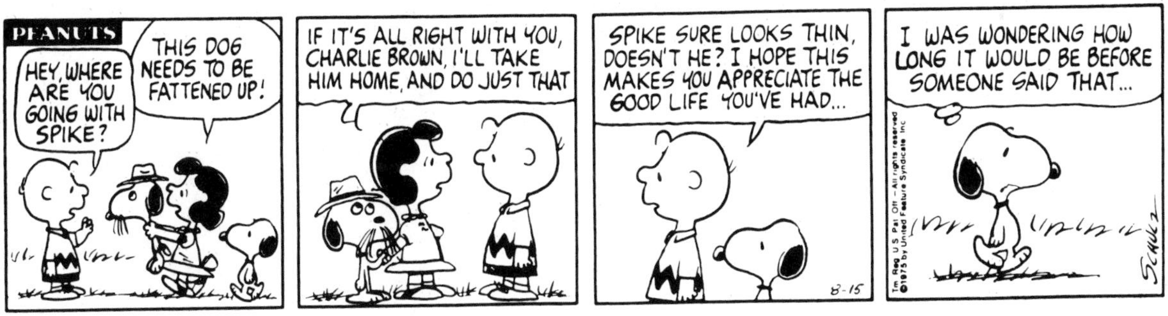

PEANUTS
HEY, WHERE ARE YOU GOING WITH SPIKE?
THIS DOG NEEDS TO BE FATTENED UP!
IF IT'S ALL RIGHT WITH YOU, CHARLIE BROWN, I'LL TAKE HIM HOME, AND DO JUST THAT
SPIKE SURE LOOKS THIN, DOESN'T HE? I HOPE THIS MAKES YOU APPRECIATE THE GOOD LIFE YOU'VE HAD...
8-15
Tm Reg U S Pat Off – All rights reserved ©1975 by United Feature Syndicate, Inc
I WAS WONDERING HOW LONG IT WOULD BE BEFORE SOMEONE SAID THAT...
SCHULZ

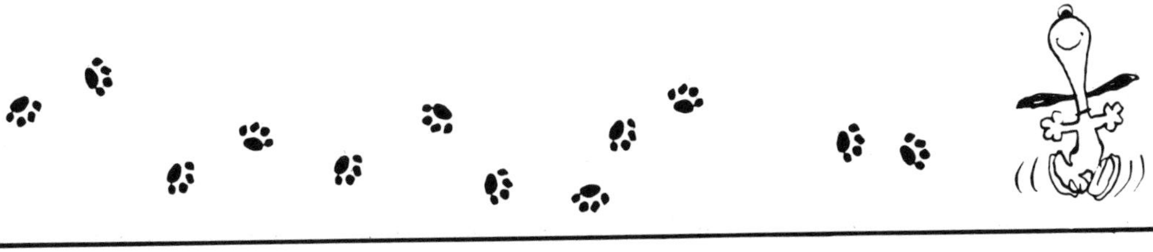

BROTHERS AND SISTERS

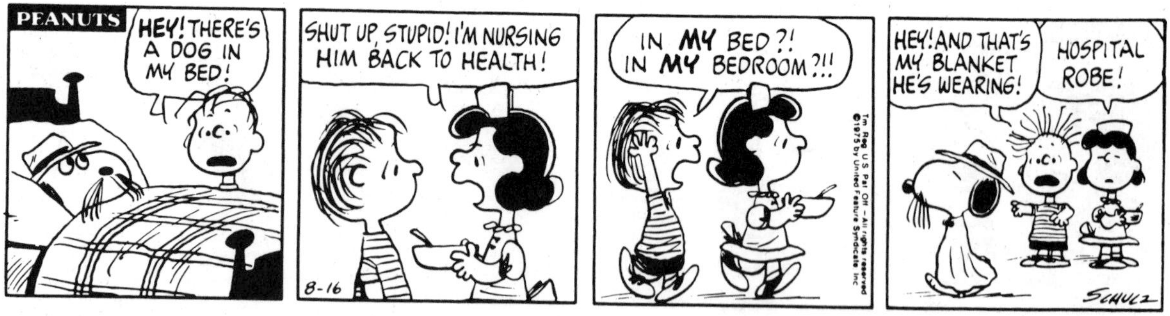
PEANUTS
HEY! THERE'S A DOG IN MY BED!
SHUT UP, STUPID! I'M NURSING HIM BACK TO HEALTH!
8-16
IN MY BED?! IN MY BEDROOM?!!
Tm Reg U S Pat Off — All rights reserved ©1975 by United Feature Syndicate Inc
HEY! AND THAT'S MY BLANKET HE'S WEARING!
HOSPITAL ROBE!
SCHULZ

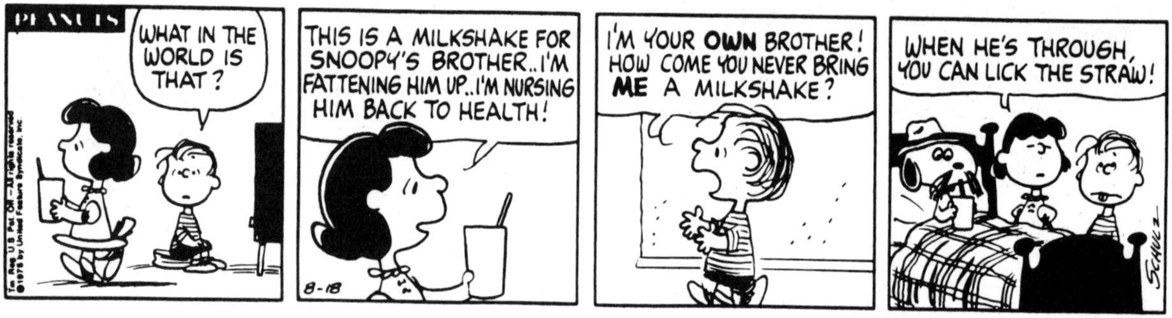
PEANUTS
WHAT IN THE WORLD IS THAT?
Tm Reg U S Pat Off — All rights reserved ©1975 by United Feature Syndicate Inc
THIS IS A MILKSHAKE FOR SNOOPY'S BROTHER.. I'M FATTENING HIM UP.. I'M NURSING HIM BACK TO HEALTH!
8-18
I'M YOUR OWN BROTHER! HOW COME YOU NEVER BRING ME A MILKSHAKE?
WHEN HE'S THROUGH, YOU CAN LICK THE STRAW!
SCHULZ

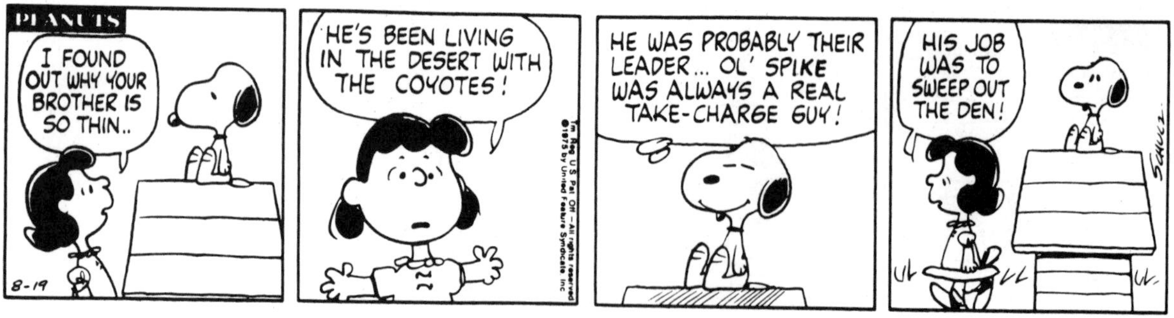
PEANUTS
I FOUND OUT WHY YOUR BROTHER IS SO THIN..
8-19
HE'S BEEN LIVING IN THE DESERT WITH THE COYOTES!
Tm Reg U S Pat Off — All rights reserved ©1975 by United Feature Syndicate Inc
HE WAS PROBABLY THEIR LEADER... OL' SPIKE WAS ALWAYS A REAL TAKE-CHARGE GUY!
HIS JOB WAS TO SWEEP OUT THE DEN!
SCHULZ

IT'S ALL RELATIVE

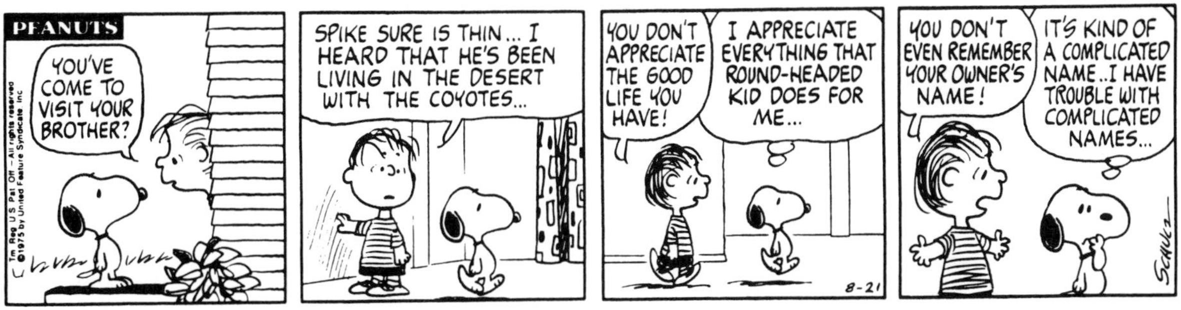
PEANUTS
Tm Reg U S Pat Off — All rights reserved ©1975 by United Feature Syndicate Inc
YOU'VE COME TO VISIT YOUR BROTHER?
SPIKE SURE IS THIN... I HEARD THAT HE'S BEEN LIVING IN THE DESERT WITH THE COYOTES...
YOU DON'T APPRECIATE THE GOOD LIFE YOU HAVE!
I APPRECIATE EVERYTHING THAT ROUND-HEADED KID DOES FOR ME...
8-21
YOU DON'T EVEN REMEMBER YOUR OWNER'S NAME!
IT'S KIND OF A COMPLICATED NAME..I HAVE TROUBLE WITH COMPLICATED NAMES...
SCHULZ

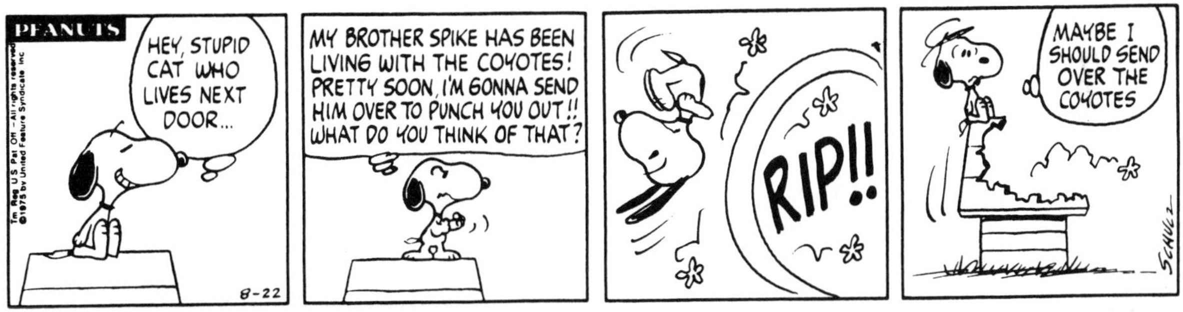
PEANUTS
Tm Reg U S Pat Off — All rights reserved ©1975 by United Feature Syndicate Inc
HEY, STUPID CAT WHO LIVES NEXT DOOR...
8-22
MY BROTHER SPIKE HAS BEEN LIVING WITH THE COYOTES! PRETTY SOON, I'M GONNA SEND HIM OVER TO PUNCH YOU OUT!! WHAT DO YOU THINK OF THAT?
RIP!!
MAYBE I SHOULD SEND OVER THE COYOTES
SCHULZ

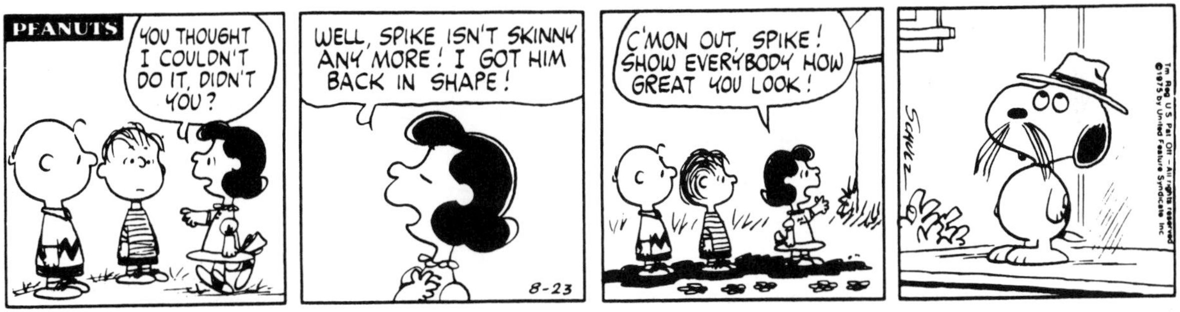
PEANUTS
YOU THOUGHT I COULDN'T DO IT, DIDN'T YOU?
WELL, SPIKE ISN'T SKINNY ANY MORE! I GOT HIM BACK IN SHAPE!
8-23
C'MON OUT, SPIKE! SHOW EVERYBODY HOW GREAT YOU LOOK!
SCHULZ
Tm Reg U S Pat Off — All rights reserved ©1975 by United Feature Syndicate Inc

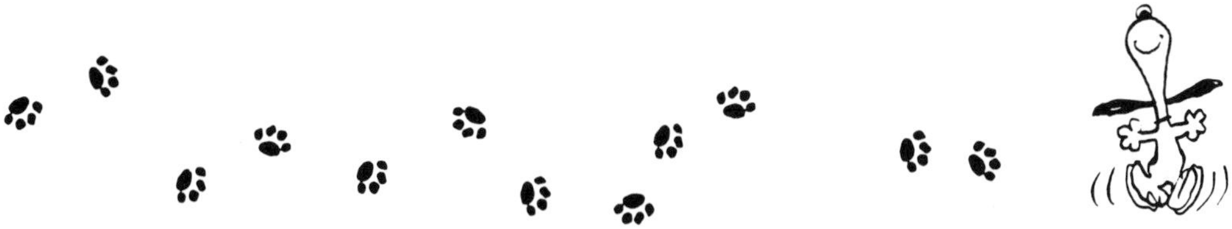

BROTHERS AND SISTERS

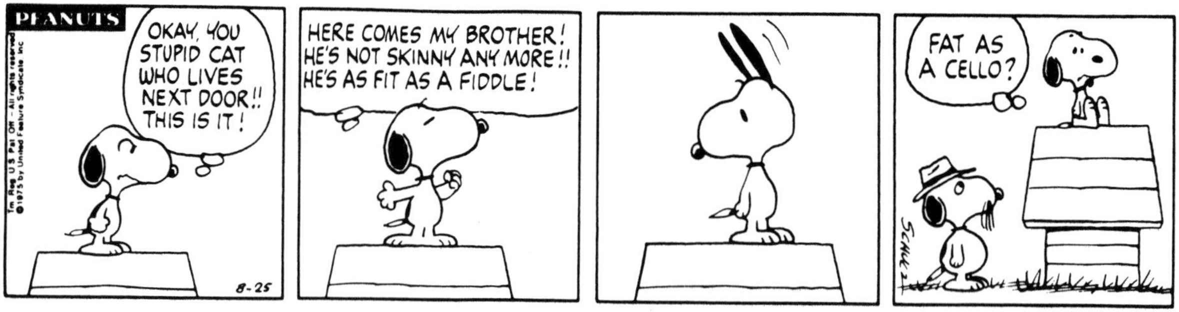
PEANUTS
OKAY, YOU STUPID CAT WHO LIVES NEXT DOOR!! THIS IS IT!
HERE COMES MY BROTHER! HE'S NOT SKINNY ANY MORE!! HE'S AS FIT AS A FIDDLE!
FAT AS A CELLO?
8-25
SCHULZ

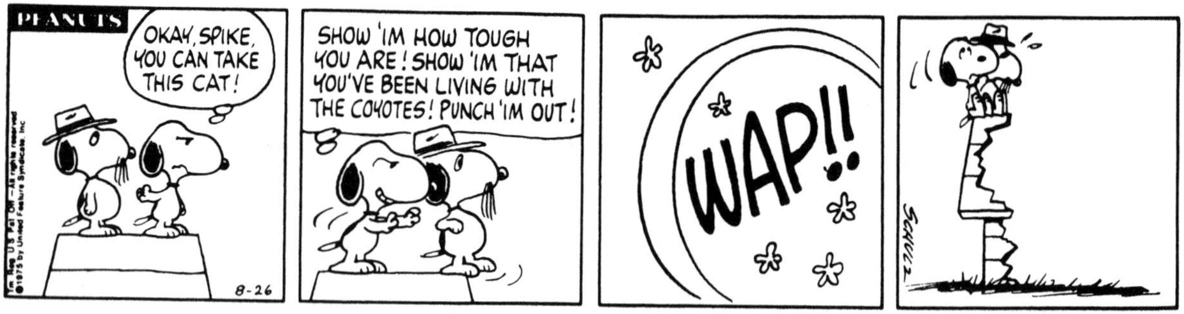
PEANUTS
OKAY, SPIKE, YOU CAN TAKE THIS CAT!
SHOW 'IM HOW TOUGH YOU ARE! SHOW 'IM THAT YOU'VE BEEN LIVING WITH THE COYOTES! PUNCH 'IM OUT!
WAP!!
8-26
SCHULZ

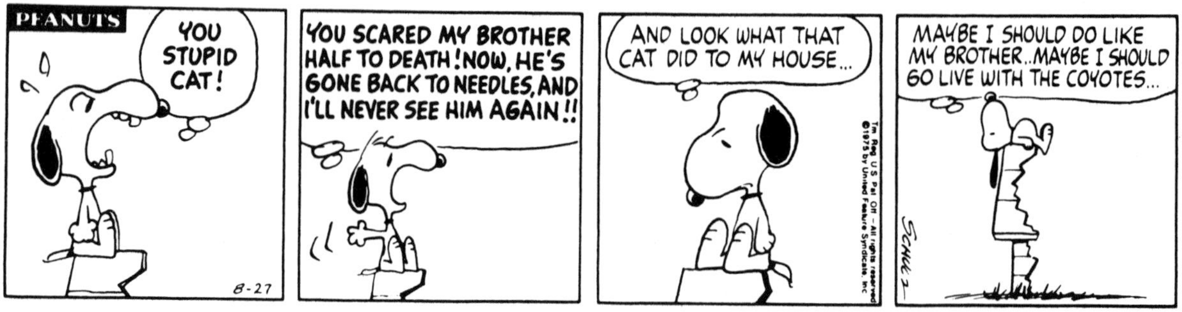
PEANUTS
YOU STUPID CAT!
YOU SCARED MY BROTHER HALF TO DEATH! NOW, HE'S GONE BACK TO NEEDLES, AND I'LL NEVER SEE HIM AGAIN!!
AND LOOK WHAT THAT CAT DID TO MY HOUSE...
MAYBE I SHOULD DO LIKE MY BROTHER.. MAYBE I SHOULD GO LIVE WITH THE COYOTES...
8-27
SCHULZ

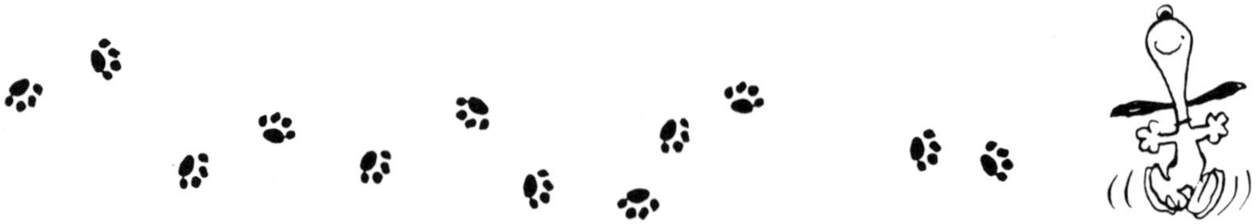

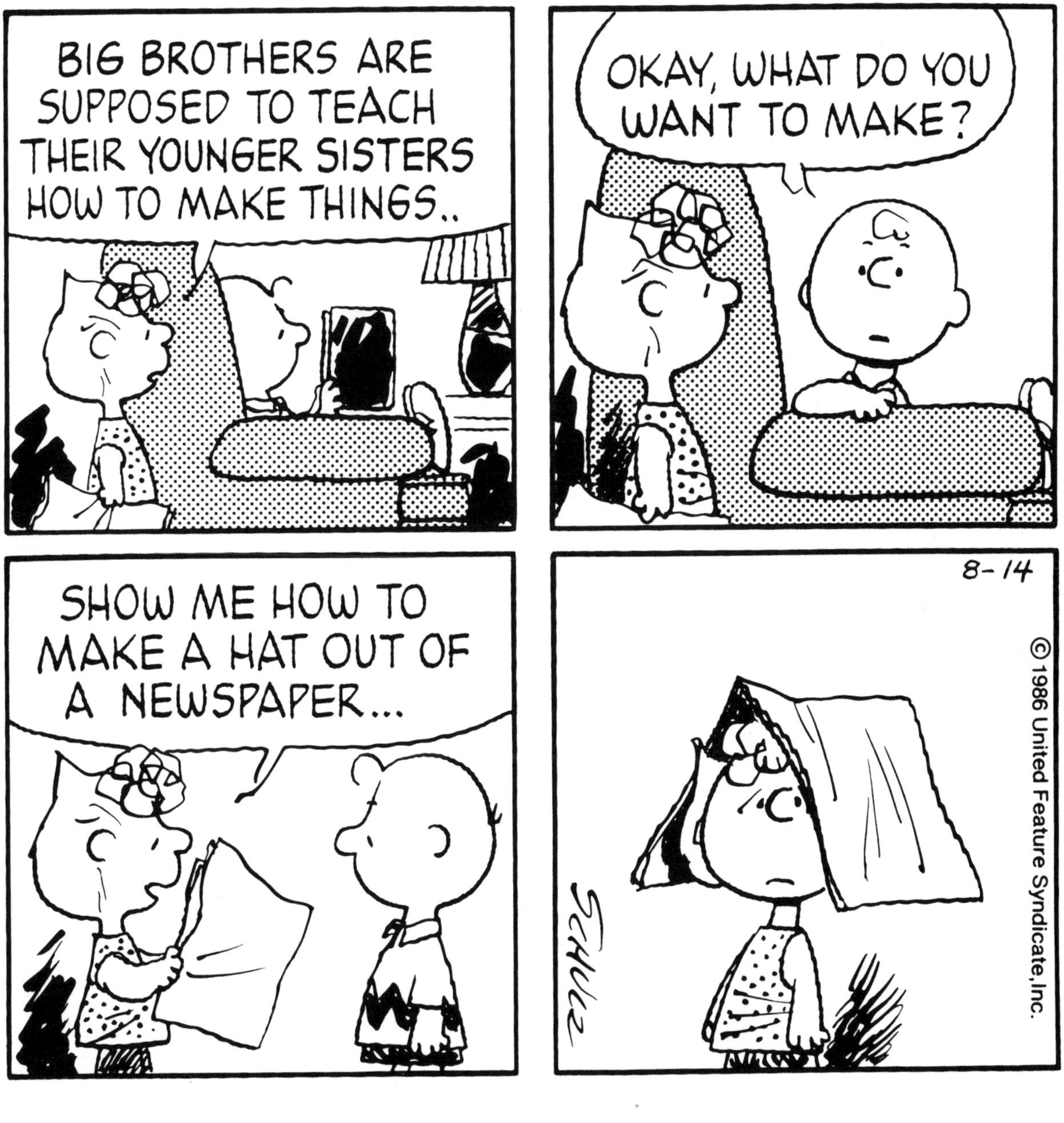
BIG BROTHERS ARE SUPPOSED TO TEACH THEIR YOUNGER SISTERS HOW TO MAKE THINGS..
OKAY, WHAT DO YOU WANT TO MAKE?
SHOW ME HOW TO MAKE A HAT OUT OF A NEWSPAPER...
8-14
SCHULZ
© 1986 United Feature Syndicate, Inc.

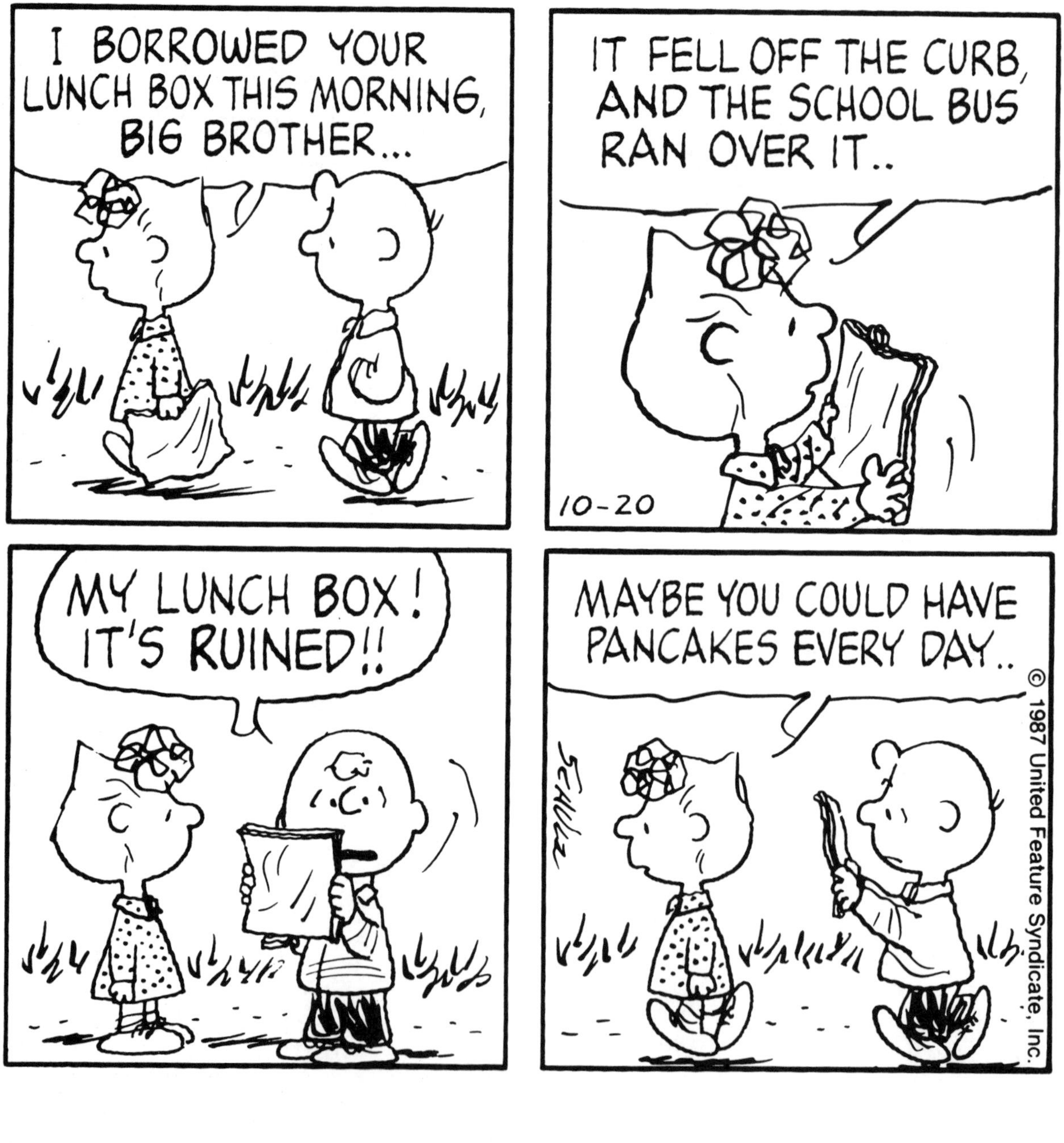
I BORROWED YOUR LUNCH BOX THIS MORNING, BIG BROTHER...
IT FELL OFF THE CURB, AND THE SCHOOL BUS RAN OVER IT..
10-20
MY LUNCH BOX! IT'S RUINED!!
MAYBE YOU COULD HAVE PANCAKES EVERY DAY..
SCHULZ
© 1987 United Feature Syndicate, Inc.

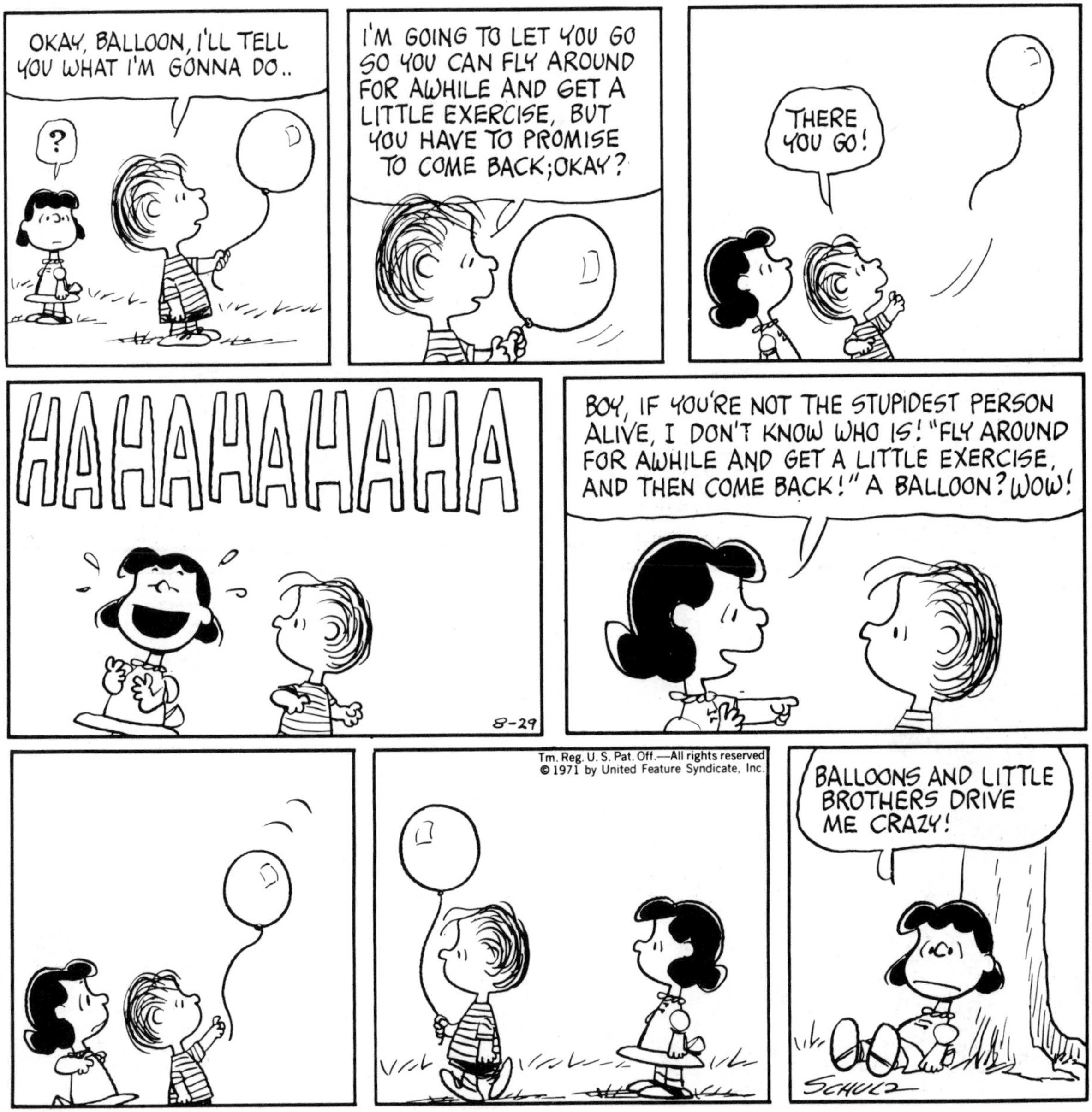
OKAY, BALLOON, I'LL TELL YOU WHAT I'M GONNA DO..
?
I'M GOING TO LET YOU GO SO YOU CAN FLY AROUND FOR AWHILE AND GET A LITTLE EXERCISE, BUT YOU HAVE TO PROMISE TO COME BACK; OKAY?
THERE YOU GO!
HAHAHAHAHAHA
8-29
BOY, IF YOU'RE NOT THE STUPIDEST PERSON ALIVE, I DON'T KNOW WHO IS! "FLY AROUND FOR AWHILE AND GET A LITTLE EXERCISE, AND THEN COME BACK!" A BALLOON? WOW!
Tm. Reg. U. S. Pat. Off.—All rights reserved
© 1971 by United Feature Syndicate, Inc.
BALLOONS AND LITTLE BROTHERS DRIVE ME CRAZY!
SCHULZ

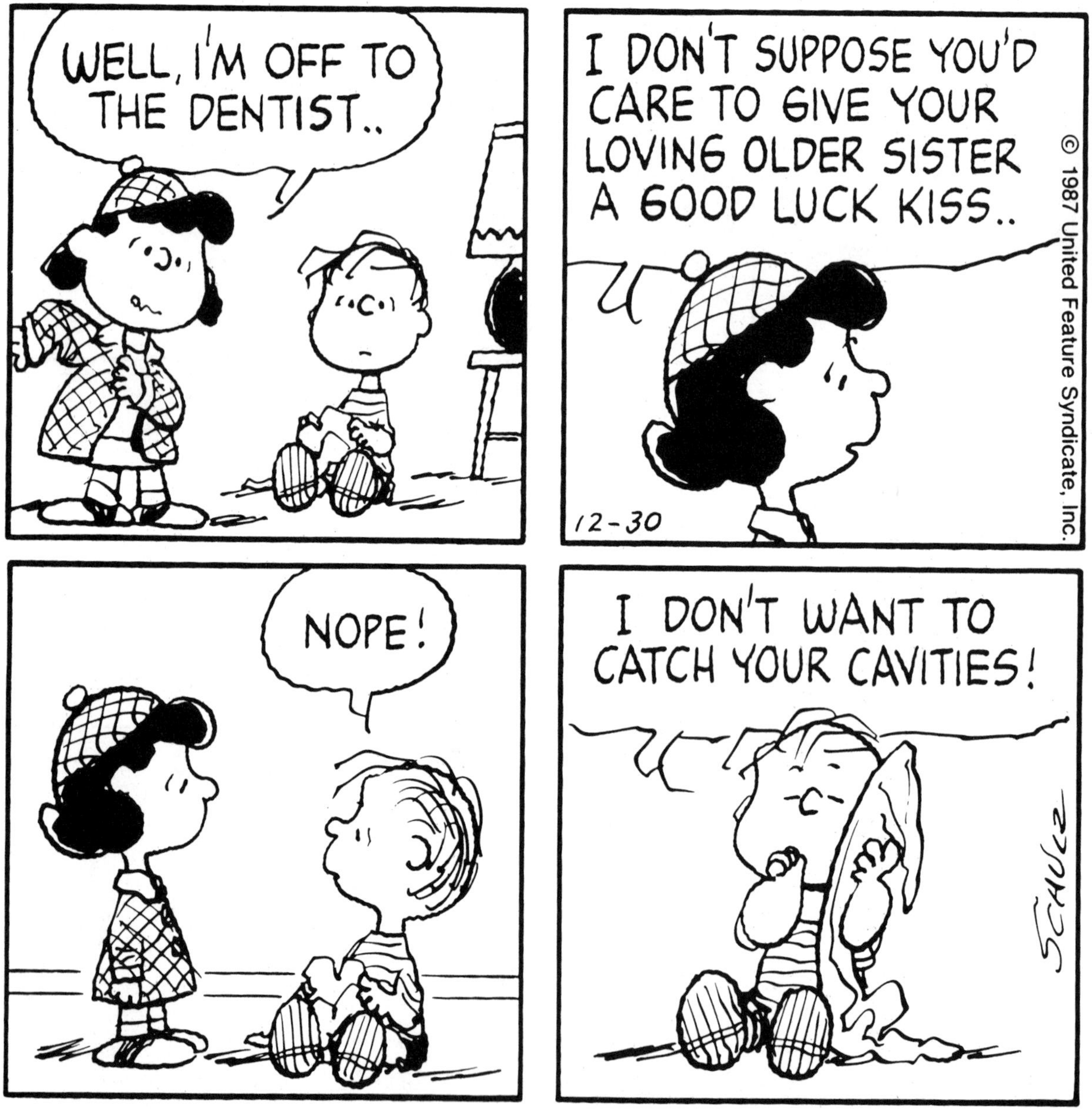
WELL, I'M OFF TO THE DENTIST..
I DON'T SUPPOSE YOU'D CARE TO GIVE YOUR LOVING OLDER SISTER A GOOD LUCK KISS..
12-30
© 1987 United Feature Syndicate, Inc.
NOPE!
I DON'T WANT TO CATCH YOUR CAVITIES!
SCHULZ

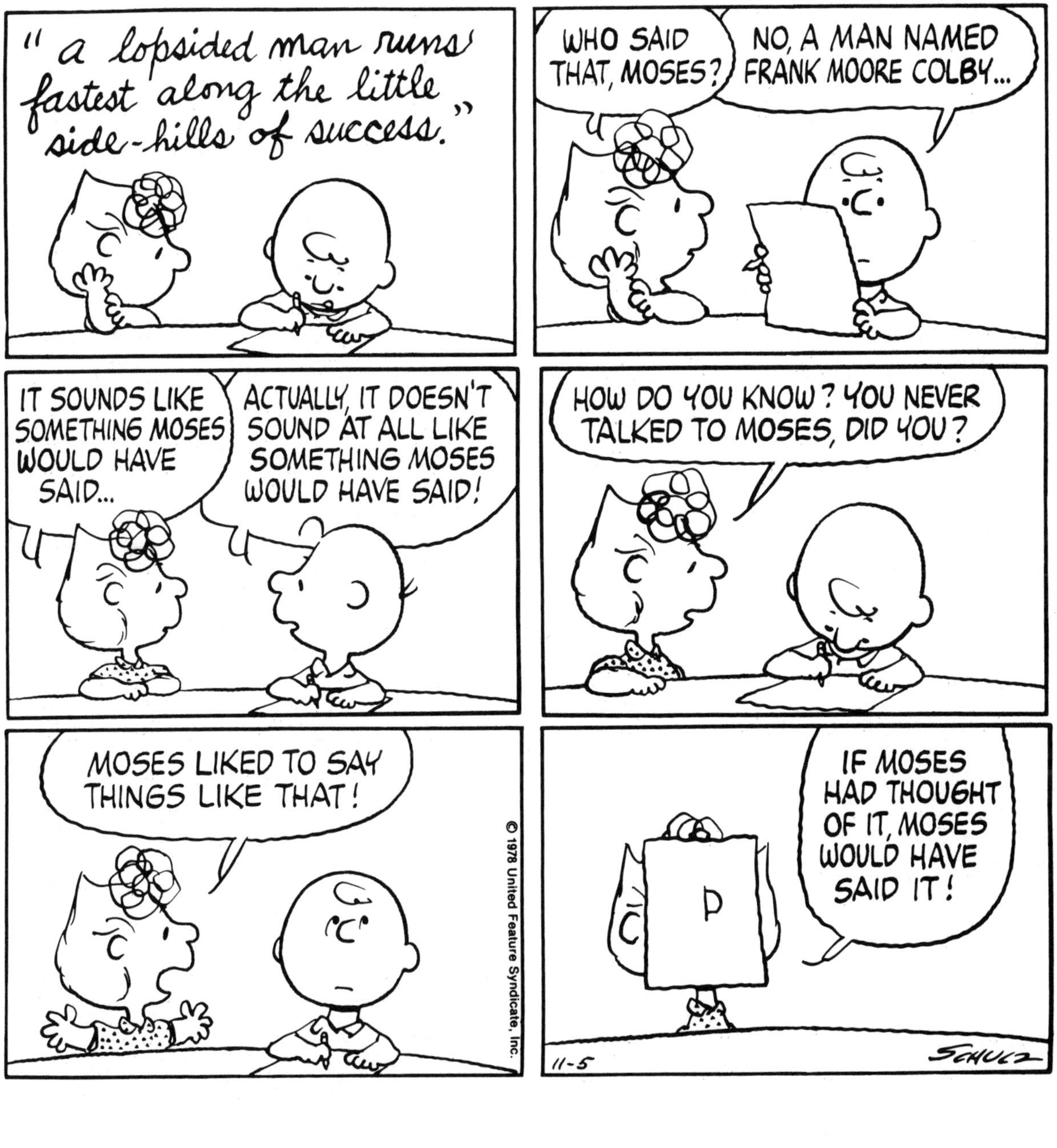
" a lopsided man runs fastest along the little side-hills of success."
WHO SAID THAT, MOSES?
NO, A MAN NAMED FRANK MOORE COLBY...
IT SOUNDS LIKE SOMETHING MOSES WOULD HAVE SAID...
ACTUALLY, IT DOESN'T SOUND AT ALL LIKE SOMETHING MOSES WOULD HAVE SAID!
HOW DO YOU KNOW? YOU NEVER TALKED TO MOSES, DID YOU?
MOSES LIKED TO SAY THINGS LIKE THAT!
© 1978 United Feature Syndicate, Inc.
IF MOSES HAD THOUGHT OF IT, MOSES WOULD HAVE SAID IT!
11-5
SCHULZ

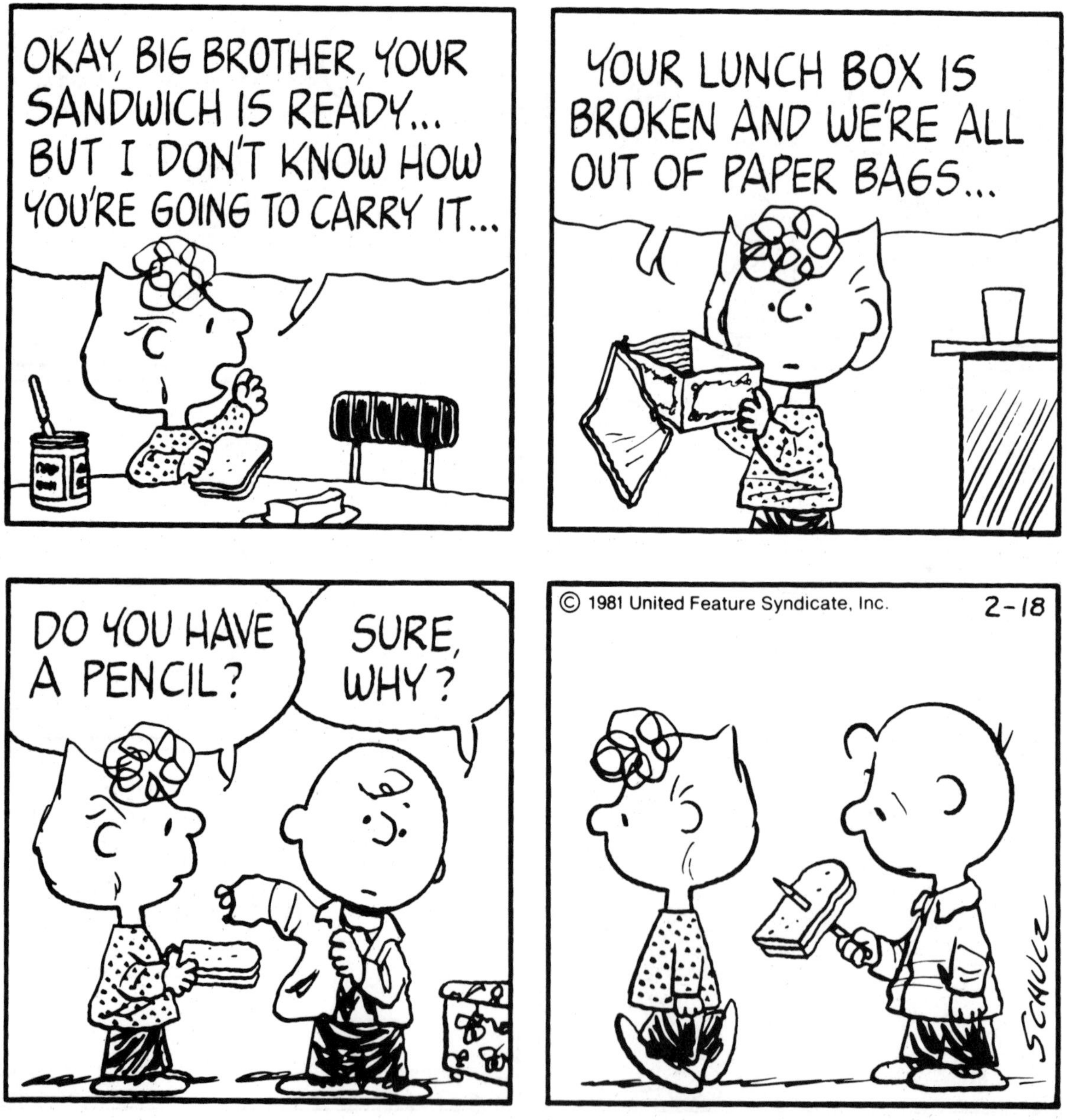
OKAY, BIG BROTHER, YOUR SANDWICH IS READY... BUT I DON'T KNOW HOW YOU'RE GOING TO CARRY IT...
YOUR LUNCH BOX IS BROKEN AND WE'RE ALL OUT OF PAPER BAGS...
DO YOU HAVE A PENCIL?
SURE, WHY?
© 1981 United Feature Syndicate, Inc.
2-18
SCHULZ

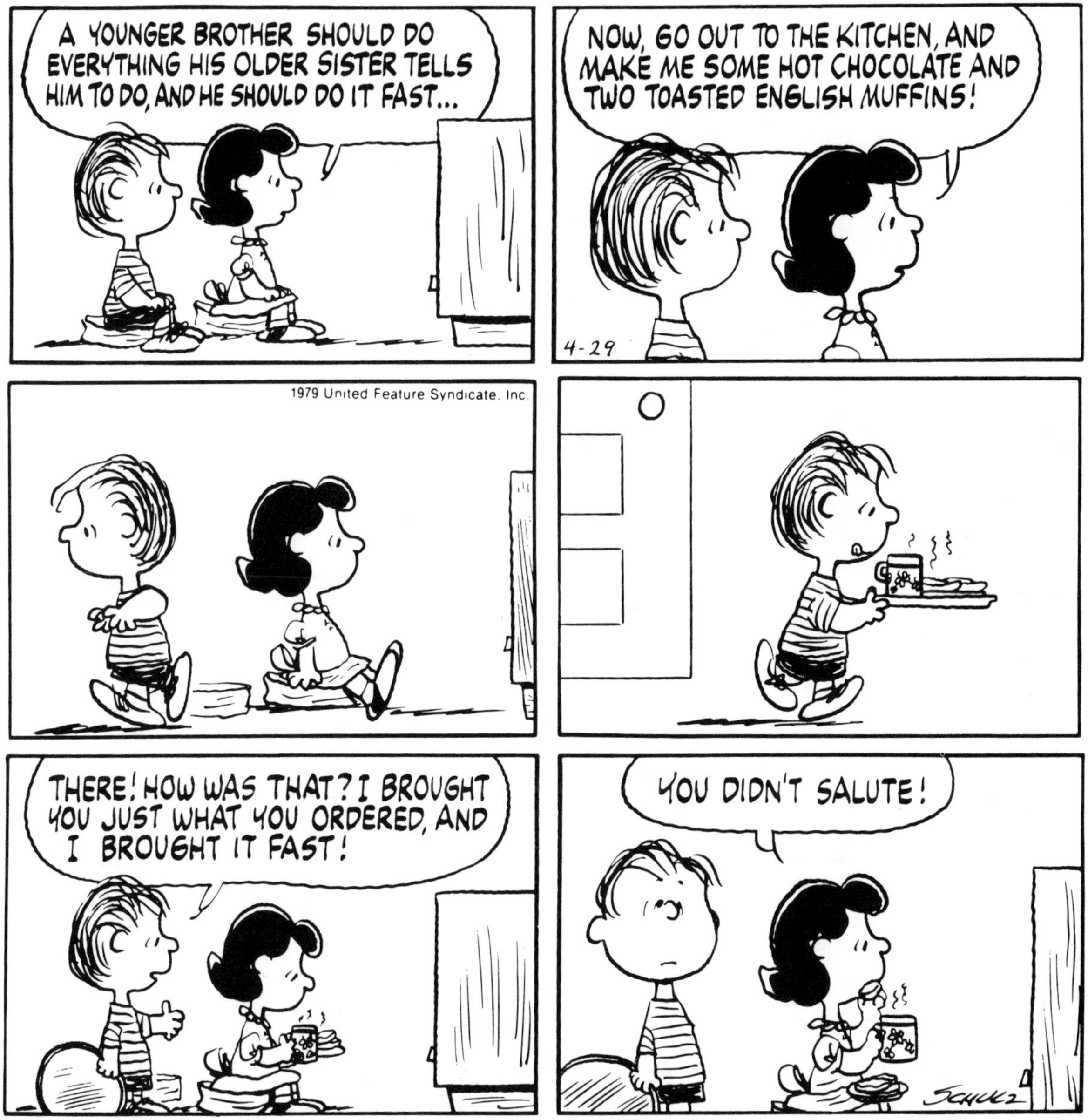
A YOUNGER BROTHER SHOULD DO EVERYTHING HIS OLDER SISTER TELLS HIM TO DO, AND HE SHOULD DO IT FAST...
NOW, GO OUT TO THE KITCHEN, AND MAKE ME SOME HOT CHOCOLATE AND TWO TOASTED ENGLISH MUFFINS!
4-29
1979 United Feature Syndicate, Inc.
THERE! HOW WAS THAT? I BROUGHT YOU JUST WHAT YOU ORDERED, AND I BROUGHT IT FAST!
YOU DIDN'T SALUTE!
SCHULZ

BROTHERS AND SISTERS

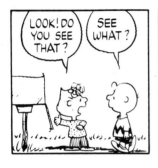

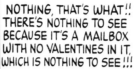

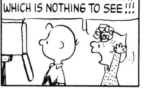

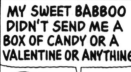

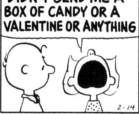

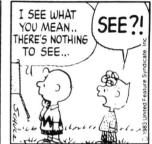

LOOK! DO YOU SEE THAT?
SEE WHAT?
NOTHING, THAT'S WHAT!! THERE'S NOTHING TO SEE BECAUSE IT'S A MAILBOX WITH NO VALENTINES IN IT, WHICH IS NOTHING TO SEE!!!
MY SWEET BABBOO DIDN'T SEND ME A BOX OF CANDY OR A VALENTINE OR ANYTHING
2-14
I SEE WHAT YOU MEAN.. THERE'S NOTHING TO SEE...
SEE?!
SCHULZ
© 1983 United Feature Syndicate, Inc.

SALLY, GET UP! YOU'RE GONNA BE LATE FOR SCHOOL!
LINUS DIDN'T SEND ME A VALENTINE, AND HE BROKE MY HEART AND I'M NEVER GOING TO SCHOOL AGAIN!
AND IF YOU SEE MY SWEET AN' SOUR BABBOO, PUNCH HIM IN THE NOSE!
"SWEET AN' SOUR"?
© 1983 United Feature Syndicate, Inc.
SCHULZ
2-15

YOU DIDN'T SEND MY SISTER A VALENTINE... YOU BROKE HER HEART..
2-16
TECHNICALLY, I SHOULD PUNCH YOU IN THE NOSE!
I HOPE YOU DON'T
© 1983 United Feature Syndicate, Inc.
YOU'D PROBABLY MISS, AND HIT ME IN THE EYE!
SCHULZ

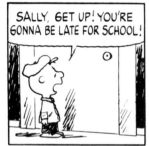

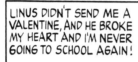

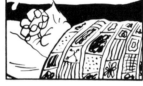

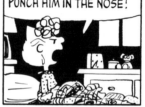

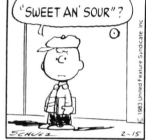

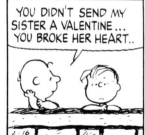

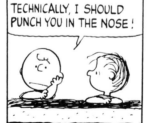

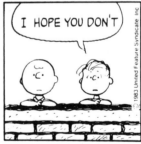

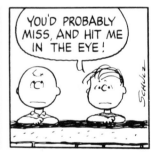

IT'S ALL RELATIVE

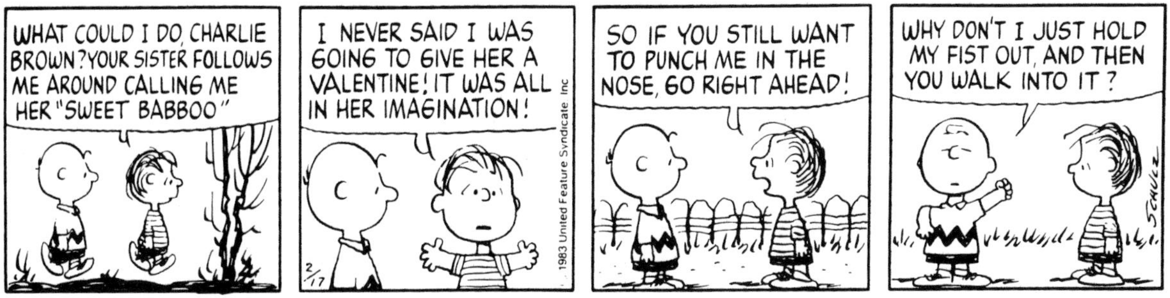
WHAT COULD I DO, CHARLIE BROWN? YOUR SISTER FOLLOWS ME AROUND CALLING ME HER "SWEET BABBOO"
I NEVER SAID I WAS GOING TO GIVE HER A VALENTINE! IT WAS ALL IN HER IMAGINATION!
2/17
© 1983 United Feature Syndicate, Inc.
SO IF YOU STILL WANT TO PUNCH ME IN THE NOSE, GO RIGHT AHEAD!
WHY DON'T I JUST HOLD MY FIST OUT, AND THEN YOU WALK INTO IT?
SCHULZ

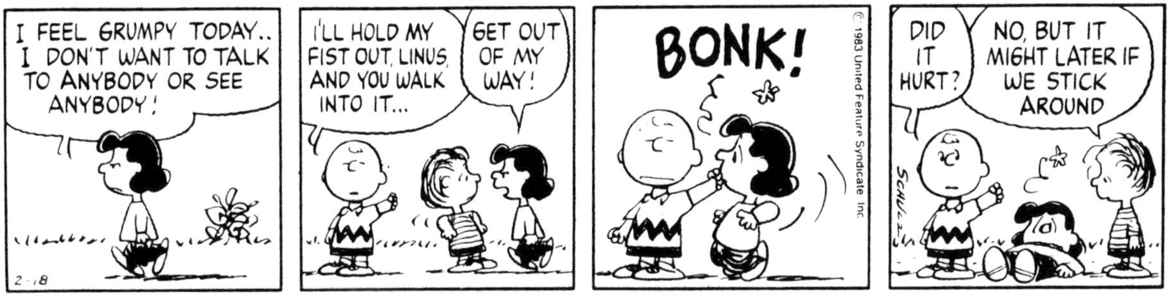
I FEEL GRUMPY TODAY.. I DON'T WANT TO TALK TO ANYBODY OR SEE ANYBODY!
2-18
I'LL HOLD MY FIST OUT, LINUS, AND YOU WALK INTO IT...
GET OUT OF MY WAY!
BONK!
© 1983 United Feature Syndicate, Inc.
DID IT HURT?
NO, BUT IT MIGHT LATER IF WE STICK AROUND
SCHULZ

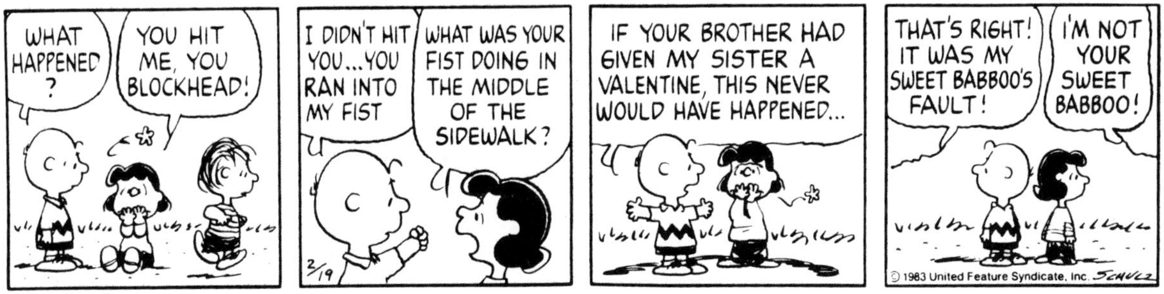
WHAT HAPPENED?
YOU HIT ME, YOU BLOCKHEAD!
I DIDN'T HIT YOU...YOU RAN INTO MY FIST
WHAT WAS YOUR FIST DOING IN THE MIDDLE OF THE SIDEWALK?
2/19
IF YOUR BROTHER HAD GIVEN MY SISTER A VALENTINE, THIS NEVER WOULD HAVE HAPPENED...
THAT'S RIGHT! IT WAS MY SWEET BABBOO'S FAULT!
I'M NOT YOUR SWEET BABBOO!
© 1983 United Feature Syndicate, Inc. SCHULZ

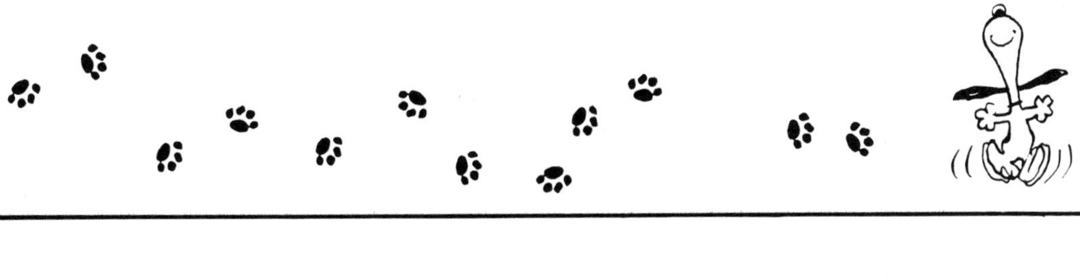

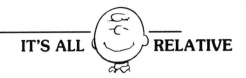

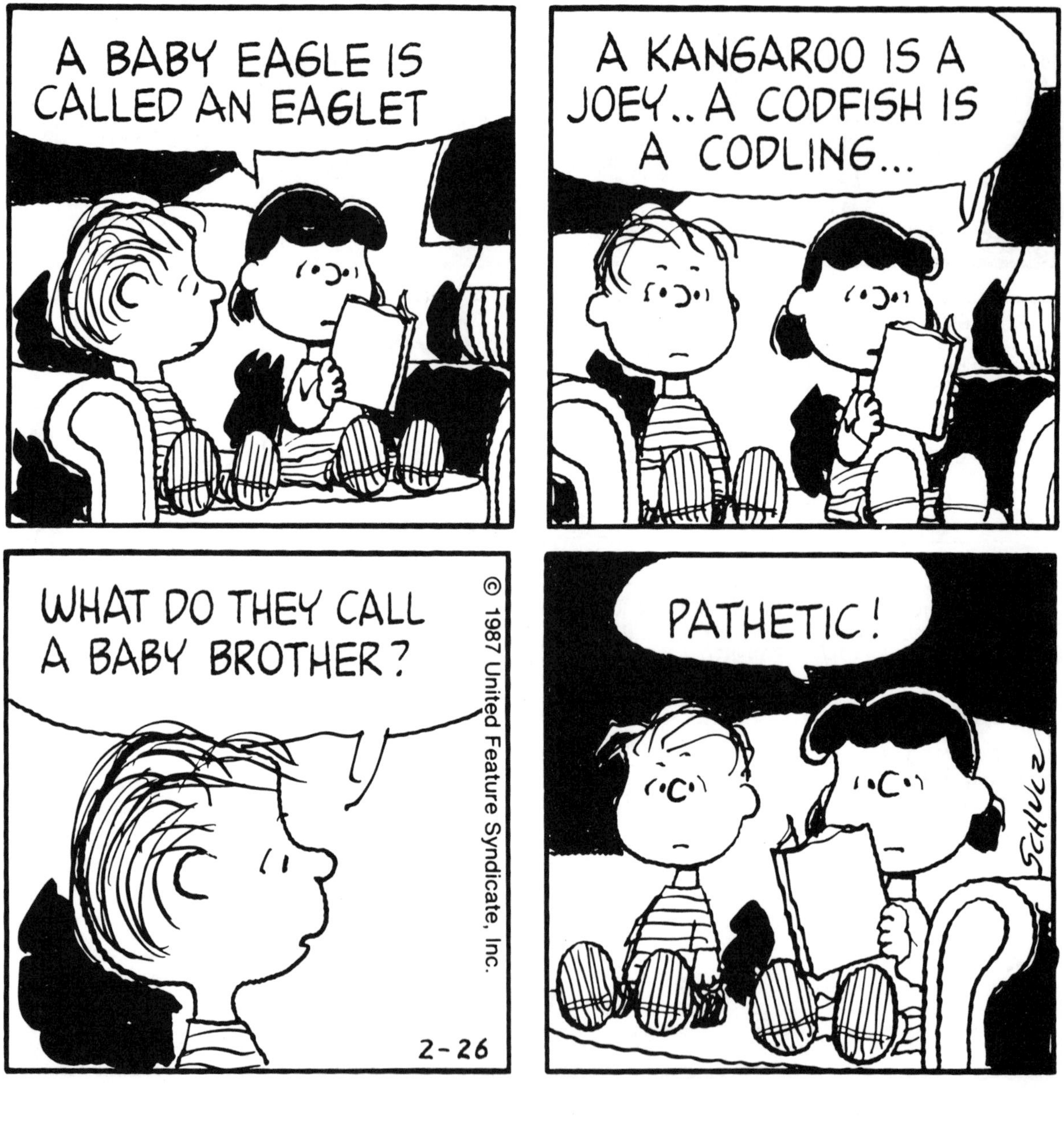
A BABY EAGLE IS CALLED AN EAGLET
A KANGAROO IS A JOEY.. A CODFISH IS A CODLING...
WHAT DO THEY CALL A BABY BROTHER?
© 1987 United Feature Syndicate, Inc.
2-26
PATHETIC!
SCHULZ

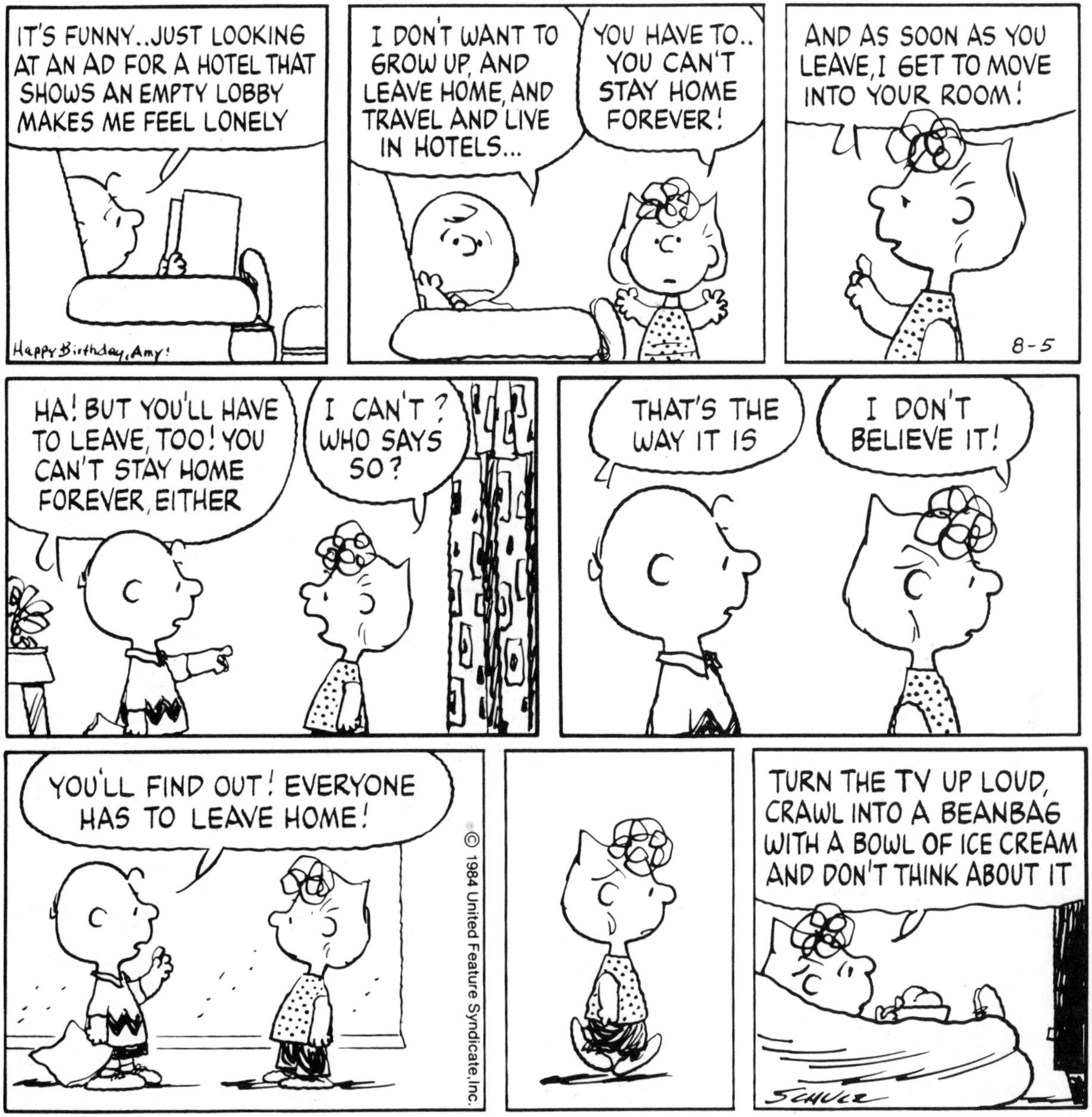
IT'S FUNNY..JUST LOOKING AT AN AD FOR A HOTEL THAT SHOWS AN EMPTY LOBBY MAKES ME FEEL LONELY
Happy Birthday, Amy!
I DON'T WANT TO GROW UP, AND LEAVE HOME, AND TRAVEL AND LIVE IN HOTELS...
YOU HAVE TO.. YOU CAN'T STAY HOME FOREVER!
AND AS SOON AS YOU LEAVE, I GET TO MOVE INTO YOUR ROOM!
8-5
HA! BUT YOU'LL HAVE TO LEAVE, TOO! YOU CAN'T STAY HOME FOREVER, EITHER
I CAN'T? WHO SAYS SO?
THAT'S THE WAY IT IS
I DON'T BELIEVE IT!
YOU'LL FIND OUT! EVERYONE HAS TO LEAVE HOME!
© 1984 United Feature Syndicate, Inc.
TURN THE TV UP LOUD, CRAWL INTO A BEANBAG WITH A BOWL OF ICE CREAM AND DON'T THINK ABOUT IT
SCHULZ

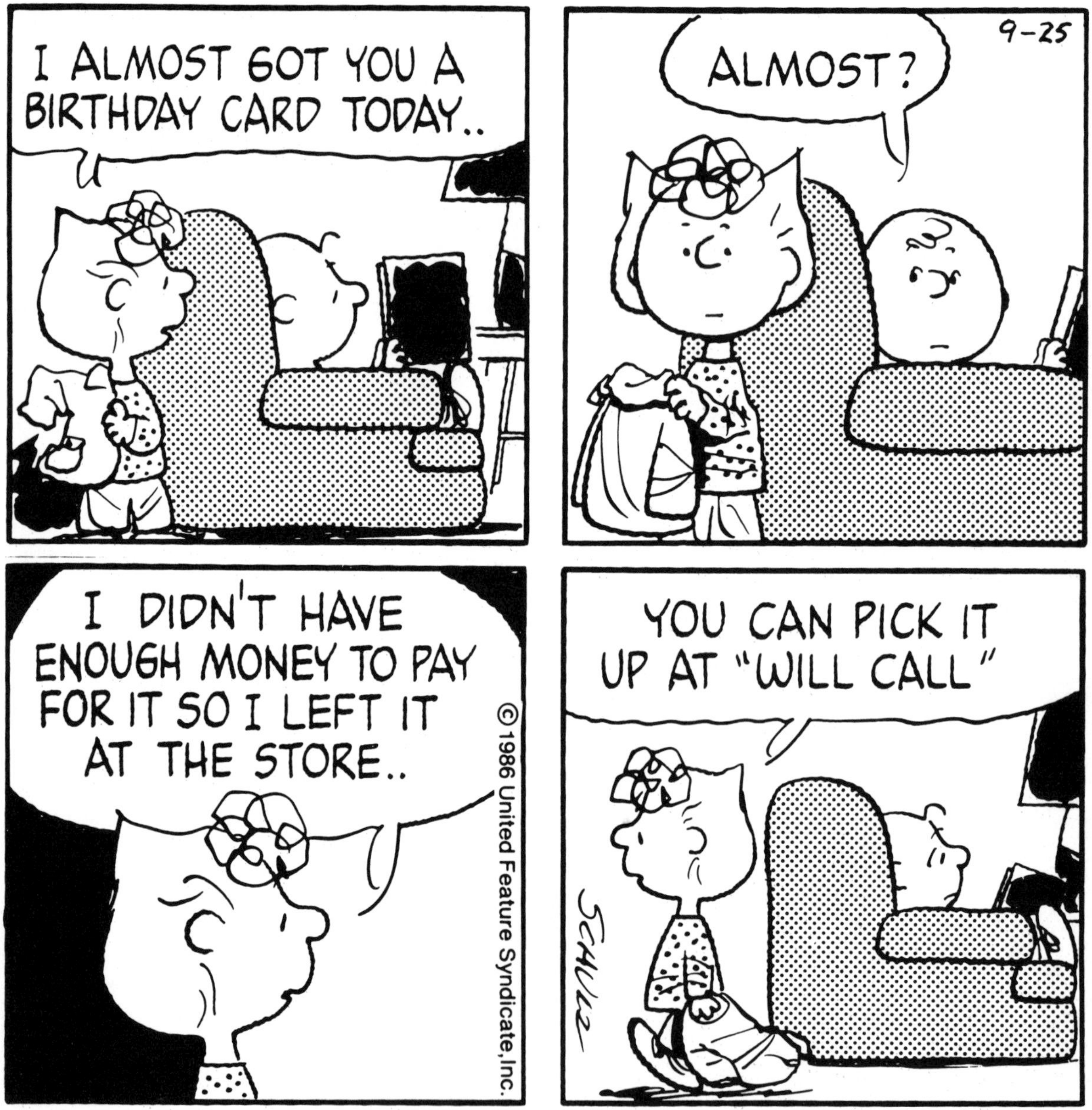
I ALMOST GOT YOU A BIRTHDAY CARD TODAY..
ALMOST?
9-25
I DIDN'T HAVE ENOUGH MONEY TO PAY FOR IT SO I LEFT IT AT THE STORE..
© 1986 United Feature Syndicate, Inc.
YOU CAN PICK IT UP AT "WILL CALL"
SCHULZ

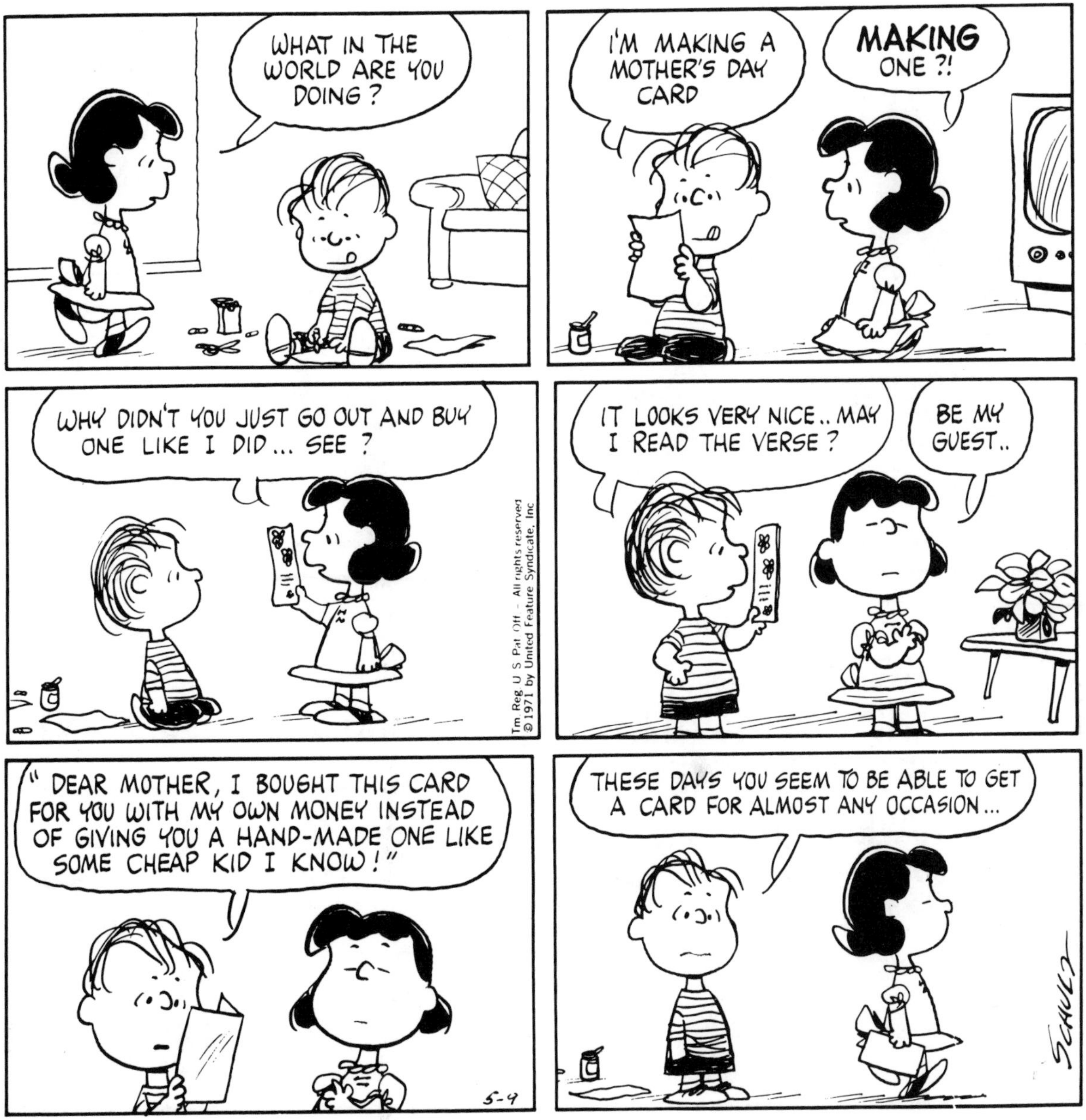
WHAT IN THE WORLD ARE YOU DOING?
I'M MAKING A MOTHER'S DAY CARD
MAKING ONE ?!
WHY DIDN'T YOU JUST GO OUT AND BUY ONE LIKE I DID... SEE ?
IT LOOKS VERY NICE.. MAY I READ THE VERSE ?
BE MY GUEST..
"DEAR MOTHER, I BOUGHT THIS CARD FOR YOU WITH MY OWN MONEY INSTEAD OF GIVING YOU A HAND-MADE ONE LIKE SOME CHEAP KID I KNOW!"
THESE DAYS YOU SEEM TO BE ABLE TO GET A CARD FOR ALMOST ANY OCCASION...
5-9
SCHULZ

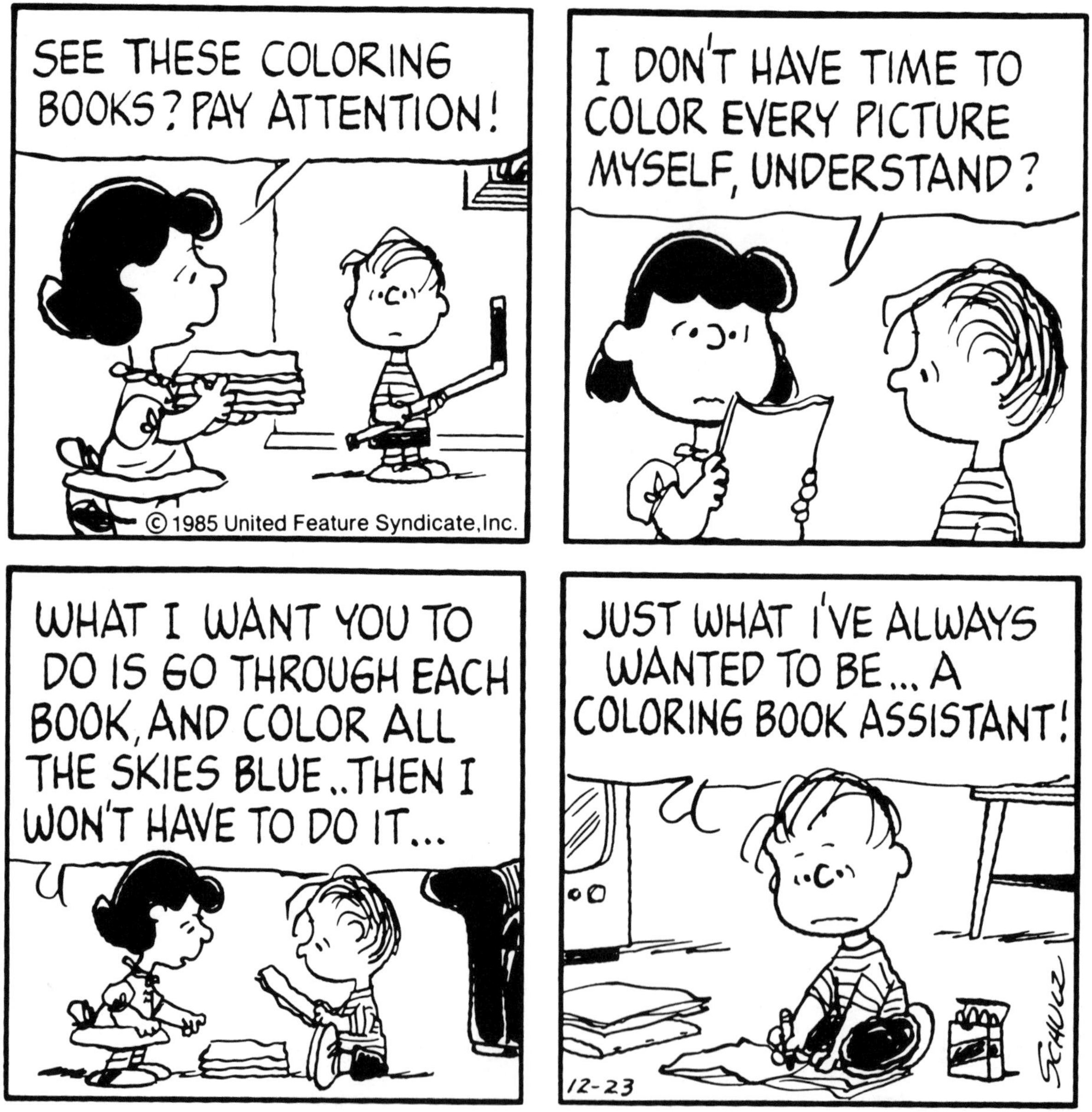
SEE THESE COLORING BOOKS? PAY ATTENTION!
© 1985 United Feature Syndicate, Inc.
I DON'T HAVE TIME TO COLOR EVERY PICTURE MYSELF, UNDERSTAND?
WHAT I WANT YOU TO DO IS GO THROUGH EACH BOOK, AND COLOR ALL THE SKIES BLUE..THEN I WON'T HAVE TO DO IT...
JUST WHAT I'VE ALWAYS WANTED TO BE... A COLORING BOOK ASSISTANT!
12-23
SCHULZ

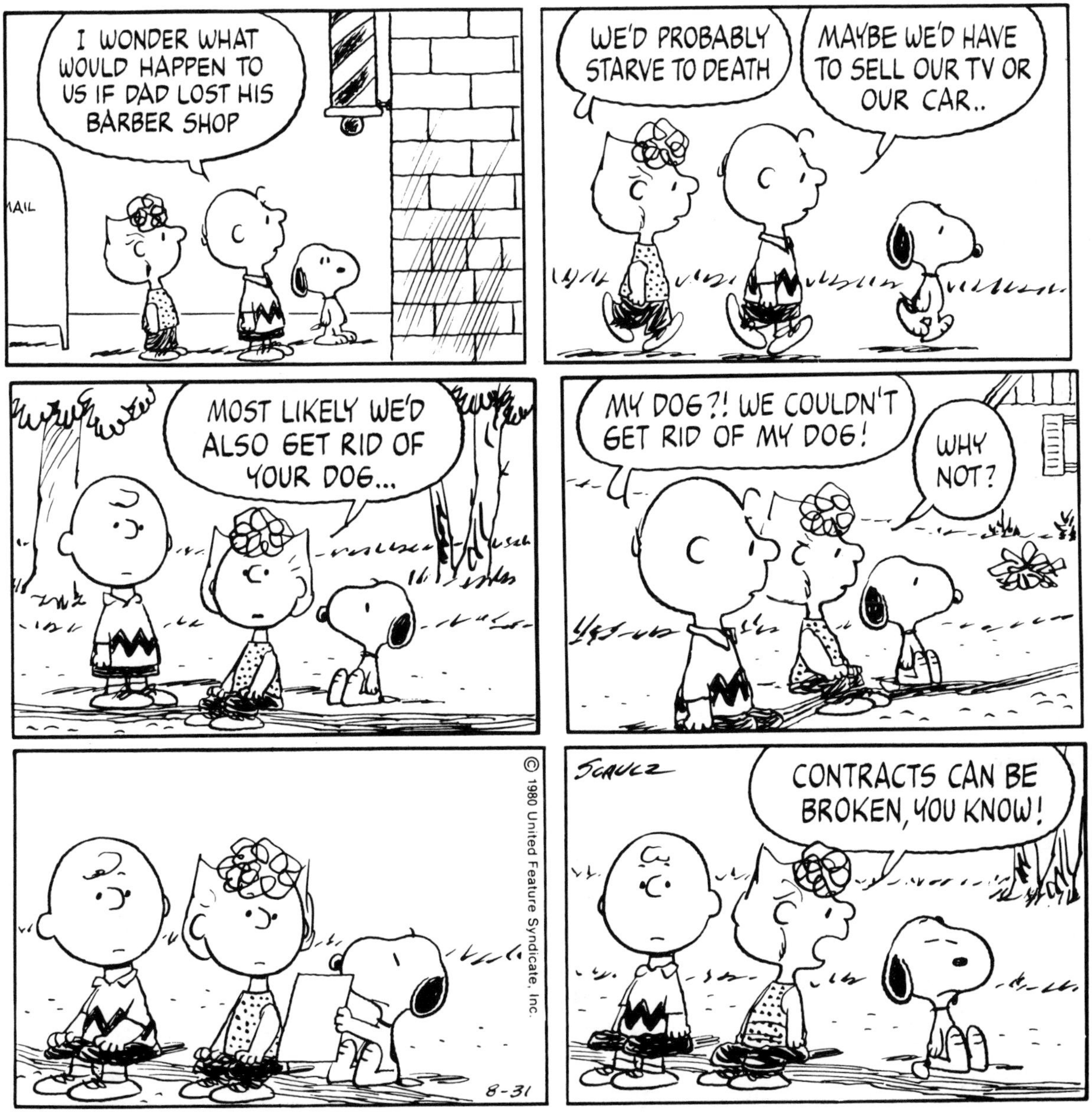
I WONDER WHAT WOULD HAPPEN TO US IF DAD LOST HIS BARBER SHOP
WE'D PROBABLY STARVE TO DEATH
MAYBE WE'D HAVE TO SELL OUR TV OR OUR CAR..
MOST LIKELY WE'D ALSO GET RID OF YOUR DOG...
MY DOG?! WE COULDN'T GET RID OF MY DOG!
WHY NOT?
© 1980 United Feature Syndicate, Inc.
8-31
SCHULZ
CONTRACTS CAN BE BROKEN, YOU KNOW!

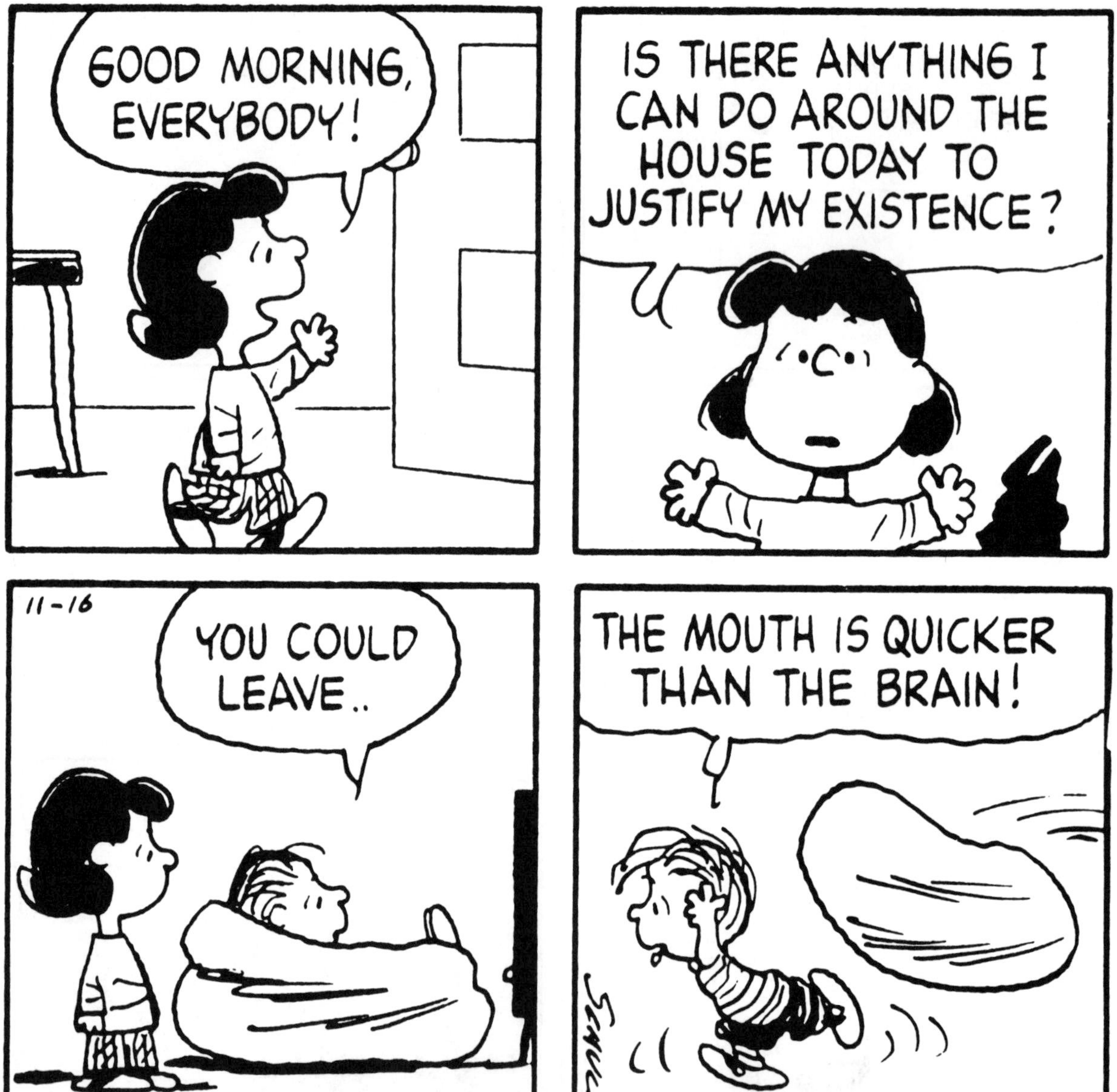
GOOD MORNING, EVERYBODY!
IS THERE ANYTHING I CAN DO AROUND THE HOUSE TODAY TO JUSTIFY MY EXISTENCE?
11-16
YOU COULD LEAVE..
THE MOUTH IS QUICKER THAN THE BRAIN!
SCHULZ
© 1985 United Feature Syndicate, Inc.

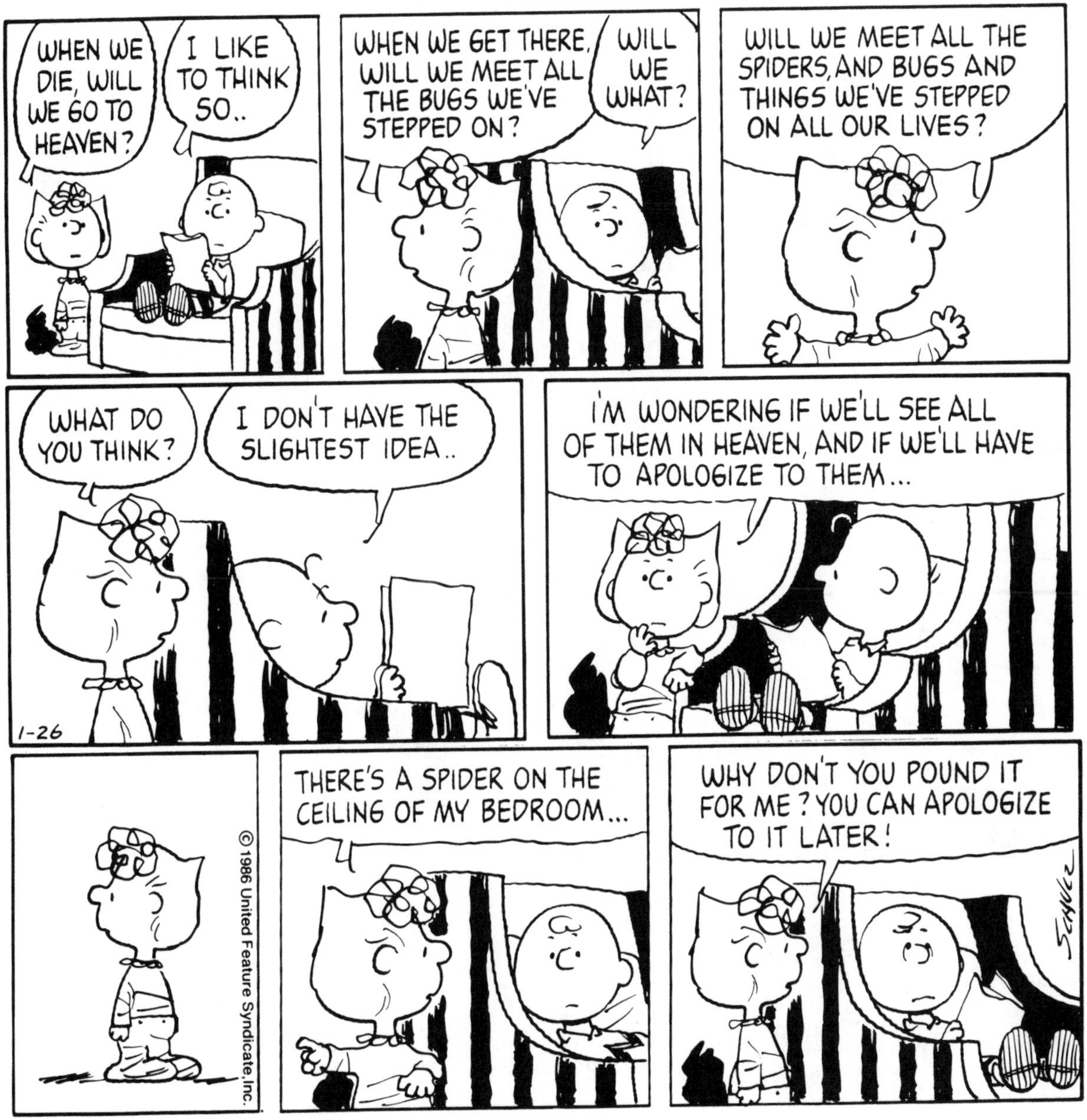
WHEN WE DIE, WILL WE GO TO HEAVEN?
I LIKE TO THINK SO..
WHEN WE GET THERE, WILL WE MEET ALL THE BUGS WE'VE STEPPED ON?
WILL WE WHAT?
WILL WE MEET ALL THE SPIDERS, AND BUGS AND THINGS WE'VE STEPPED ON ALL OUR LIVES?
WHAT DO YOU THINK?
I DON'T HAVE THE SLIGHTEST IDEA..
1-26
I'M WONDERING IF WE'LL SEE ALL OF THEM IN HEAVEN, AND IF WE'LL HAVE TO APOLOGIZE TO THEM...
© 1986 United Feature Syndicate, Inc.
THERE'S A SPIDER ON THE CEILING OF MY BEDROOM...
WHY DON'T YOU POUND IT FOR ME? YOU CAN APOLOGIZE TO IT LATER!
SCHULZ

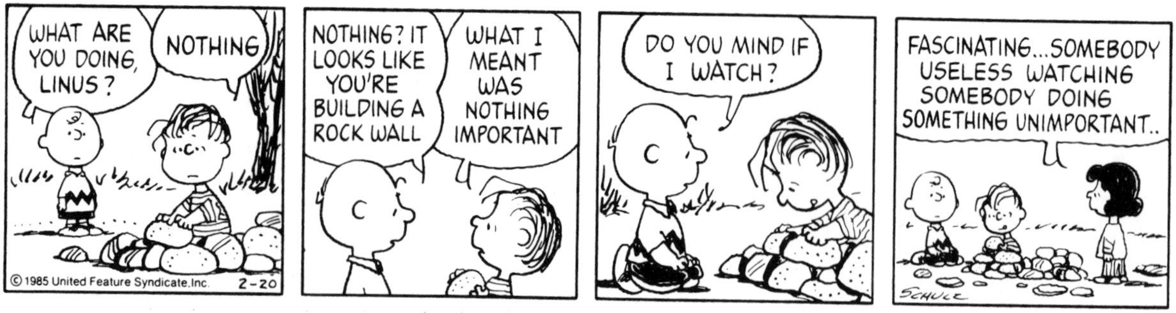
WHAT ARE YOU DOING, LINUS?
NOTHING
© 1985 United Feature Syndicate, Inc.
2-20
NOTHING? IT LOOKS LIKE YOU'RE BUILDING A ROCK WALL
WHAT I MEANT WAS NOTHING IMPORTANT
DO YOU MIND IF I WATCH?
FASCINATING...SOMEBODY USELESS WATCHING SOMEBODY DOING SOMETHING UNIMPORTANT..
SCHULZ

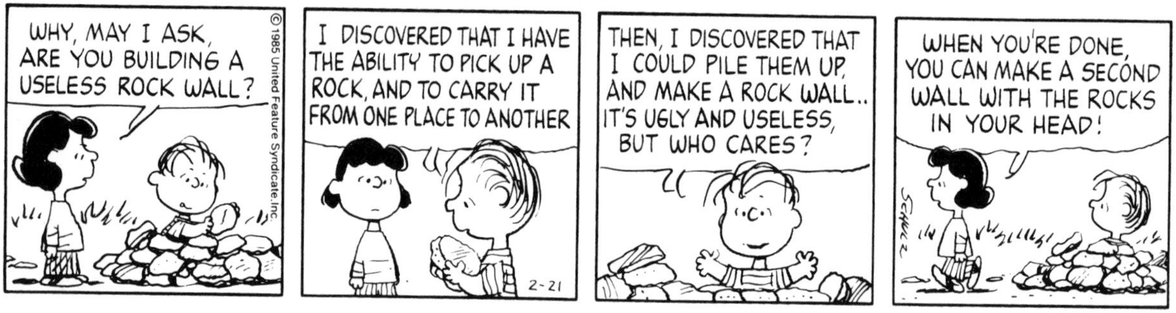
WHY, MAY I ASK, ARE YOU BUILDING A USELESS ROCK WALL?
© 1985 United Feature Syndicate, Inc.
I DISCOVERED THAT I HAVE THE ABILITY TO PICK UP A ROCK, AND TO CARRY IT FROM ONE PLACE TO ANOTHER
2-21
THEN, I DISCOVERED THAT I COULD PILE THEM UP, AND MAKE A ROCK WALL.. IT'S UGLY AND USELESS, BUT WHO CARES?
WHEN YOU'RE DONE, YOU CAN MAKE A SECOND WALL WITH THE ROCKS IN YOUR HEAD!
SCHULZ

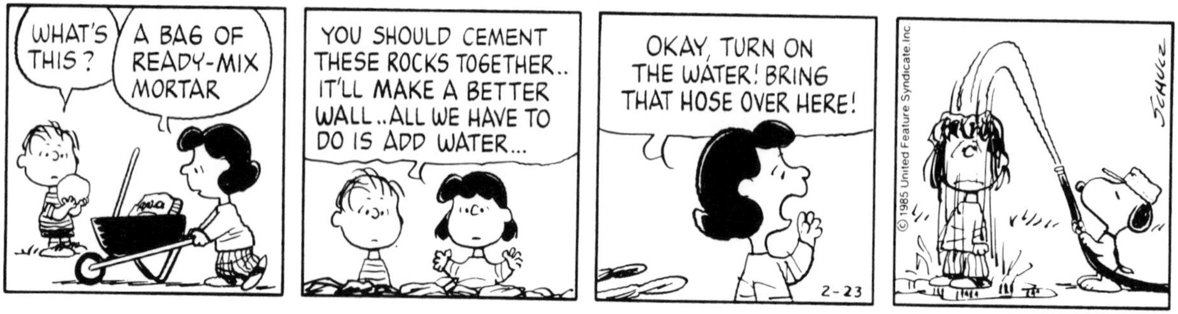
WHAT'S THIS?
A BAG OF READY-MIX MORTAR
YOU SHOULD CEMENT THESE ROCKS TOGETHER.. IT'LL MAKE A BETTER WALL..ALL WE HAVE TO DO IS ADD WATER...
OKAY, TURN ON THE WATER! BRING THAT HOSE OVER HERE!
2-23
© 1985 United Feature Syndicate, Inc.
SCHULZ

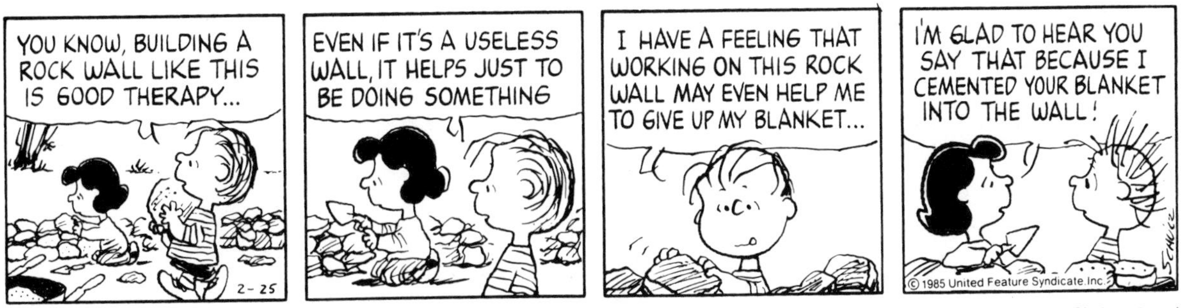
YOU KNOW, BUILDING A ROCK WALL LIKE THIS IS GOOD THERAPY...
2-25
EVEN IF IT'S A USELESS WALL, IT HELPS JUST TO BE DOING SOMETHING
I HAVE A FEELING THAT WORKING ON THIS ROCK WALL MAY EVEN HELP ME TO GIVE UP MY BLANKET...
I'M GLAD TO HEAR YOU SAY THAT BECAUSE I CEMENTED YOUR BLANKET INTO THE WALL!
SCHULZ
© 1985 United Feature Syndicate, Inc.

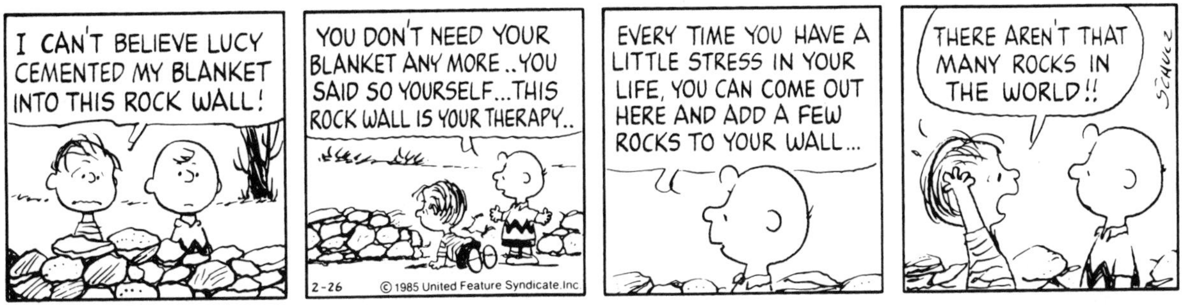
I CAN'T BELIEVE LUCY CEMENTED MY BLANKET INTO THIS ROCK WALL!
YOU DON'T NEED YOUR BLANKET ANY MORE..YOU SAID SO YOURSELF...THIS ROCK WALL IS YOUR THERAPY..
2-26
© 1985 United Feature Syndicate, Inc.
EVERY TIME YOU HAVE A LITTLE STRESS IN YOUR LIFE, YOU CAN COME OUT HERE AND ADD A FEW ROCKS TO YOUR WALL...
THERE AREN'T THAT MANY ROCKS IN THE WORLD!!
SCHULZ

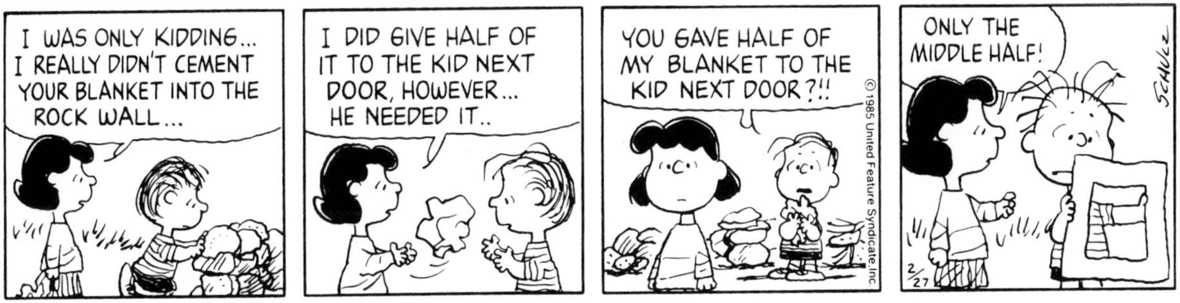
I WAS ONLY KIDDING... I REALLY DIDN'T CEMENT YOUR BLANKET INTO THE ROCK WALL...
I DID GIVE HALF OF IT TO THE KID NEXT DOOR, HOWEVER... HE NEEDED IT..
YOU GAVE HALF OF MY BLANKET TO THE KID NEXT DOOR?!!
© 1985 United Feature Syndicate, Inc.
ONLY THE MIDDLE HALF!
SCHULZ
2/27

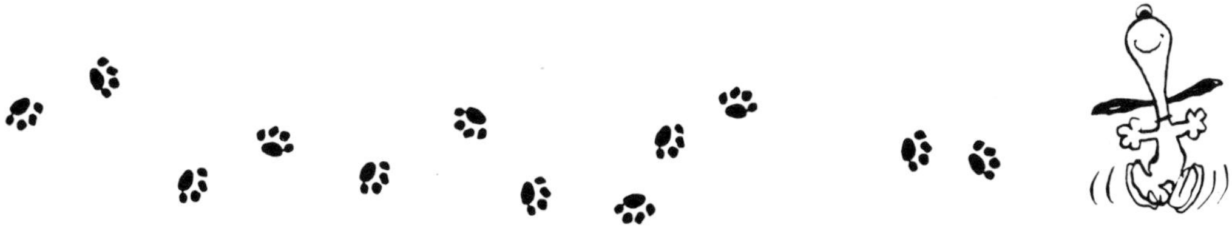

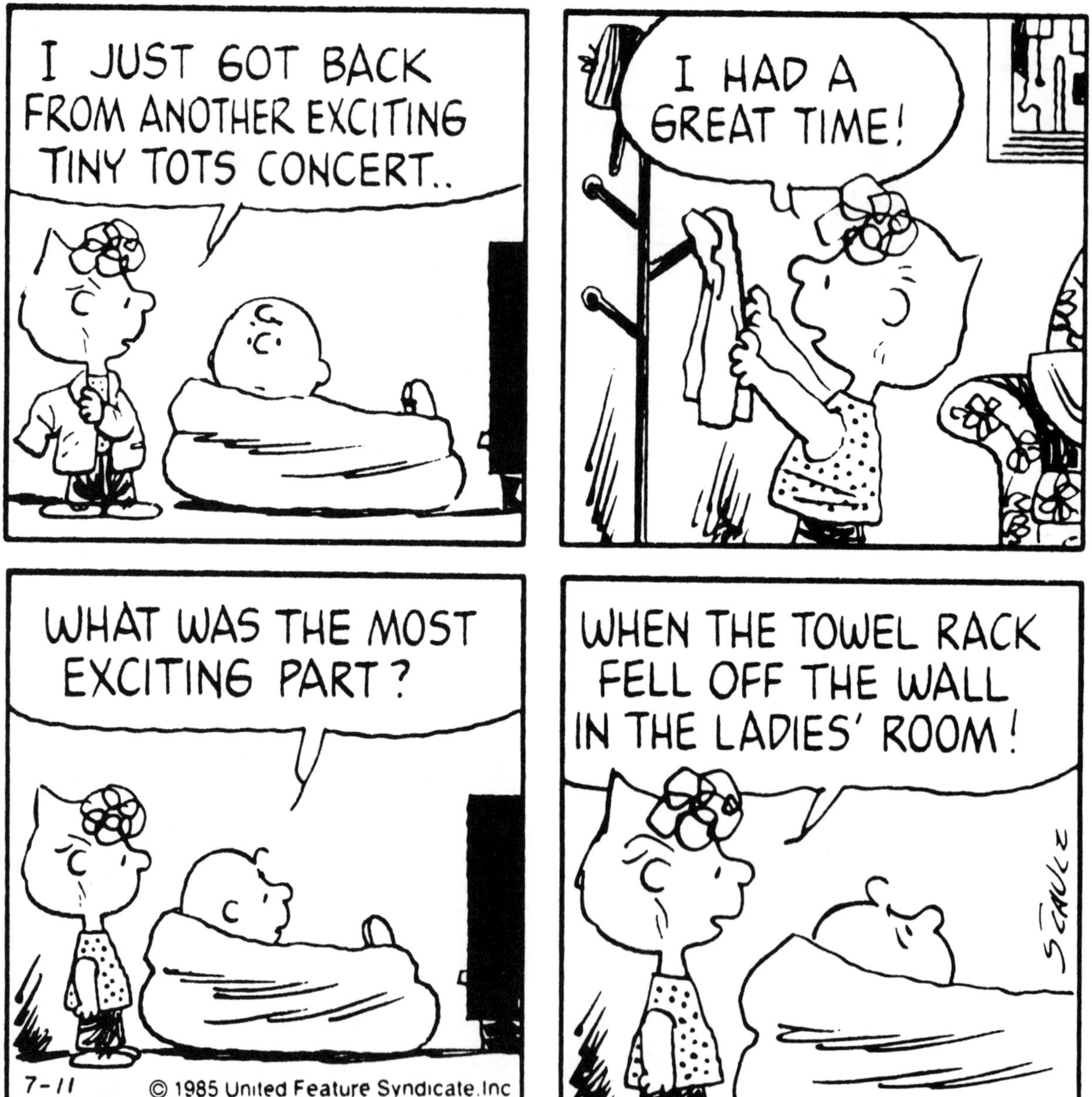
I JUST GOT BACK FROM ANOTHER EXCITING TINY TOTS CONCERT..
I HAD A GREAT TIME!
WHAT WAS THE MOST EXCITING PART?
WHEN THE TOWEL RACK FELL OFF THE WALL IN THE LADIES' ROOM!
SCHULZ
7-11
© 1985 United Feature Syndicate, Inc

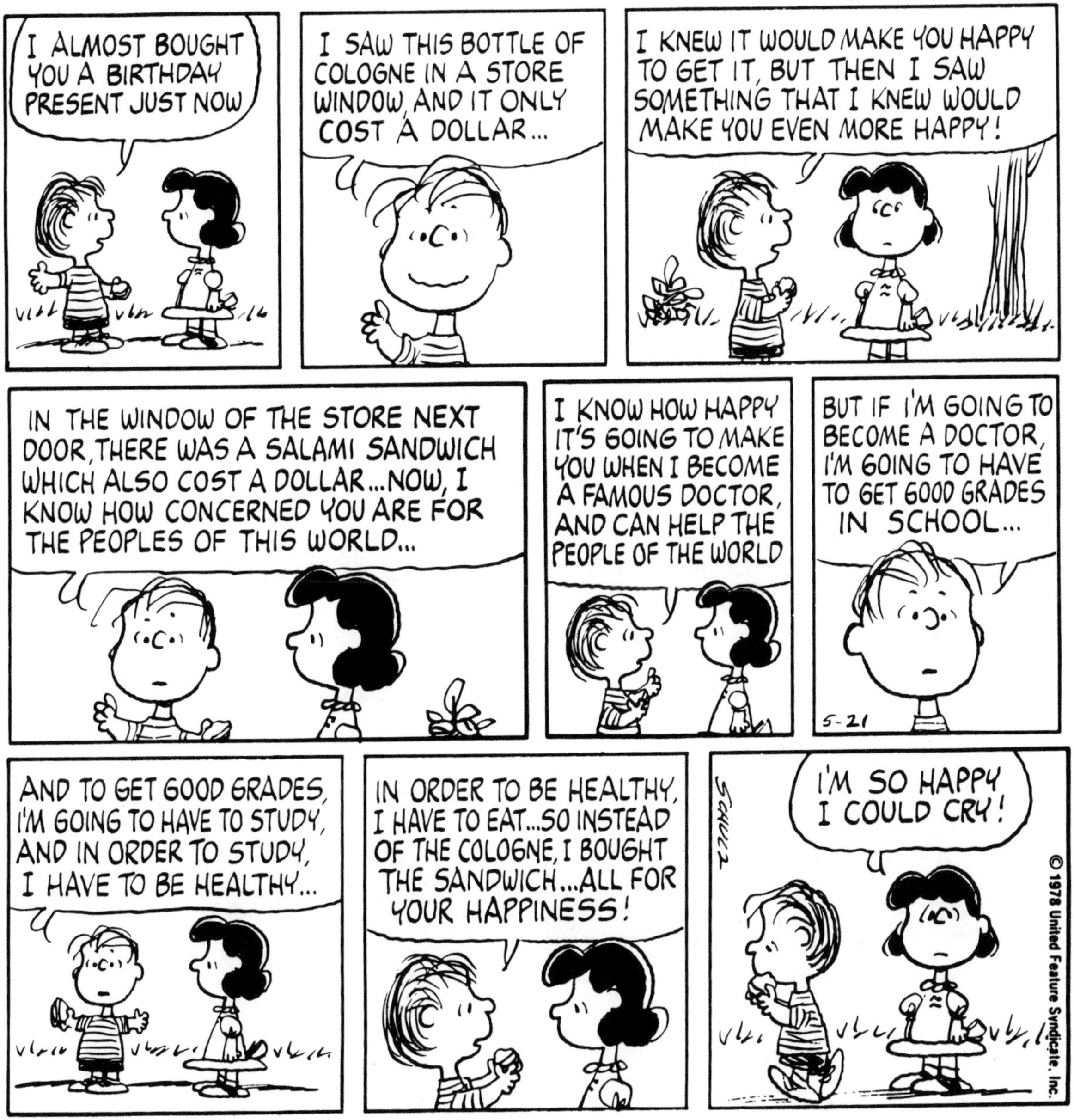
I ALMOST BOUGHT YOU A BIRTHDAY PRESENT JUST NOW
I SAW THIS BOTTLE OF COLOGNE IN A STORE WINDOW, AND IT ONLY COST A DOLLAR...
I KNEW IT WOULD MAKE YOU HAPPY TO GET IT, BUT THEN I SAW SOMETHING THAT I KNEW WOULD MAKE YOU EVEN MORE HAPPY!
IN THE WINDOW OF THE STORE NEXT DOOR, THERE WAS A SALAMI SANDWICH WHICH ALSO COST A DOLLAR...NOW, I KNOW HOW CONCERNED YOU ARE FOR THE PEOPLES OF THIS WORLD...
I KNOW HOW HAPPY IT'S GOING TO MAKE YOU WHEN I BECOME A FAMOUS DOCTOR, AND CAN HELP THE PEOPLE OF THE WORLD
BUT IF I'M GOING TO BECOME A DOCTOR, I'M GOING TO HAVE TO GET GOOD GRADES IN SCHOOL...
5-21
AND TO GET GOOD GRADES, I'M GOING TO HAVE TO STUDY, AND IN ORDER TO STUDY, I HAVE TO BE HEALTHY...
IN ORDER TO BE HEALTHY, I HAVE TO EAT...SO INSTEAD OF THE COLOGNE, I BOUGHT THE SANDWICH...ALL FOR YOUR HAPPINESS!
SCHULZ
I'M SO HAPPY I COULD CRY!
© 1978 United Feature Syndicate, Inc.

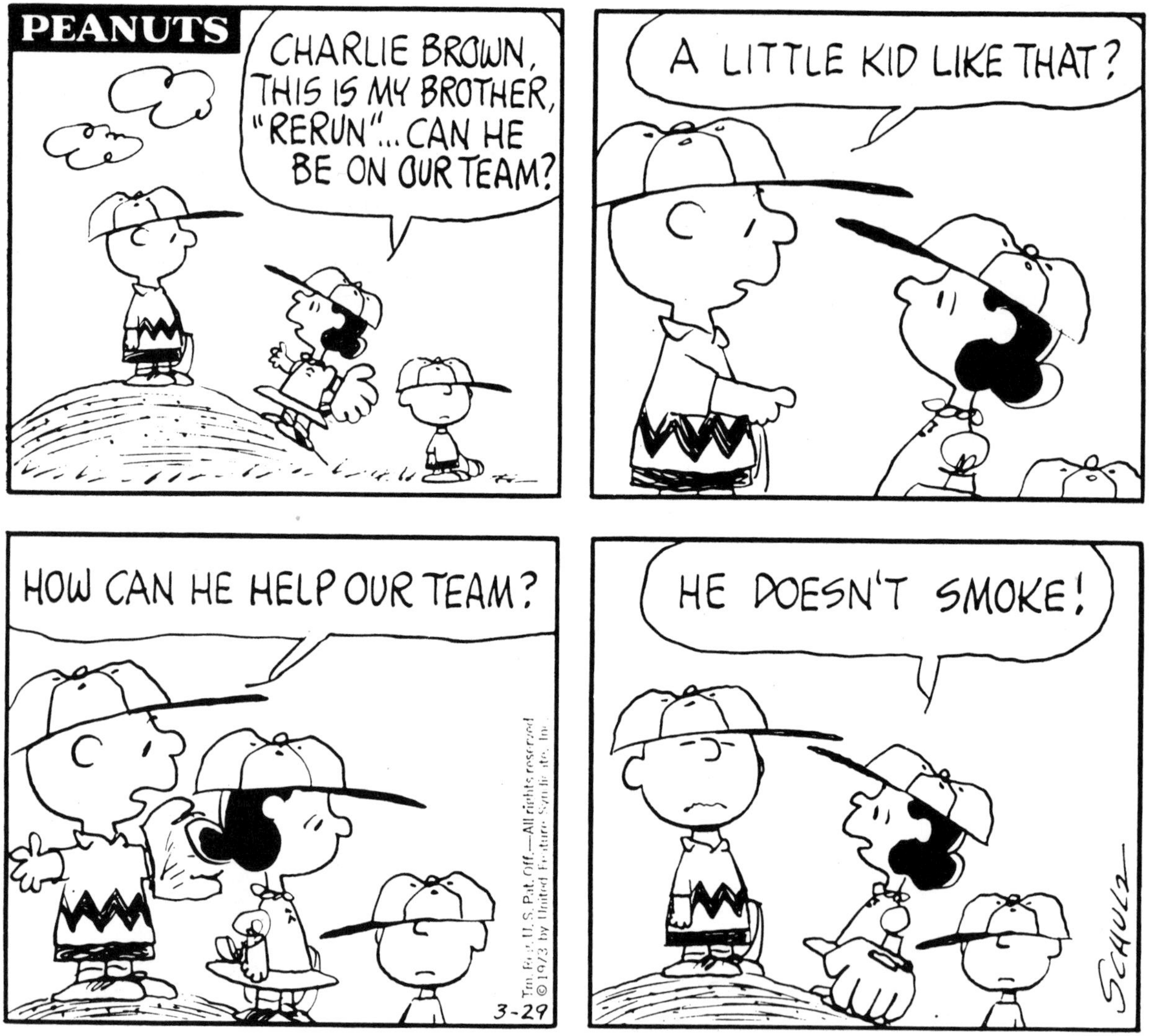
PEANUTS
CHARLIE BROWN, THIS IS MY BROTHER, "RERUN"... CAN HE BE ON OUR TEAM?
A LITTLE KID LIKE THAT?
HOW CAN HE HELP OUR TEAM?
Tm. Reg. U.S. Pat. Off.—All rights reserved
© 1973 by United Feature Syndicate, Inc.
3-29
HE DOESN'T SMOKE!
SCHULZ

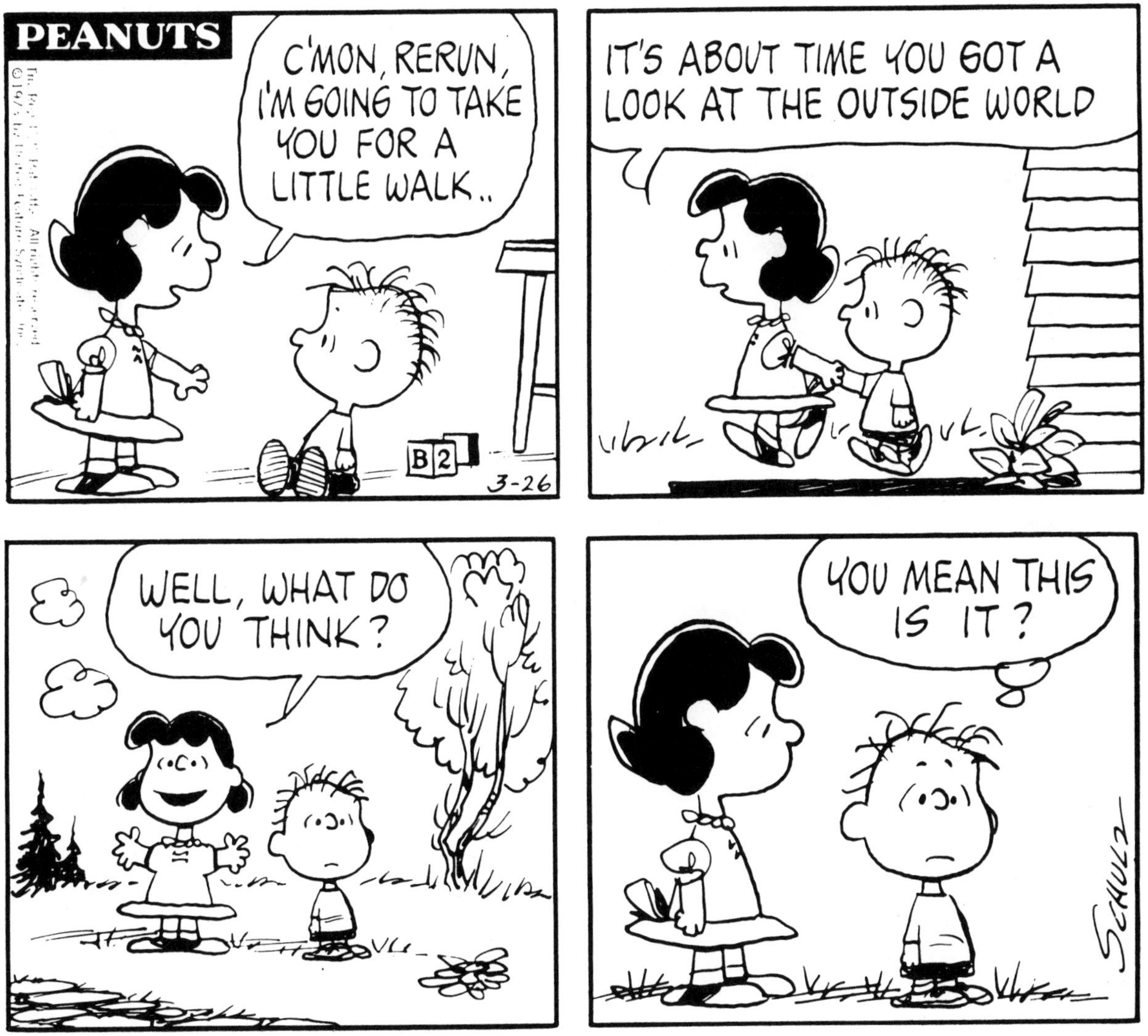
PEANUTS
C'MON, RERUN, I'M GOING TO TAKE YOU FOR A LITTLE WALK..
B 2
3-26
IT'S ABOUT TIME YOU GOT A LOOK AT THE OUTSIDE WORLD
WELL, WHAT DO YOU THINK?
YOU MEAN THIS IS IT?
SCHULZ

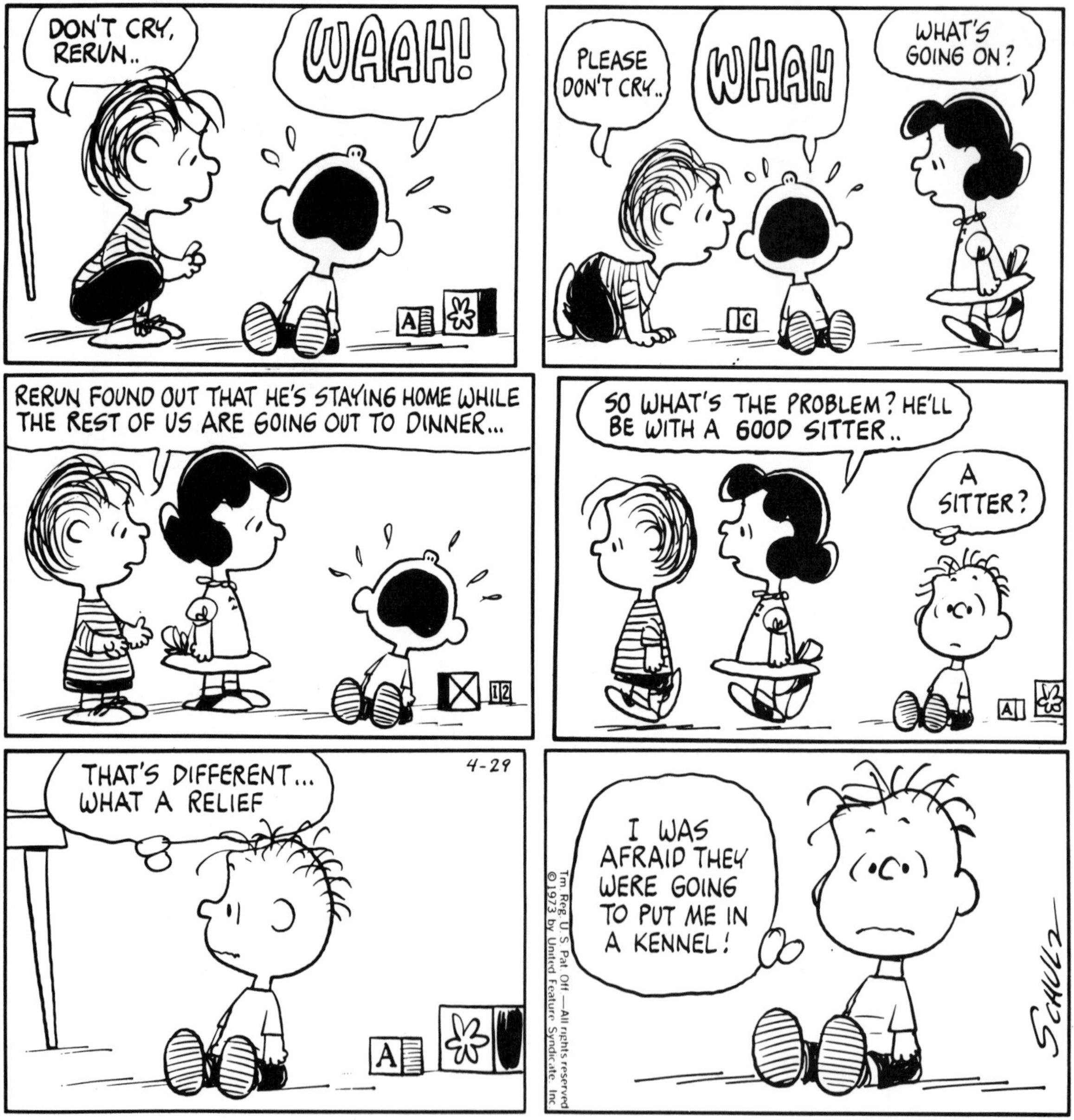
DON'T CRY, RERUN..
WAAH!
PLEASE DON'T CRY..
WHAH
WHAT'S GOING ON?
RERUN FOUND OUT THAT HE'S STAYING HOME WHILE THE REST OF US ARE GOING OUT TO DINNER...
SO WHAT'S THE PROBLEM? HE'LL BE WITH A GOOD SITTER..
A SITTER?
4-29
THAT'S DIFFERENT... WHAT A RELIEF
I WAS AFRAID THEY WERE GOING TO PUT ME IN A KENNEL!
Tm. Reg. U.S. Pat. Off.—All rights reserved
© 1973 by United Feature Syndicate, Inc.
SCHULZ

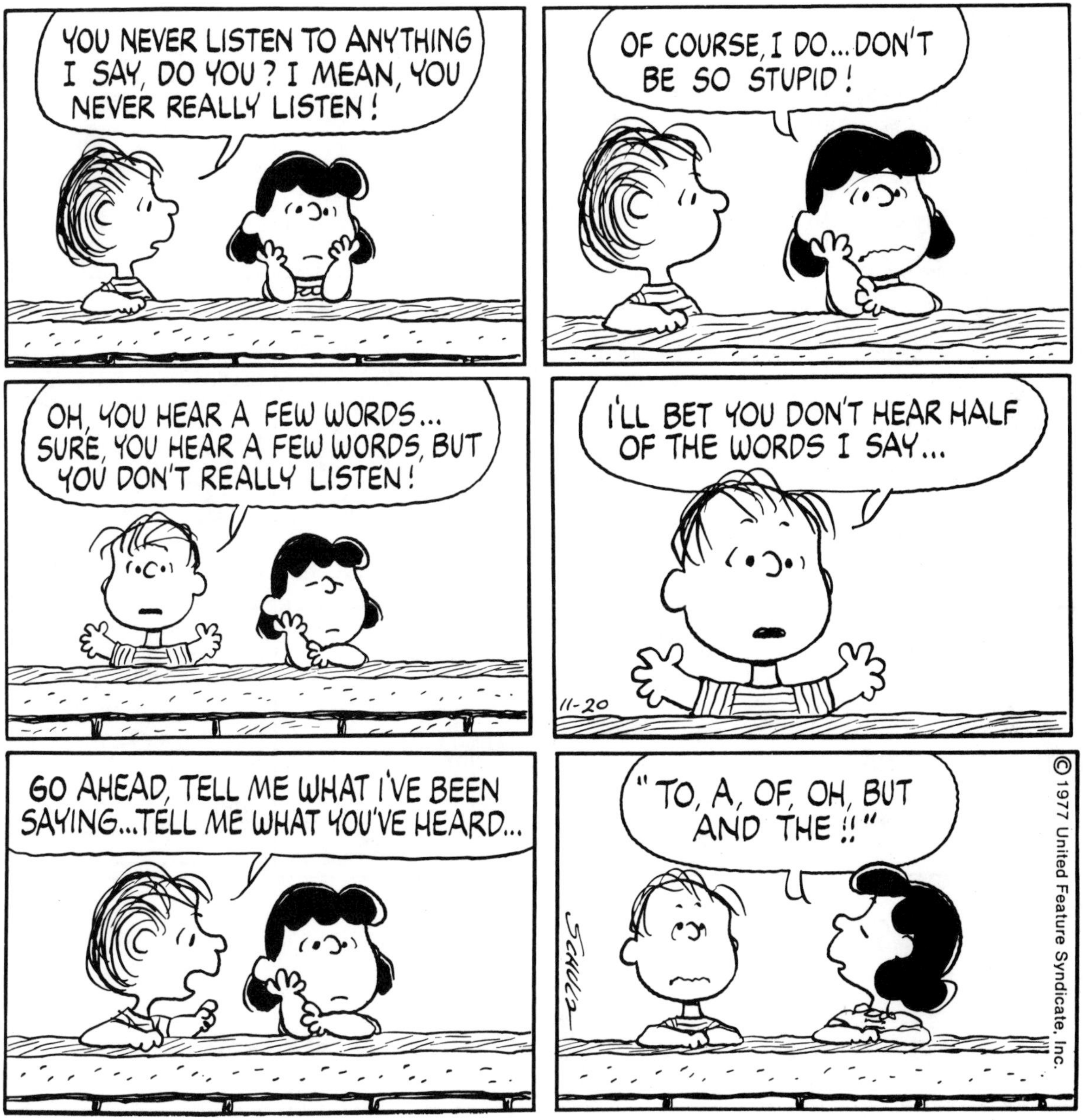
YOU NEVER LISTEN TO ANYTHING I SAY, DO YOU? I MEAN, YOU NEVER REALLY LISTEN!
OF COURSE, I DO... DON'T BE SO STUPID!
OH, YOU HEAR A FEW WORDS... SURE, YOU HEAR A FEW WORDS, BUT YOU DON'T REALLY LISTEN!
I'LL BET YOU DON'T HEAR HALF OF THE WORDS I SAY...
11-20
GO AHEAD, TELL ME WHAT I'VE BEEN SAYING... TELL ME WHAT YOU'VE HEARD...
"TO, A, OF, OH, BUT AND THE!!"
SCHULZ
© 1977 United Feature Syndicate, Inc.

PEANUTS
KANSAS CITY!
WOW! WHAT A PLACE!
Tm Reg U S Pat Off — All rights reserved © 1976 by United Feature Syndicate Inc
I SHOULD SEND THAT ROUND-HEADED KID ANOTHER NOTE OR A CARD TO LET HIM KNOW I'M ALL RIGHT...
6-21
I WONDER IF YOU CAN GET GREETING CARDS IN KANSAS CITY...
SCHULZ

PEANUTS
"DEAR ROUND-HEADED KID..."
Tm Reg U S Pat Off — All rights reserved © 1976 by United Feature Syndicate Inc
"TODAY I ARRIVED IN KANSAS CITY... WHILE I'M HERE, I'M GOING TO TRY TO SEE BELLE"
BELLE?!!
WHO IN THE WORLD IS BELLE?
6-22
"P.S. SAY HELLO TO WOODSTOCK FOR ME"
DO YOU KNOW WHO BELLE IS?
?
SCHULZ

PEANUTS
BELLE?
HEY, LOOK AT THE FUNNY DOG!
6-23
GET AWAY FROM ME, KID, OR I'LL REARRANGE YOUR LANDSCAPE!!
THAT DOG WAS WEARING A TENNIS VISOR...
STUPID KID! HE LIVES IN KANSAS CITY, AND HE'S NEVER SEEN A TENNIS VISOR!
SCHULZ
Tm Reg U S Pat Off — All rights reserved © 1976 by United Feature Syndicate Inc

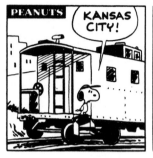

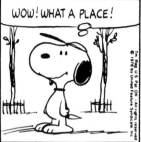

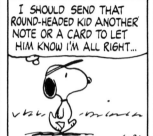

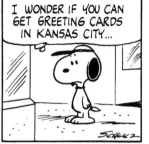

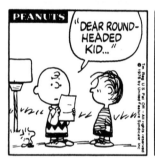

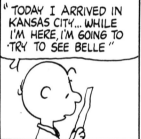

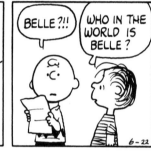

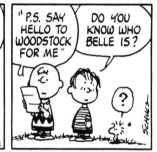

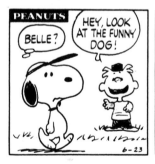

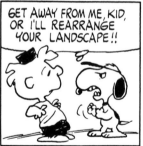

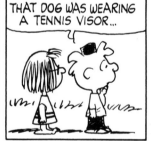

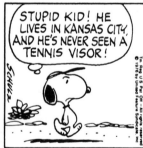

IT'S ALL RELATIVE

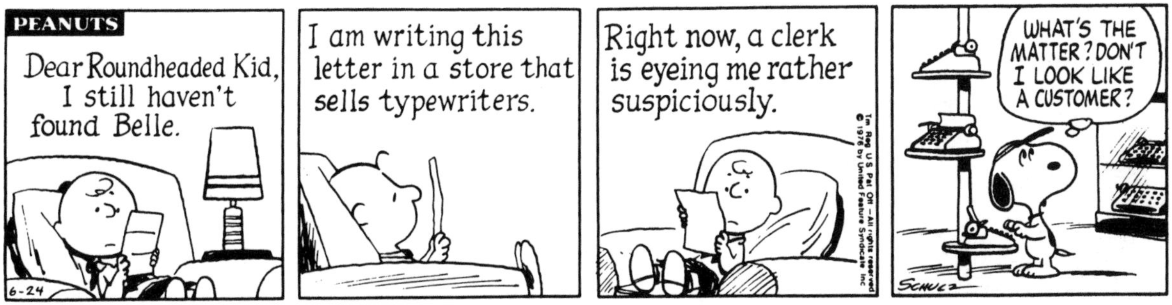
PEANUTS
Dear Roundheaded Kid, I still haven't found Belle.
6-24
I am writing this letter in a store that sells typewriters.
Right now, a clerk is eyeing me rather suspiciously.
Tm Reg U S Pat Off —All rights reserved © 1976 by United Feature Syndicate Inc
WHAT'S THE MATTER? DON'T I LOOK LIKE A CUSTOMER?
SCHULZ

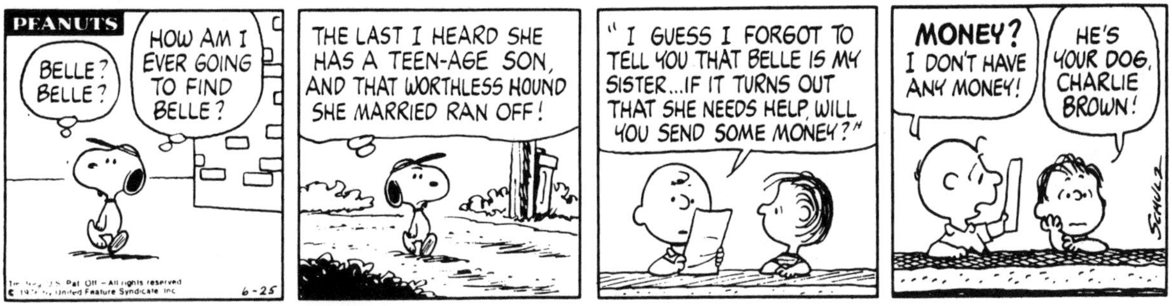
PEANUTS
BELLE? BELLE?
HOW AM I EVER GOING TO FIND BELLE?
6-25
THE LAST I HEARD SHE HAS A TEEN-AGE SON, AND THAT WORTHLESS HOUND SHE MARRIED RAN OFF!
"I GUESS I FORGOT TO TELL YOU THAT BELLE IS MY SISTER...IF IT TURNS OUT THAT SHE NEEDS HELP, WILL YOU SEND SOME MONEY?"
MONEY? I DON'T HAVE ANY MONEY!
HE'S YOUR DOG, CHARLIE BROWN!
SCHULZ

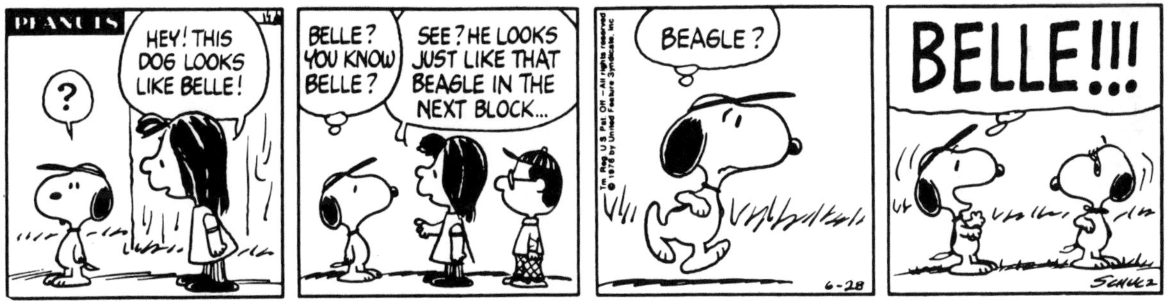
PEANUTS
?
HEY! THIS DOG LOOKS LIKE BELLE!
BELLE? YOU KNOW BELLE?
SEE? HE LOOKS JUST LIKE THAT BEAGLE IN THE NEXT BLOCK...
Tm Reg U S Pat Off —All rights reserved © 1976 by United Feature Syndicate Inc
BEAGLE?
6-28
BELLE!!!
SCHULZ

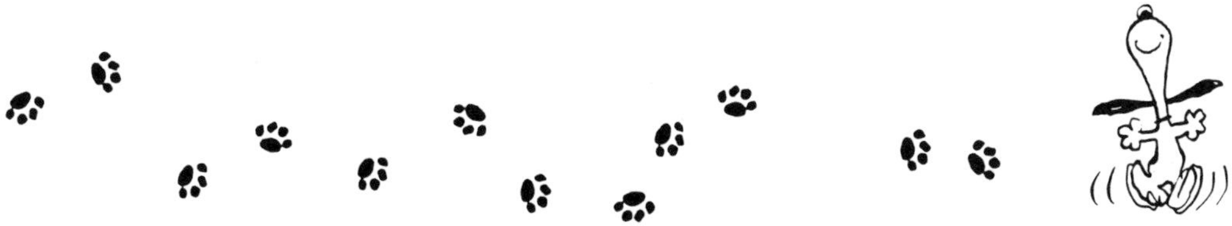

BROTHERS AND SISTERS

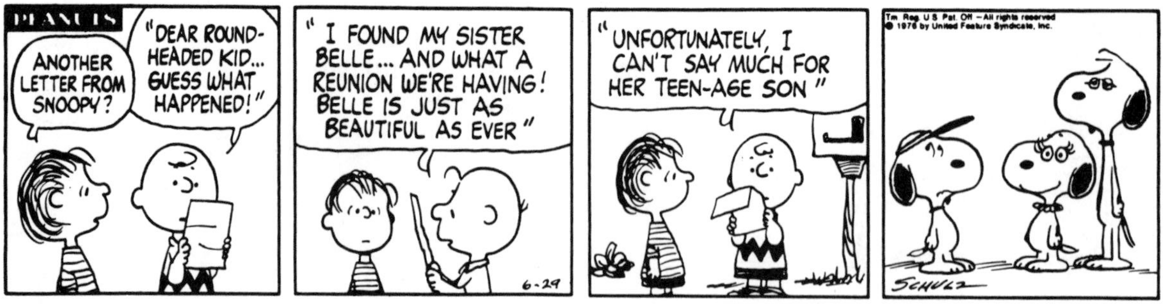
PEANUTS
ANOTHER LETTER FROM SNOOPY?
"DEAR ROUND-HEADED KID... GUESS WHAT HAPPENED!"
"I FOUND MY SISTER BELLE... AND WHAT A REUNION WE'RE HAVING! BELLE IS JUST AS BEAUTIFUL AS EVER"
6-29
"UNFORTUNATELY, I CAN'T SAY MUCH FOR HER TEEN-AGE SON"
Tm. Reg. U.S. Pat. Off.—All rights reserved © 1976 by United Feature Syndicate, Inc.
SCHULZ

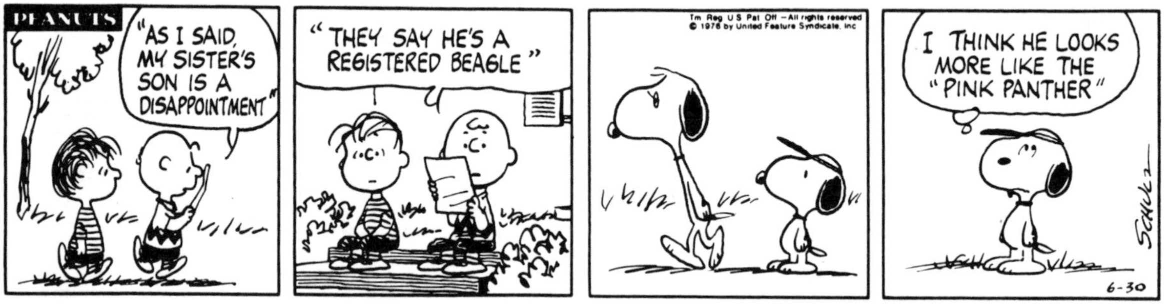
PEANUTS
"AS I SAID, MY SISTER'S SON IS A DISAPPOINTMENT"
"THEY SAY HE'S A REGISTERED BEAGLE"
Tm. Reg. U.S. Pat. Off.—All rights reserved © 1976 by United Feature Syndicate, Inc.
I THINK HE LOOKS MORE LIKE THE "PINK PANTHER"
SCHULZ
6-30

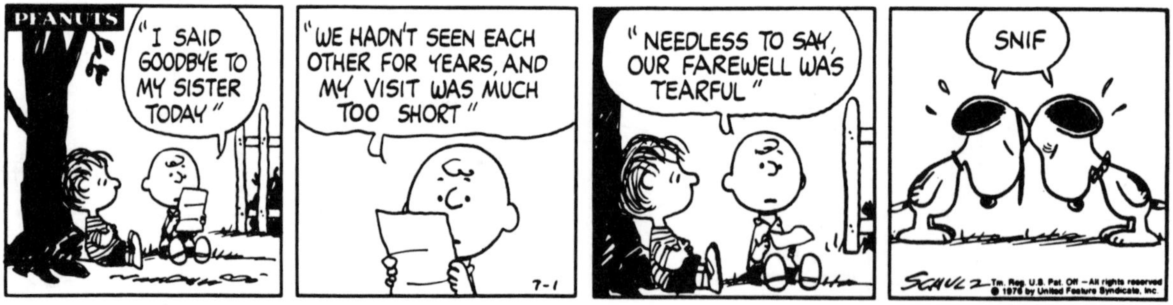
PEANUTS
"I SAID GOODBYE TO MY SISTER TODAY"
"WE HADN'T SEEN EACH OTHER FOR YEARS, AND MY VISIT WAS MUCH TOO SHORT"
7-1
"NEEDLESS TO SAY, OUR FAREWELL WAS TEARFUL"
SNIF
SCHULZ
Tm. Reg. U.S. Pat. Off.—All rights reserved © 1976 by United Feature Syndicate, Inc.

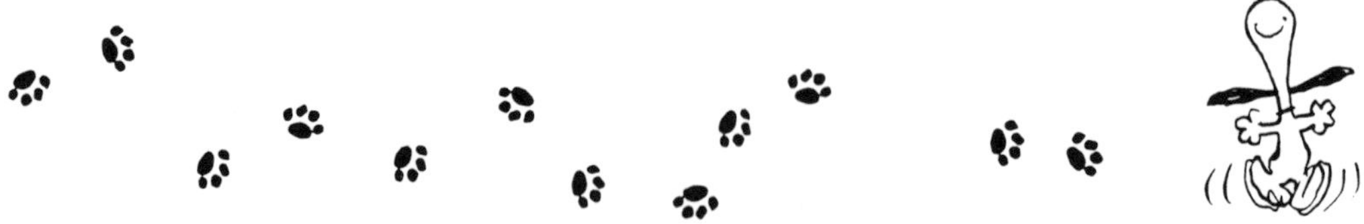

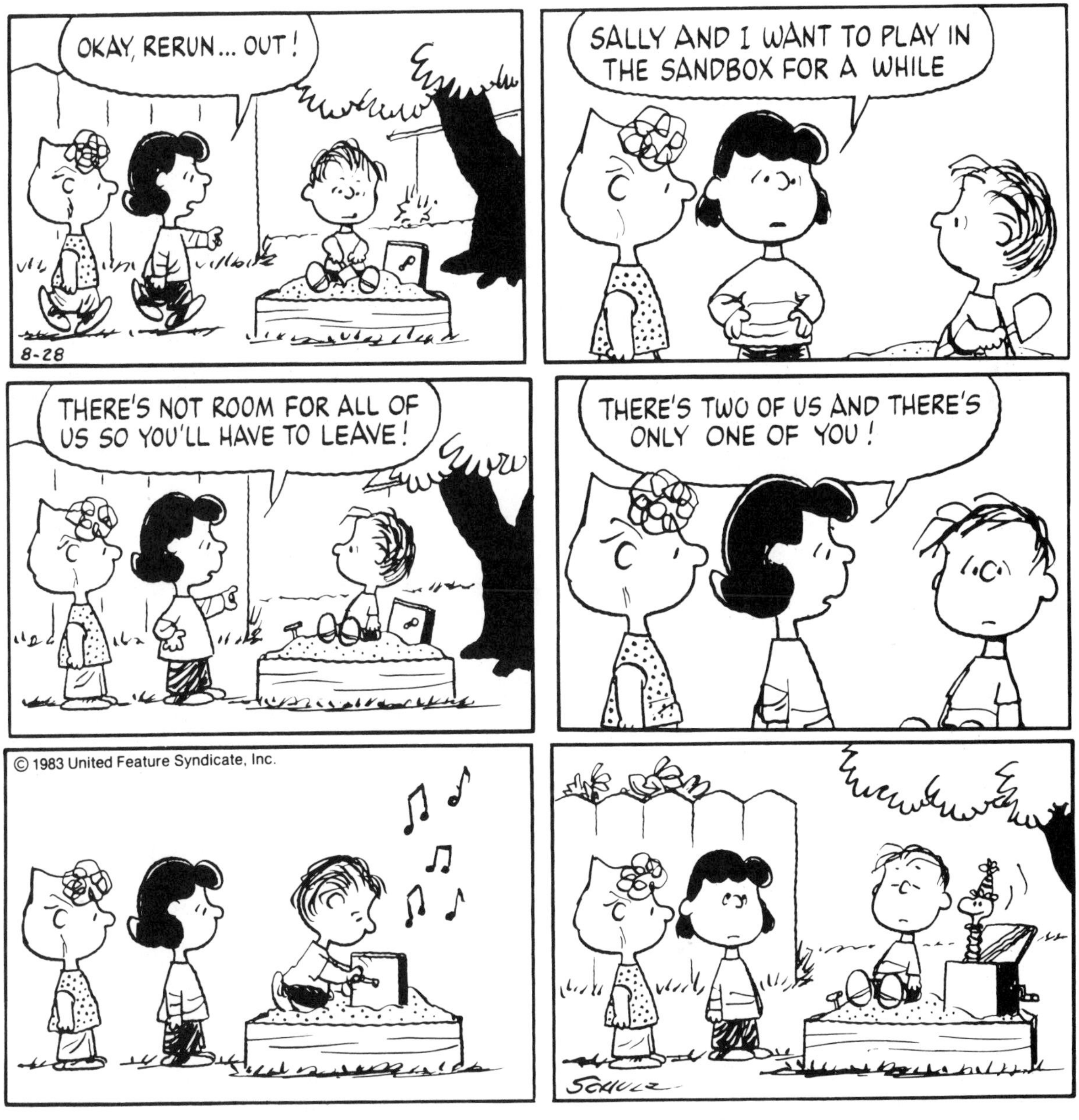
OKAY, RERUN... OUT!
8-28
SALLY AND I WANT TO PLAY IN THE SANDBOX FOR A WHILE
THERE'S NOT ROOM FOR ALL OF US SO YOU'LL HAVE TO LEAVE!
THERE'S TWO OF US AND THERE'S ONLY ONE OF YOU!
SCHULZ

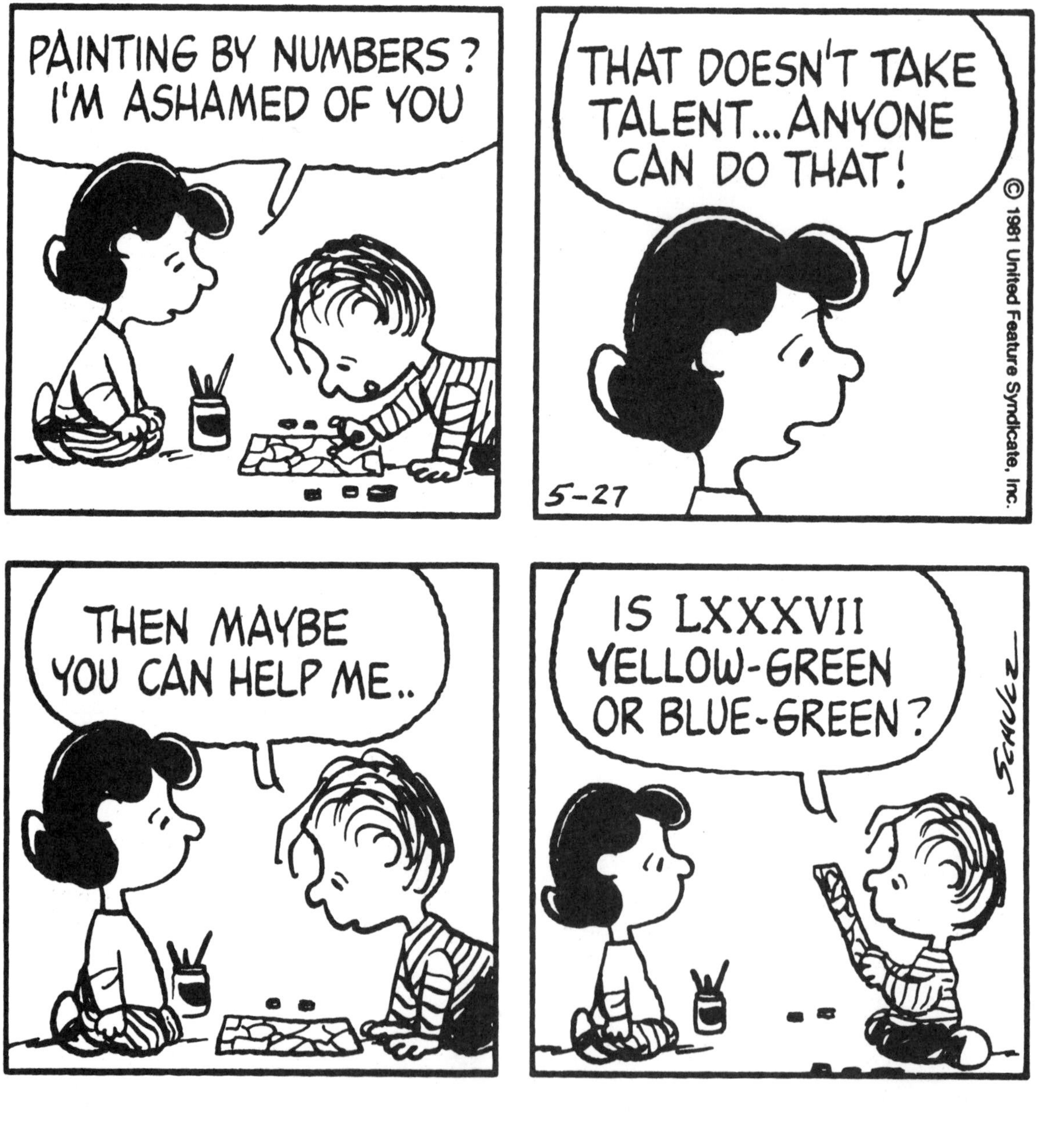
PAINTING BY NUMBERS? I'M ASHAMED OF YOU
THAT DOESN'T TAKE TALENT...ANYONE CAN DO THAT!
5-27
© 1981 United Feature Syndicate, Inc.
THEN MAYBE YOU CAN HELP ME..
IS LXXXVII YELLOW-GREEN OR BLUE-GREEN?
SCHULZ

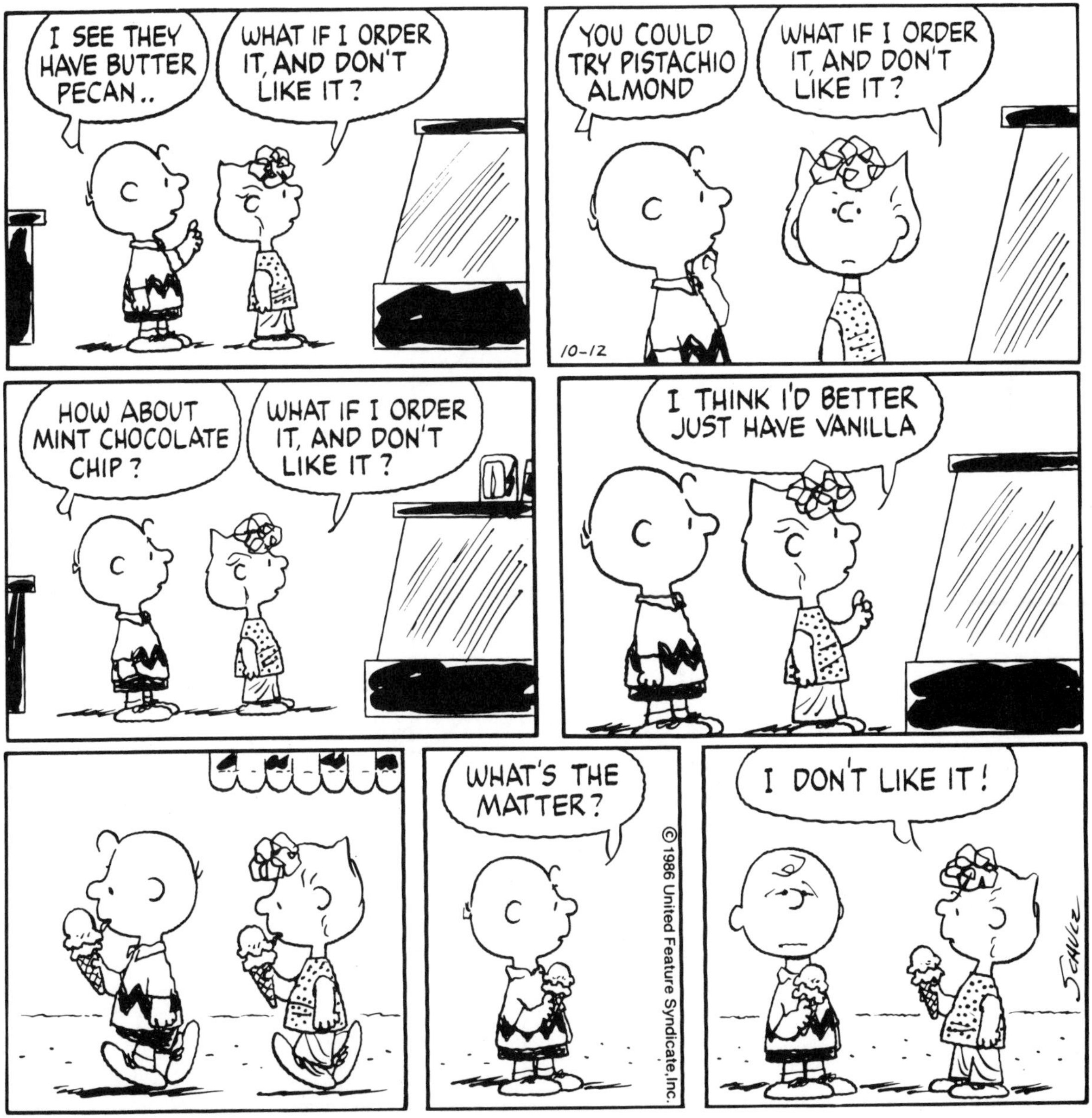
I SEE THEY HAVE BUTTER PECAN..
WHAT IF I ORDER IT, AND DON'T LIKE IT?
YOU COULD TRY PISTACHIO ALMOND
WHAT IF I ORDER IT, AND DON'T LIKE IT?
10-12
HOW ABOUT MINT CHOCOLATE CHIP?
WHAT IF I ORDER IT, AND DON'T LIKE IT?
I THINK I'D BETTER JUST HAVE VANILLA
WHAT'S THE MATTER?
© 1986 United Feature Syndicate, Inc.
I DON'T LIKE IT!
SCHULZ

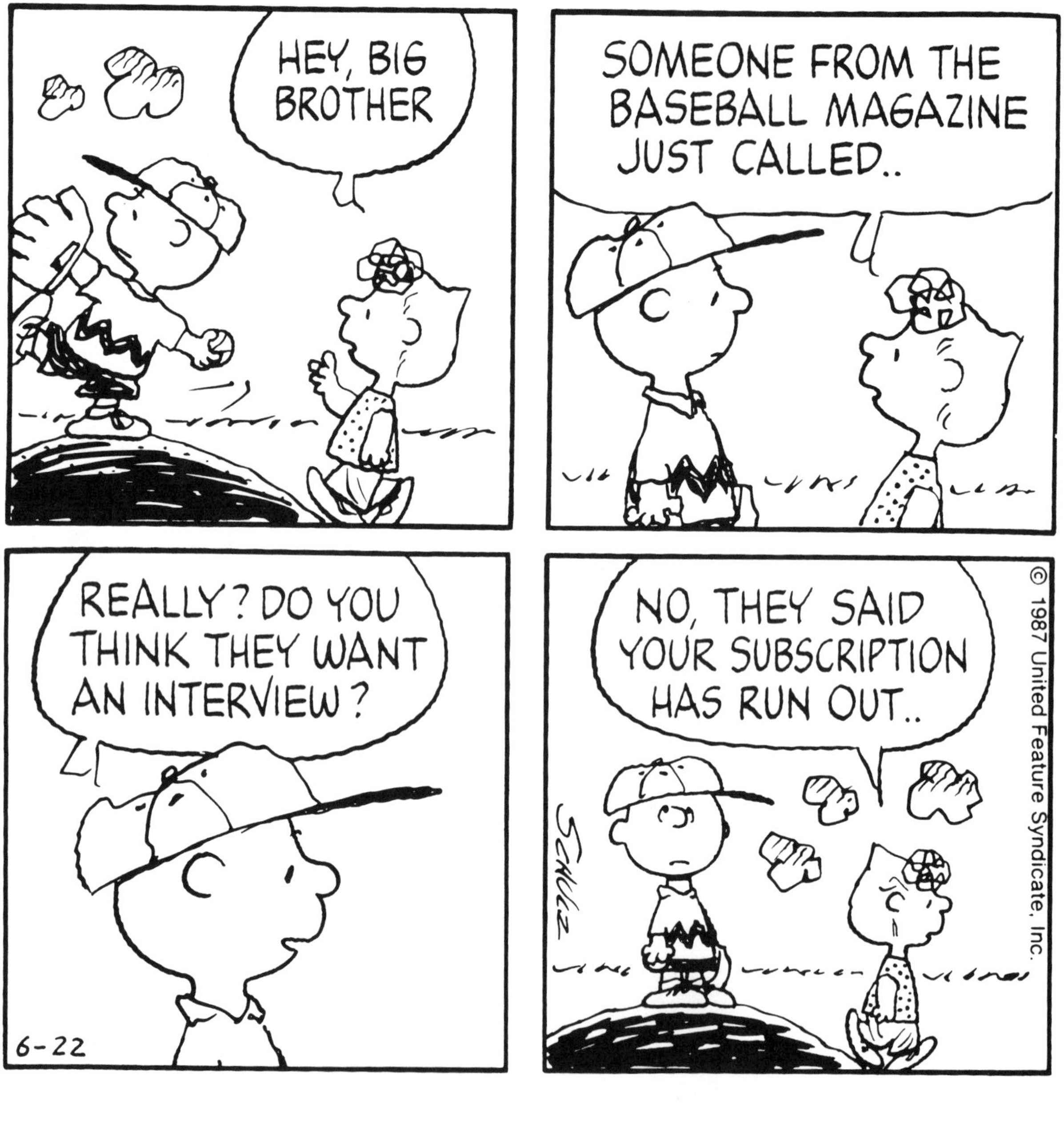
HEY, BIG BROTHER
SOMEONE FROM THE BASEBALL MAGAZINE JUST CALLED..
REALLY? DO YOU THINK THEY WANT AN INTERVIEW?
6-22
NO, THEY SAID YOUR SUBSCRIPTION HAS RUN OUT..
SCHULZ
© 1987 United Feature Syndicate, Inc.

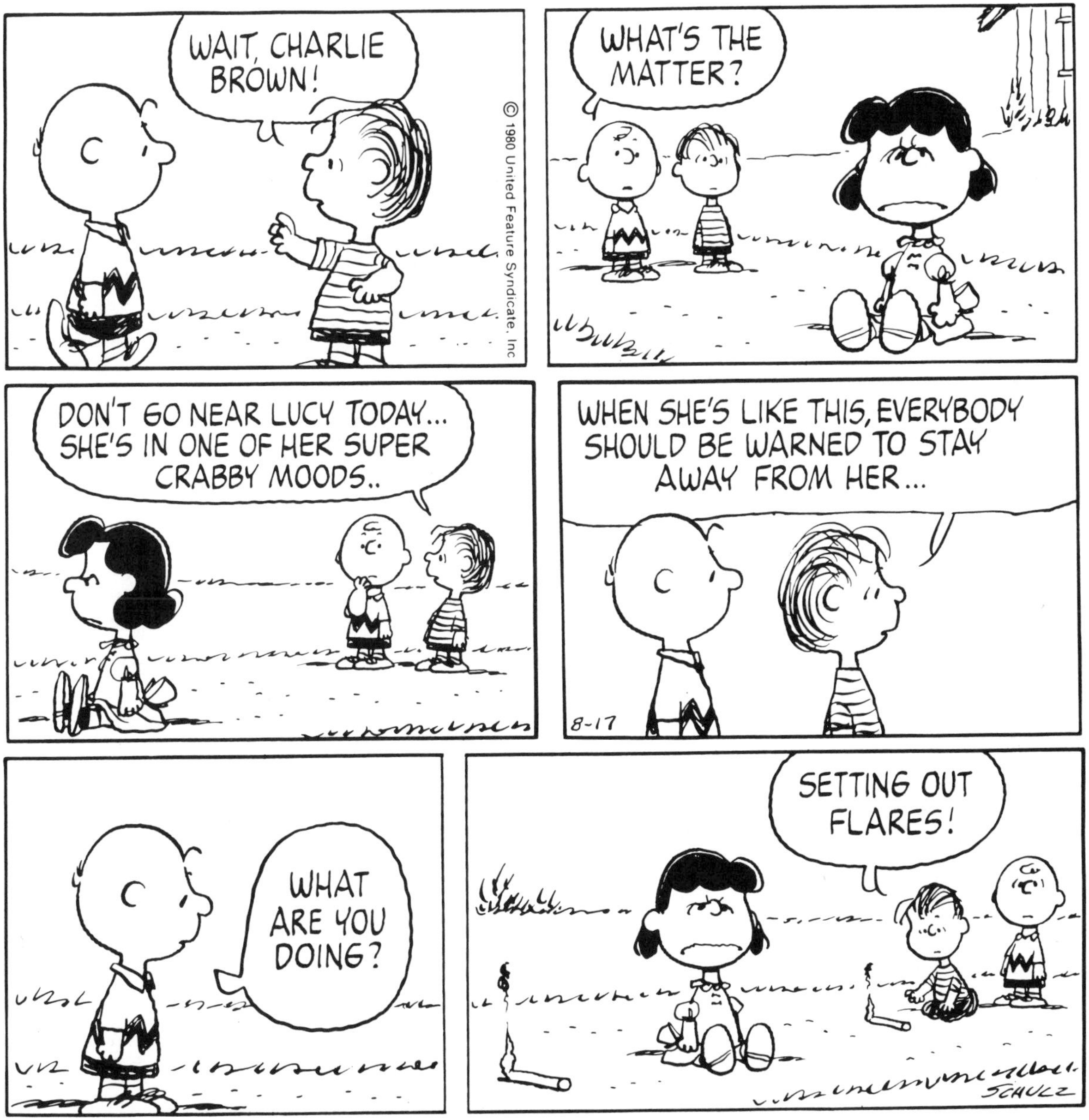
WAIT, CHARLIE BROWN!
© 1980 United Feature Syndicate, Inc
WHAT'S THE MATTER?
DON'T GO NEAR LUCY TODAY... SHE'S IN ONE OF HER SUPER CRABBY MOODS..
WHEN SHE'S LIKE THIS, EVERYBODY SHOULD BE WARNED TO STAY AWAY FROM HER...
8-17
WHAT ARE YOU DOING?
SETTING OUT FLARES!
SCHULZ

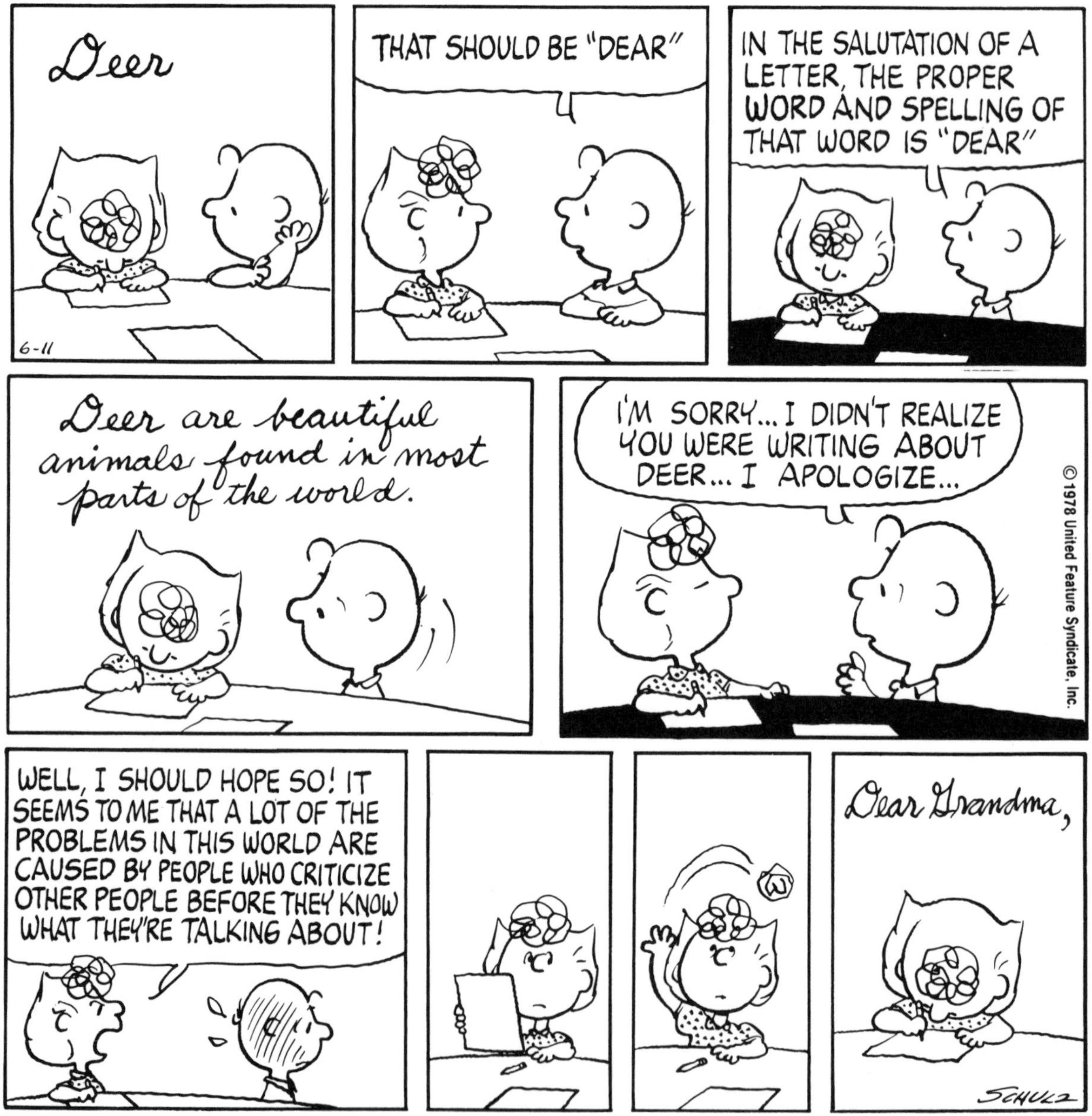
Deer
6-11
THAT SHOULD BE "DEAR"
IN THE SALUTATION OF A LETTER, THE PROPER WORD AND SPELLING OF THAT WORD IS "DEAR"
Deer are beautiful animals found in most parts of the world.
I'M SORRY... I DIDN'T REALIZE YOU WERE WRITING ABOUT DEER... I APOLOGIZE...
© 1978 United Feature Syndicate, Inc.
WELL, I SHOULD HOPE SO! IT SEEMS TO ME THAT A LOT OF THE PROBLEMS IN THIS WORLD ARE CAUSED BY PEOPLE WHO CRITICIZE OTHER PEOPLE BEFORE THEY KNOW WHAT THEY'RE TALKING ABOUT!
Dear Grandma,
SCHULZ

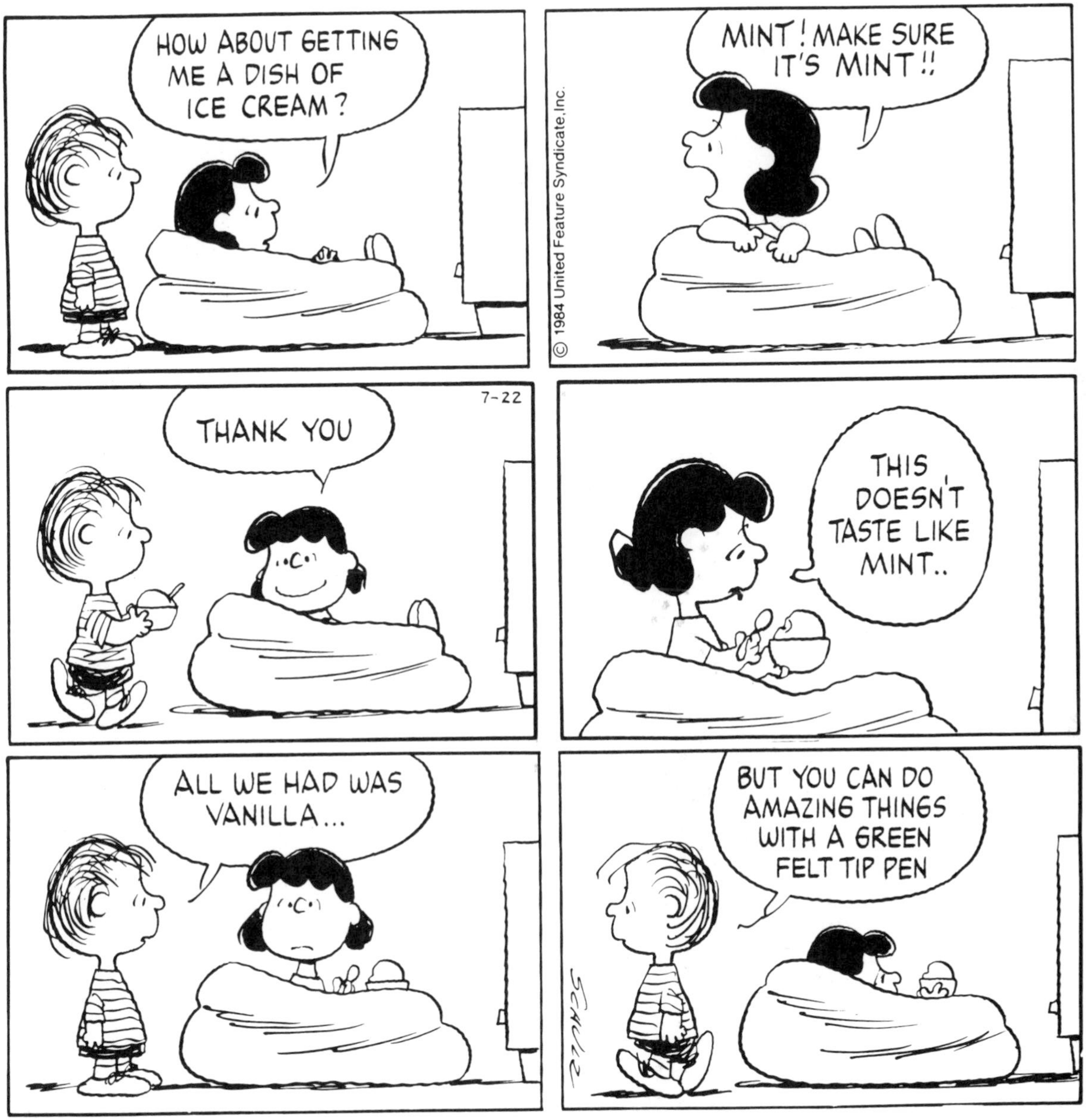
HOW ABOUT GETTING ME A DISH OF ICE CREAM?
MINT! MAKE SURE IT'S MINT!!
© 1984 United Feature Syndicate, Inc.
7-22
THANK YOU
THIS DOESN'T TASTE LIKE MINT..
ALL WE HAD WAS VANILLA...
BUT YOU CAN DO AMAZING THINGS WITH A GREEN FELT TIP PEN
SCHULZ

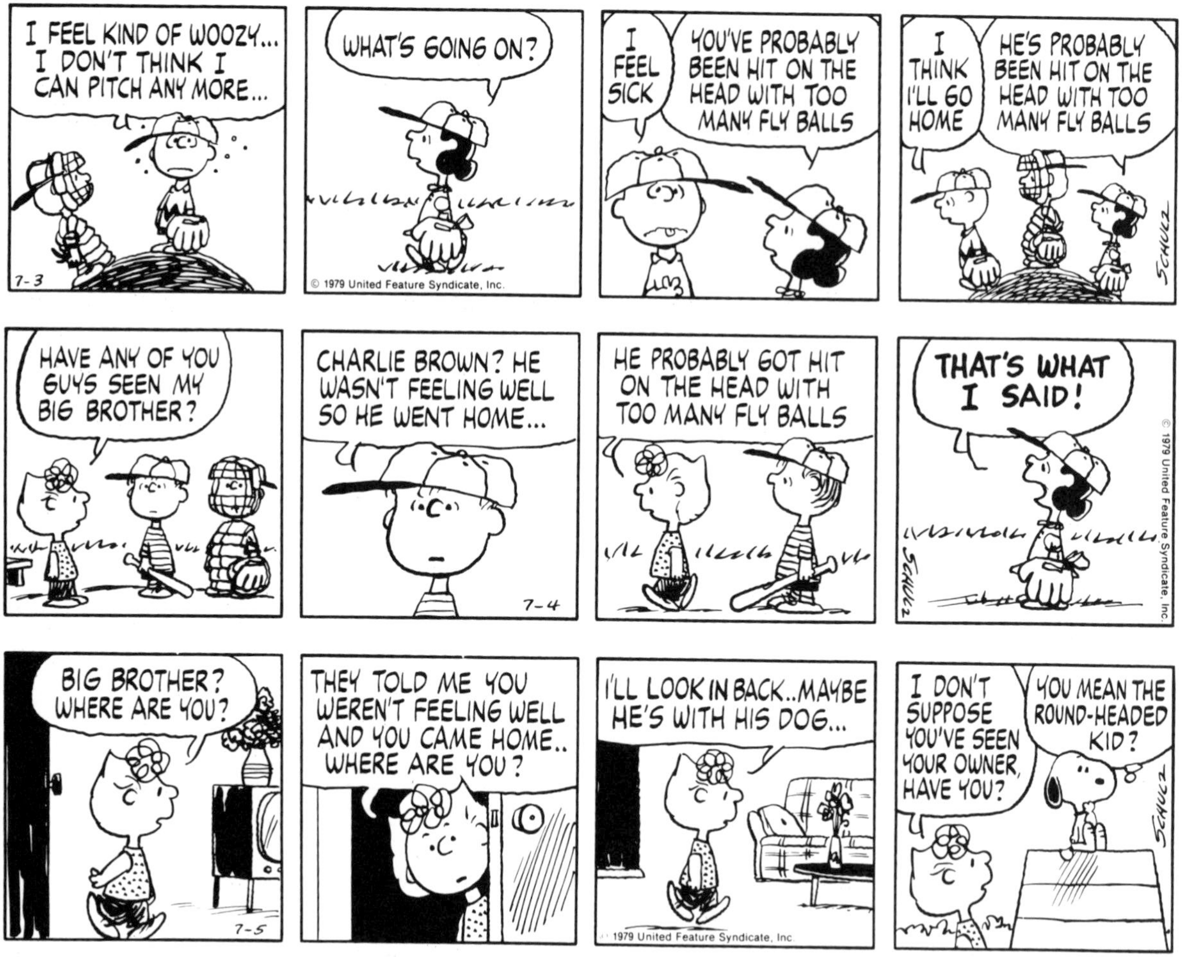
I FEEL KIND OF WOOZY... I DON'T THINK I CAN PITCH ANY MORE...
WHAT'S GOING ON?
© 1979 United Feature Syndicate, Inc.
I FEEL SICK
YOU'VE PROBABLY BEEN HIT ON THE HEAD WITH TOO MANY FLY BALLS
I THINK I'LL GO HOME
HE'S PROBABLY BEEN HIT ON THE HEAD WITH TOO MANY FLY BALLS
HAVE ANY OF YOU GUYS SEEN MY BIG BROTHER?
CHARLIE BROWN? HE WASN'T FEELING WELL SO HE WENT HOME...
HE PROBABLY GOT HIT ON THE HEAD WITH TOO MANY FLY BALLS
THAT'S WHAT I SAID!
© 1979 United Feature Syndicate, Inc.
BIG BROTHER? WHERE ARE YOU?
THEY TOLD ME YOU WEREN'T FEELING WELL AND YOU CAME HOME.. WHERE ARE YOU?
I'LL LOOK IN BACK..MAYBE HE'S WITH HIS DOG...
© 1979 United Feature Syndicate, Inc.
I DON'T SUPPOSE YOU'VE SEEN YOUR OWNER, HAVE YOU?
YOU MEAN THE ROUND-HEADED KID?

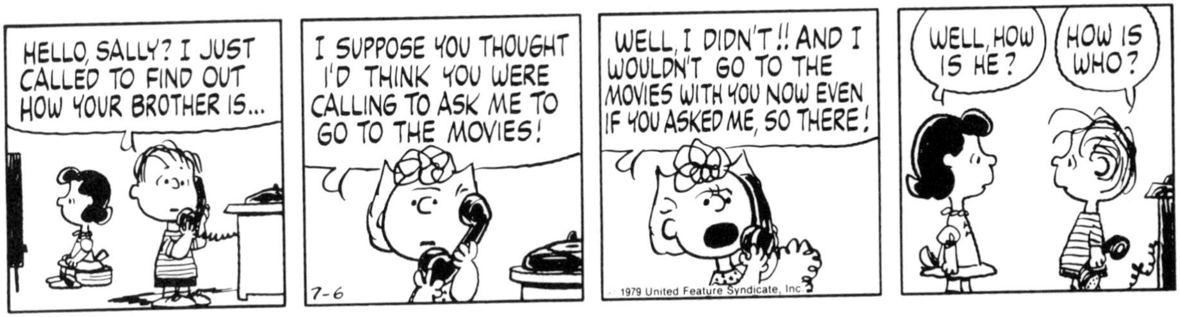
HELLO, SALLY? I JUST CALLED TO FIND OUT HOW YOUR BROTHER IS...
I SUPPOSE YOU THOUGHT I'D THINK YOU WERE CALLING TO ASK ME TO GO TO THE MOVIES!
7-6
WELL, I DIDN'T!! AND I WOULDN'T GO TO THE MOVIES WITH YOU NOW EVEN IF YOU ASKED ME, SO THERE!
1979 United Feature Syndicate, Inc.
WELL, HOW IS HE?
HOW IS WHO?

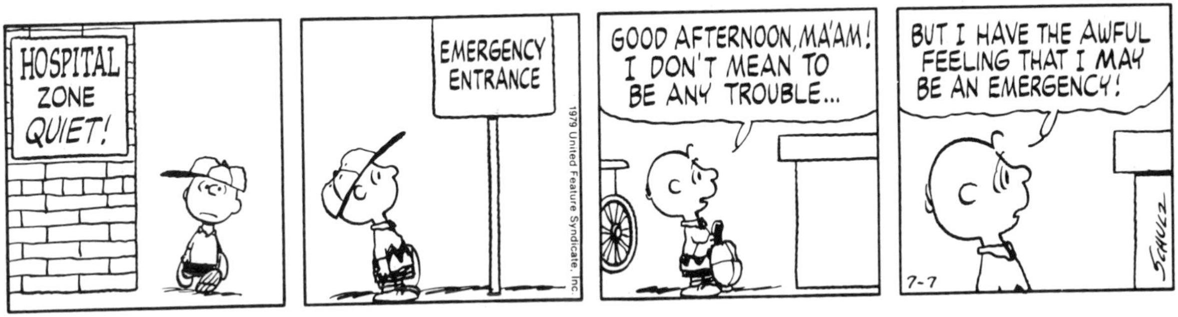
HOSPITAL ZONE QUIET!
EMERGENCY ENTRANCE
1979 United Feature Syndicate, Inc.
GOOD AFTERNOON, MA'AM! I DON'T MEAN TO BE ANY TROUBLE...
BUT I HAVE THE AWFUL FEELING THAT I MAY BE AN EMERGENCY!
7-7
SCHULZ

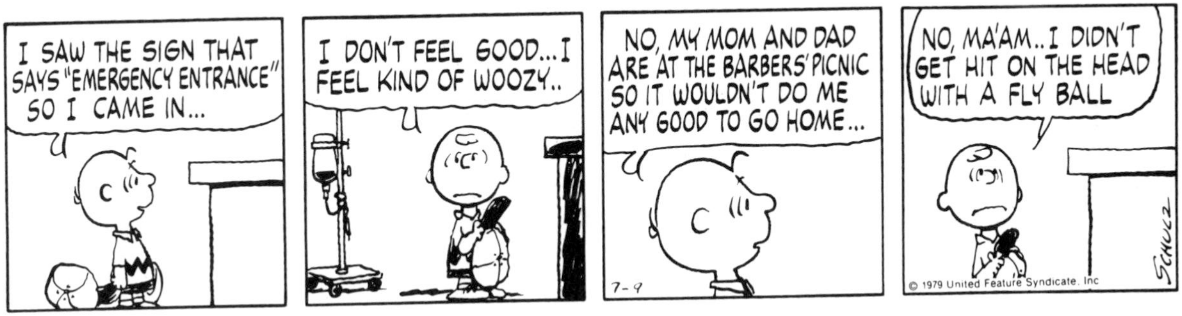
I SAW THE SIGN THAT SAYS "EMERGENCY ENTRANCE" SO I CAME IN...
I DON'T FEEL GOOD...I FEEL KIND OF WOOZY..
NO, MY MOM AND DAD ARE AT THE BARBERS' PICNIC SO IT WOULDN'T DO ME ANY GOOD TO GO HOME...
7-9
NO, MA'AM..I DIDN'T GET HIT ON THE HEAD WITH A FLY BALL
© 1979 United Feature Syndicate, Inc
SCHULZ

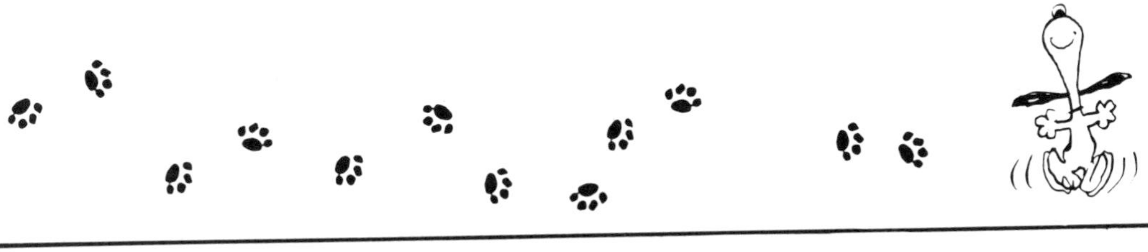

BROTHERS AND SISTERS

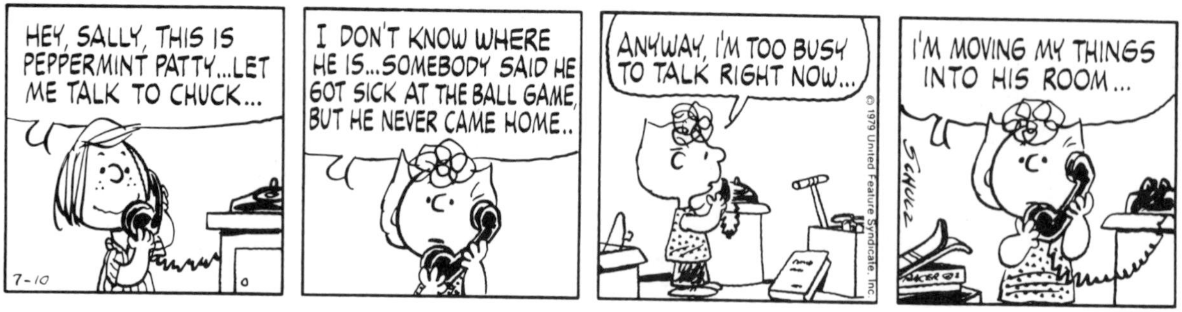
HEY, SALLY, THIS IS PEPPERMINT PATTY...LET ME TALK TO CHUCK...
7-10
I DON'T KNOW WHERE HE IS...SOMEBODY SAID HE GOT SICK AT THE BALL GAME, BUT HE NEVER CAME HOME..
ANYWAY, I'M TOO BUSY TO TALK RIGHT NOW...
© 1979 United Feature Syndicate, Inc.
I'M MOVING MY THINGS INTO HIS ROOM...
SCHULZ

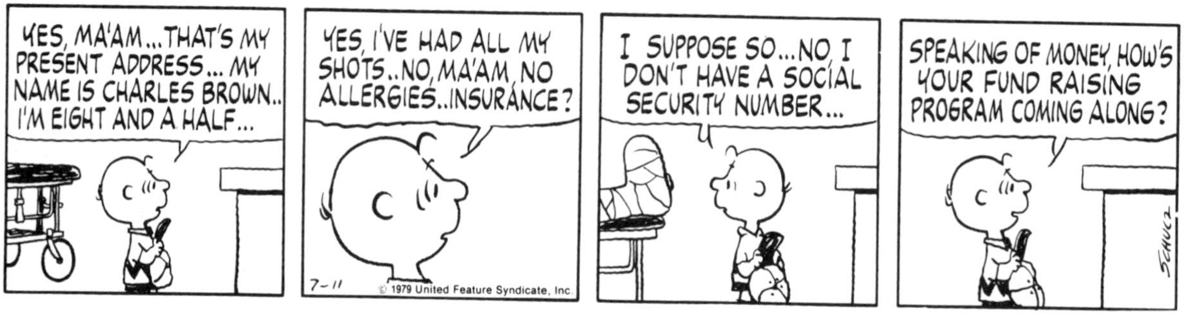
YES, MA'AM...THAT'S MY PRESENT ADDRESS... MY NAME IS CHARLES BROWN.. I'M EIGHT AND A HALF...
YES, I'VE HAD ALL MY SHOTS..NO, MA'AM, NO ALLERGIES..INSURANCE?
7-11
© 1979 United Feature Syndicate, Inc.
I SUPPOSE SO...NO, I DON'T HAVE A SOCIAL SECURITY NUMBER...
SPEAKING OF MONEY, HOW'S YOUR FUND RAISING PROGRAM COMING ALONG?
SCHULZ

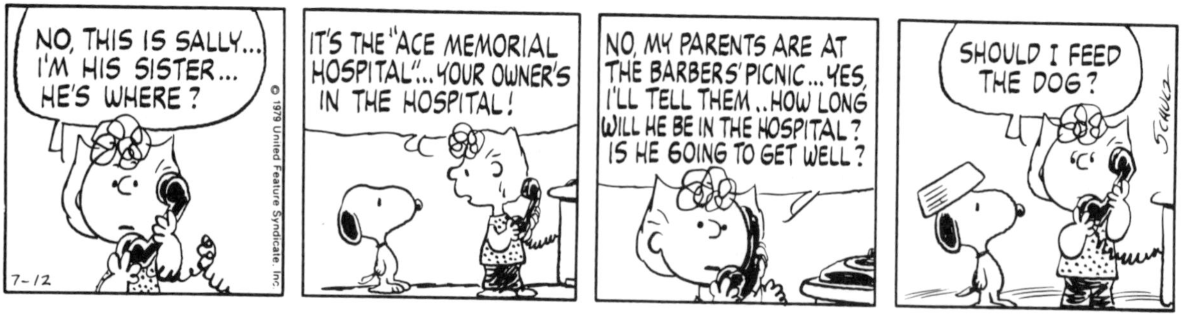
NO, THIS IS SALLY... I'M HIS SISTER... HE'S WHERE?
7-12
© 1979 United Feature Syndicate, Inc.
IT'S THE "ACE MEMORIAL HOSPITAL"...YOUR OWNER'S IN THE HOSPITAL!
NO, MY PARENTS ARE AT THE BARBERS' PICNIC...YES, I'LL TELL THEM..HOW LONG WILL HE BE IN THE HOSPITAL? IS HE GOING TO GET WELL?
SHOULD I FEED THE DOG?
SCHULZ

IT'S ALL RELATIVE

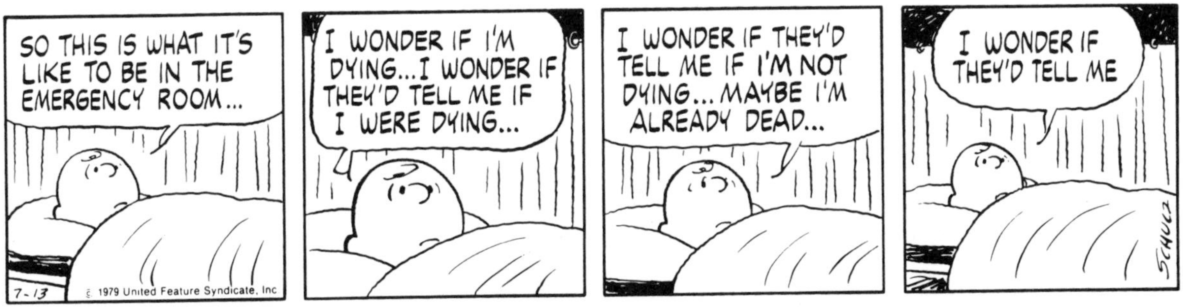
SO THIS IS WHAT IT'S LIKE TO BE IN THE EMERGENCY ROOM...
7-13
© 1979 United Feature Syndicate, Inc.
I WONDER IF I'M DYING...I WONDER IF THEY'D TELL ME IF I WERE DYING...
I WONDER IF THEY'D TELL ME IF I'M NOT DYING... MAYBE I'M ALREADY DEAD...
I WONDER IF THEY'D TELL ME
SCHULZ

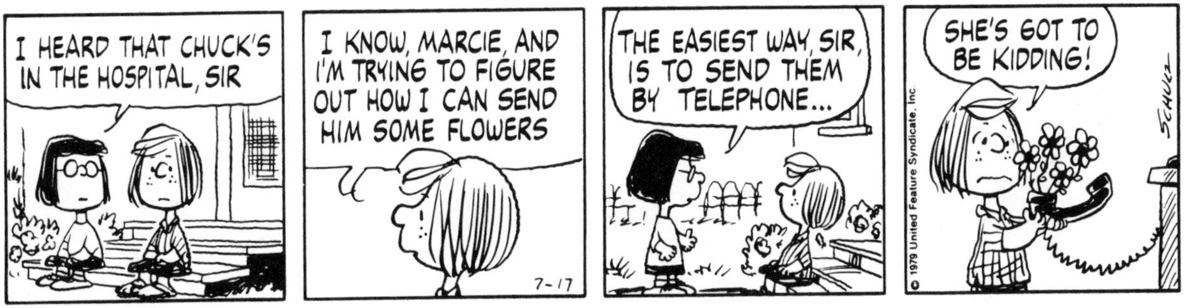
I HEARD THAT CHUCK'S IN THE HOSPITAL, SIR
I KNOW, MARCIE, AND I'M TRYING TO FIGURE OUT HOW I CAN SEND HIM SOME FLOWERS
7-17
THE EASIEST WAY, SIR, IS TO SEND THEM BY TELEPHONE...
© 1979 United Feature Syndicate, Inc.
SHE'S GOT TO BE KIDDING!
SCHULZ

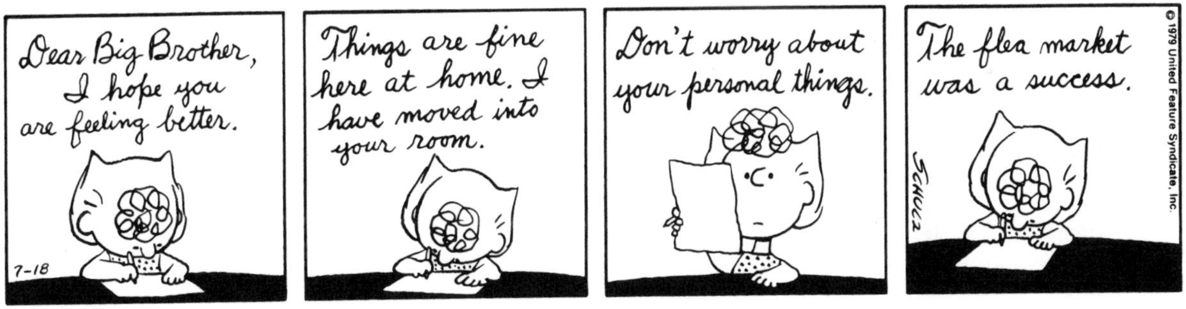
Dear Big Brother, I hope you are feeling better.
7-18
Things are fine here at home. I have moved into your room.
Don't worry about your personal things.
SCHULZ
The flea market was a success.
© 1979 United Feature Syndicate, Inc.

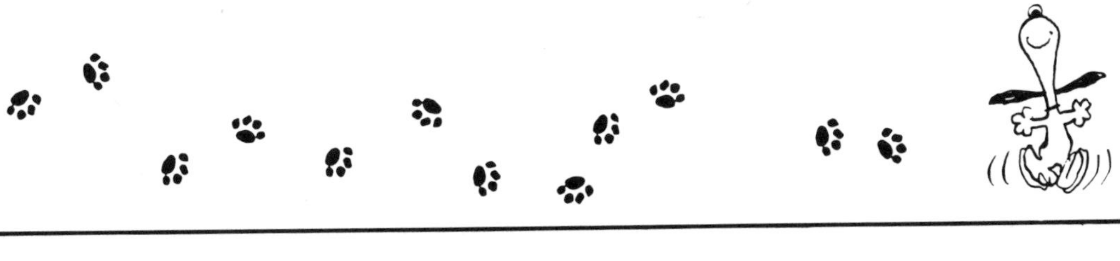

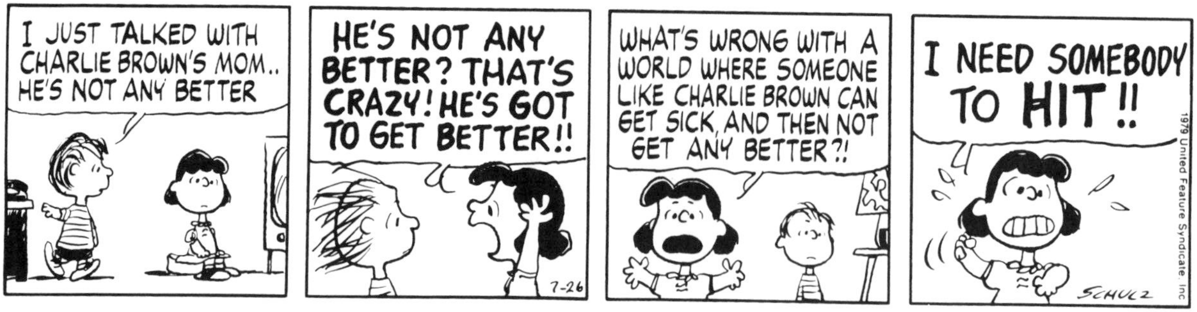
I JUST TALKED WITH CHARLIE BROWN'S MOM.. HE'S NOT ANY BETTER
HE'S NOT ANY BETTER? THAT'S CRAZY! HE'S GOT TO GET BETTER!!
7-26
WHAT'S WRONG WITH A WORLD WHERE SOMEONE LIKE CHARLIE BROWN CAN GET SICK, AND THEN NOT GET ANY BETTER?!
I NEED SOMEBODY TO HIT!!
SCHULZ
1979 United Feature Syndicate, Inc

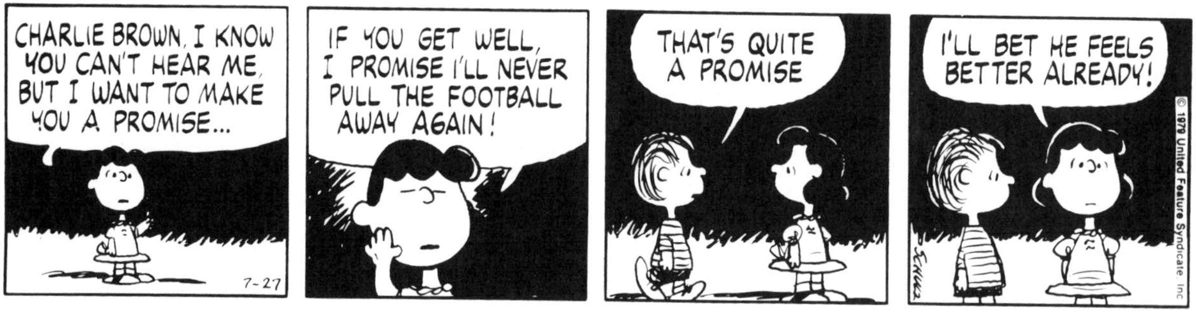
CHARLIE BROWN, I KNOW YOU CAN'T HEAR ME, BUT I WANT TO MAKE YOU A PROMISE...
7-27
IF YOU GET WELL, I PROMISE I'LL NEVER PULL THE FOOTBALL AWAY AGAIN!
THAT'S QUITE A PROMISE
I'LL BET HE FEELS BETTER ALREADY!
SCHULZ
© 1979 United Feature Syndicate, Inc

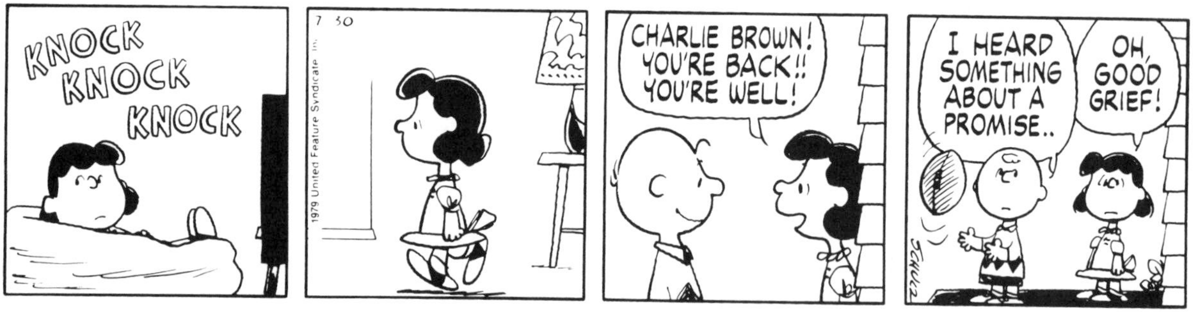
KNOCK
KNOCK
KNOCK
7 30
1979 United Feature Syndicate, Inc
CHARLIE BROWN! YOU'RE BACK!! YOU'RE WELL!
I HEARD SOMETHING ABOUT A PROMISE..
OH, GOOD GRIEF!
SCHULZ

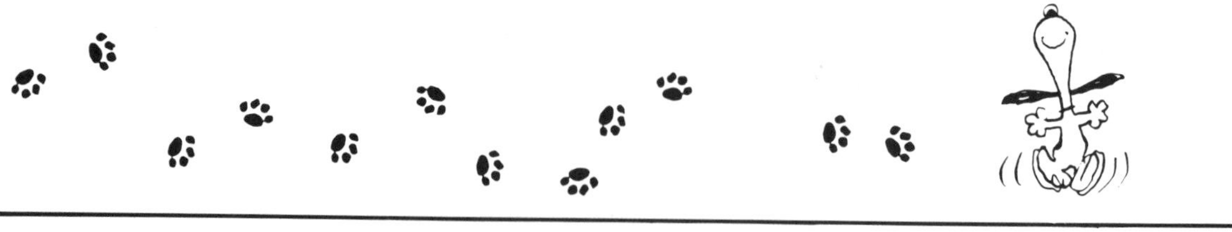

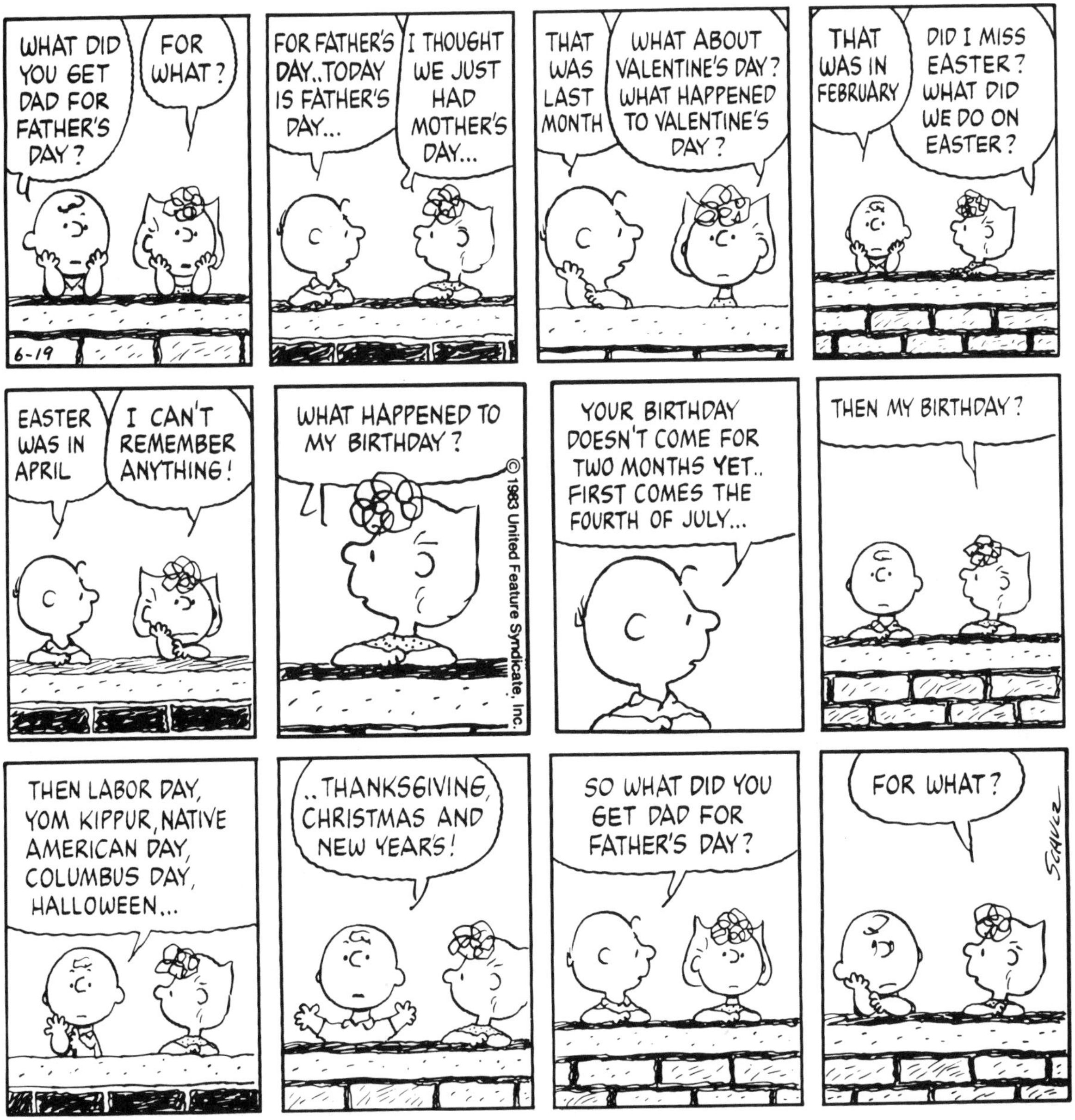
WHAT DID YOU GET DAD FOR FATHER'S DAY?
FOR WHAT?
6-19
FOR FATHER'S DAY..TODAY IS FATHER'S DAY...
I THOUGHT WE JUST HAD MOTHER'S DAY...
THAT WAS LAST MONTH
WHAT ABOUT VALENTINE'S DAY? WHAT HAPPENED TO VALENTINE'S DAY?
THAT WAS IN FEBRUARY
DID I MISS EASTER? WHAT DID WE DO ON EASTER?
EASTER WAS IN APRIL
I CAN'T REMEMBER ANYTHING!
WHAT HAPPENED TO MY BIRTHDAY?
© 1983 United Feature Syndicate, Inc.
YOUR BIRTHDAY DOESN'T COME FOR TWO MONTHS YET.. FIRST COMES THE FOURTH OF JULY...
THEN MY BIRTHDAY?
THEN LABOR DAY, YOM KIPPUR, NATIVE AMERICAN DAY, COLUMBUS DAY, HALLOWEEN...
..THANKSGIVING, CHRISTMAS AND NEW YEAR'S!
SO WHAT DID YOU GET DAD FOR FATHER'S DAY?
FOR WHAT?
SCHULZ

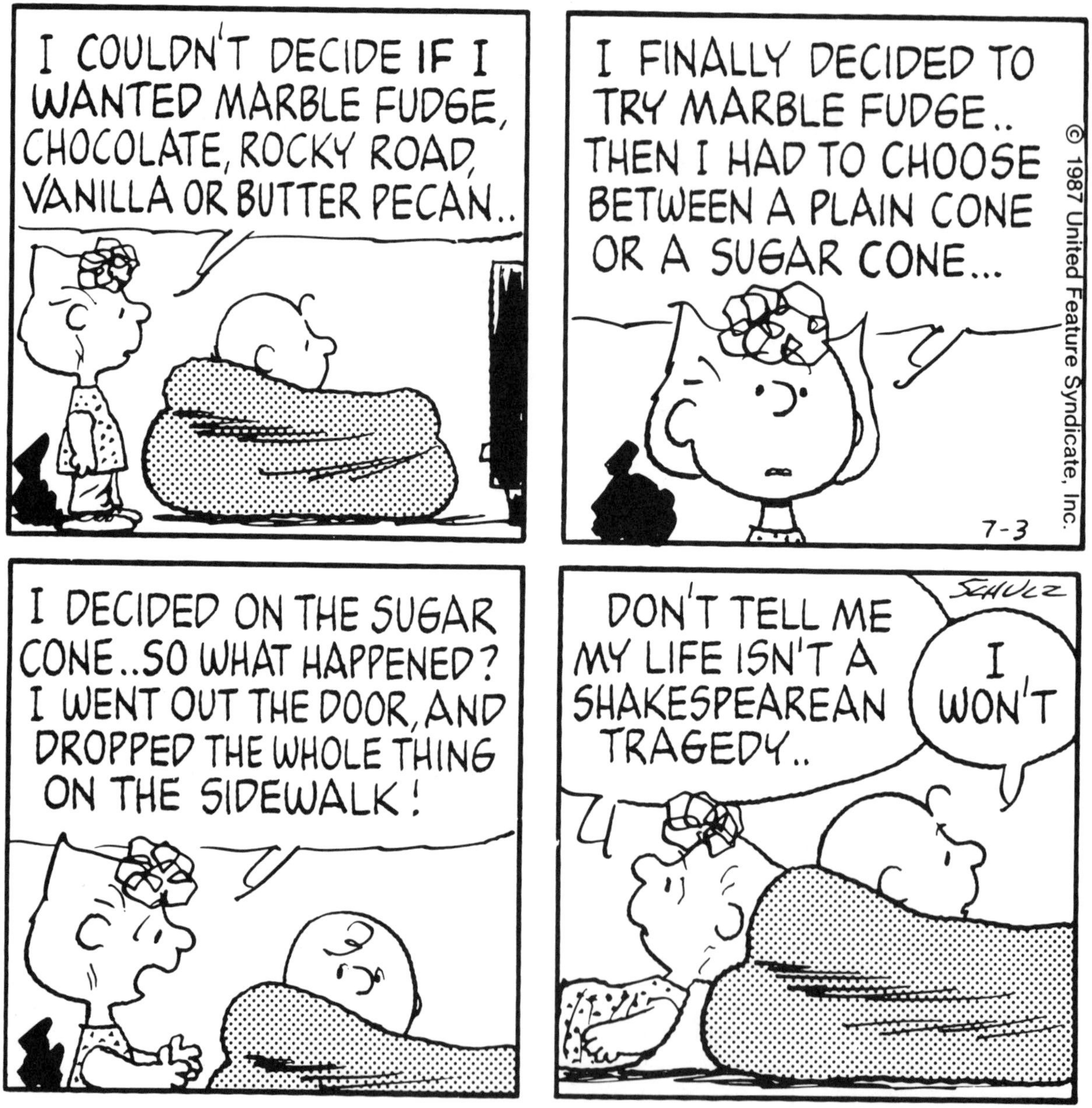
I COULDN'T DECIDE IF I WANTED MARBLE FUDGE, CHOCOLATE, ROCKY ROAD, VANILLA OR BUTTER PECAN..
I FINALLY DECIDED TO TRY MARBLE FUDGE.. THEN I HAD TO CHOOSE BETWEEN A PLAIN CONE OR A SUGAR CONE...
© 1987 United Feature Syndicate, Inc.
7-3
I DECIDED ON THE SUGAR CONE..SO WHAT HAPPENED? I WENT OUT THE DOOR, AND DROPPED THE WHOLE THING ON THE SIDEWALK!
SCHULZ
DON'T TELL ME MY LIFE ISN'T A SHAKESPEAREAN TRAGEDY..
I WON'T

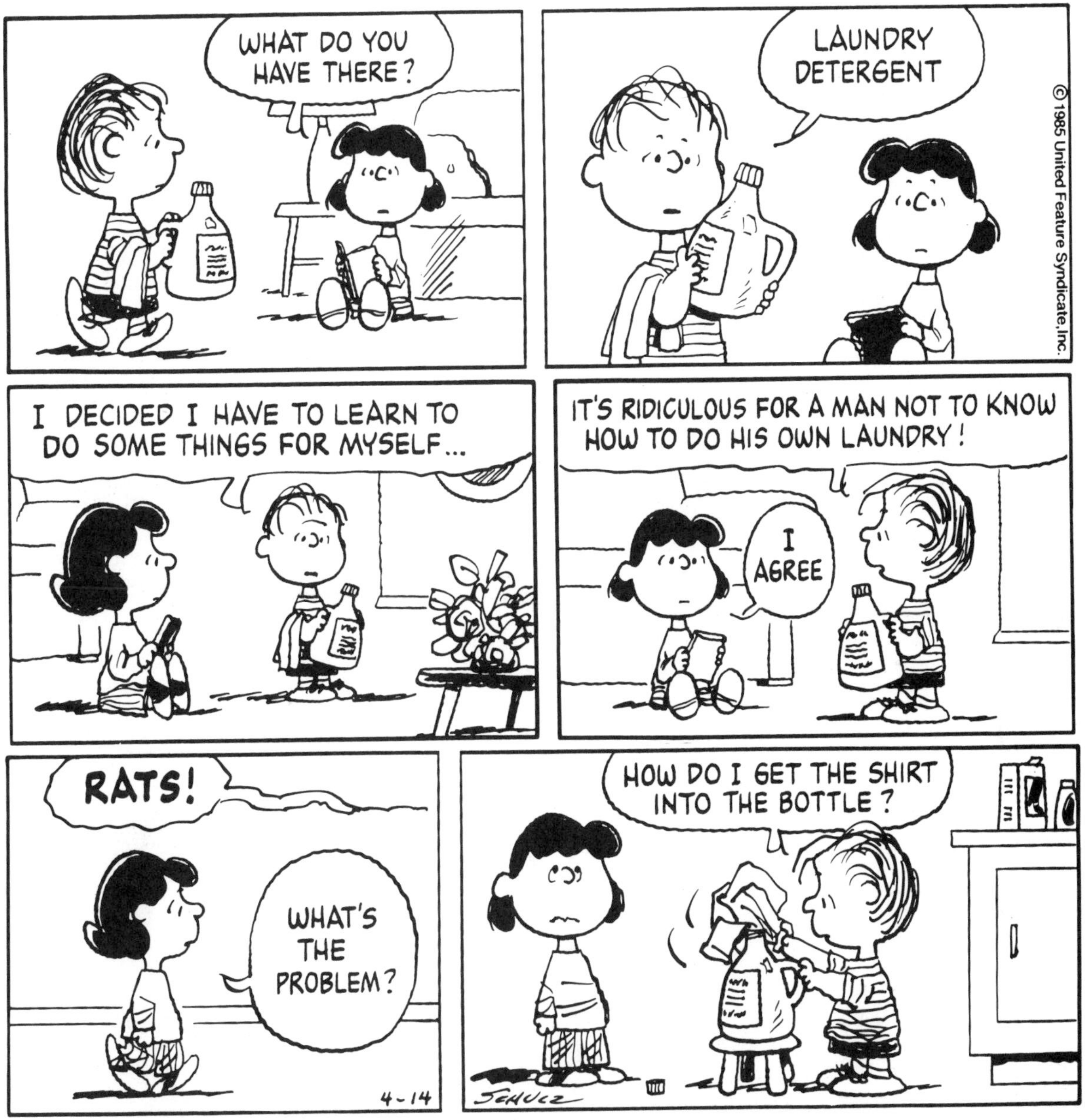
WHAT DO YOU HAVE THERE?
LAUNDRY DETERGENT
© 1985 United Feature Syndicate, Inc.
I DECIDED I HAVE TO LEARN TO DO SOME THINGS FOR MYSELF...
IT'S RIDICULOUS FOR A MAN NOT TO KNOW HOW TO DO HIS OWN LAUNDRY!
I AGREE
RATS!
WHAT'S THE PROBLEM?
HOW DO I GET THE SHIRT INTO THE BOTTLE?
4-14
SCHULZ

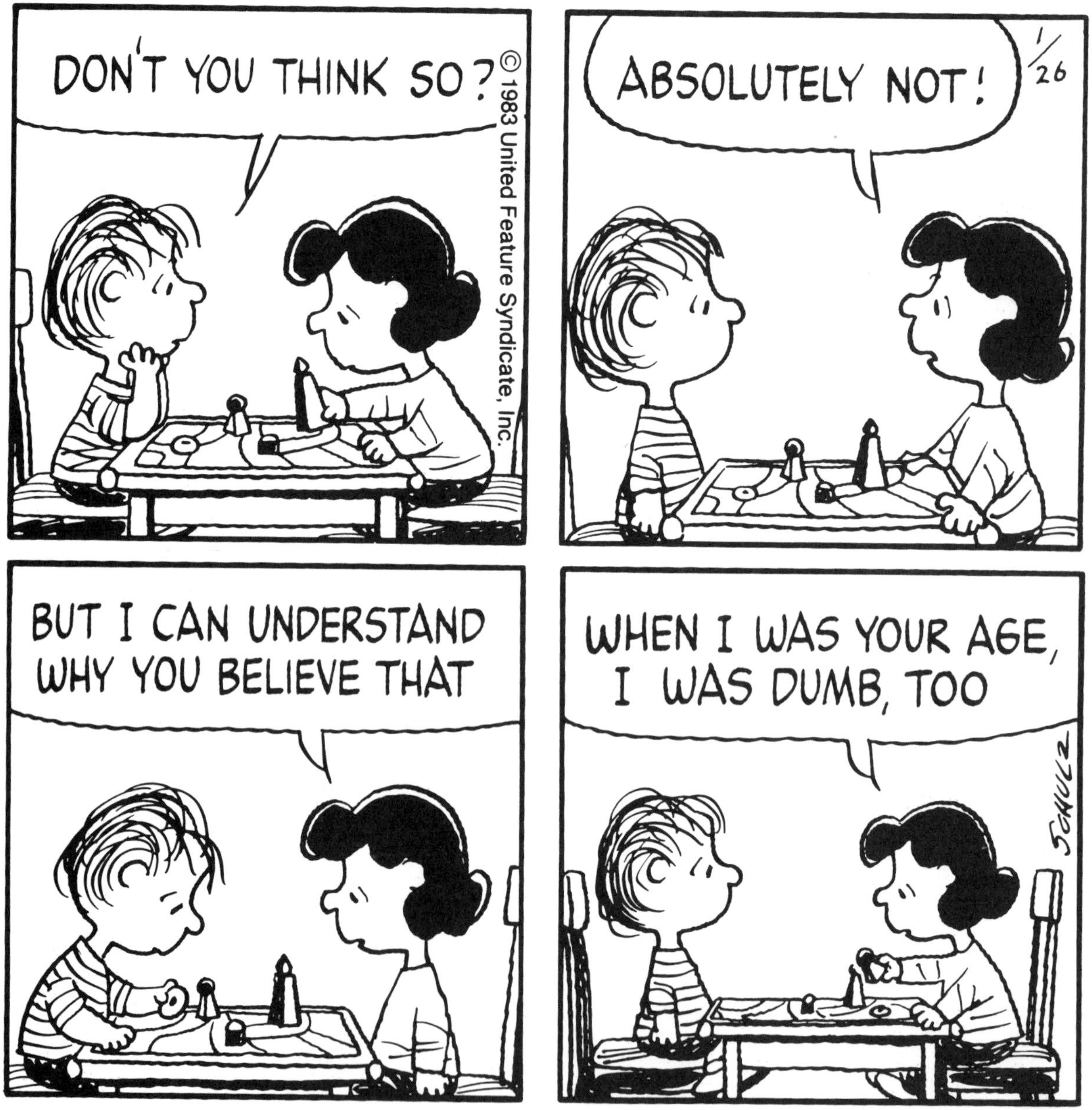
DON'T YOU THINK SO?
© 1983 United Feature Syndicate, Inc.
ABSOLUTELY NOT!
1/26
BUT I CAN UNDERSTAND WHY YOU BELIEVE THAT
WHEN I WAS YOUR AGE, I WAS DUMB, TOO
SCHULZ

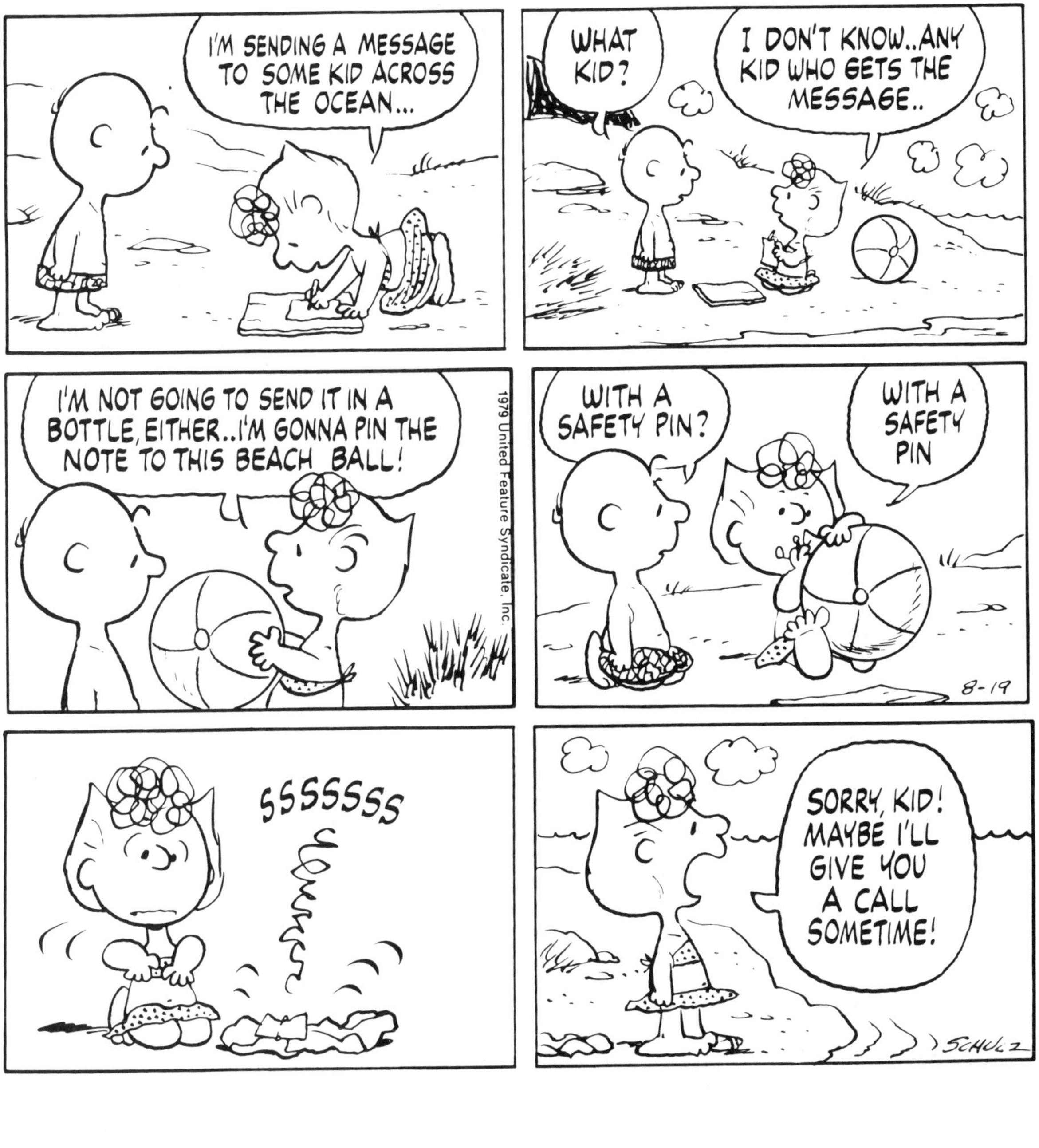
I'M SENDING A MESSAGE TO SOME KID ACROSS THE OCEAN...
WHAT KID?
I DON'T KNOW..ANY KID WHO GETS THE MESSAGE..
I'M NOT GOING TO SEND IT IN A BOTTLE, EITHER..I'M GONNA PIN THE NOTE TO THIS BEACH BALL!
1979 United Feature Syndicate, Inc.
WITH A SAFETY PIN?
WITH A SAFETY PIN
8-19
SSSSSSS
SORRY, KID! MAYBE I'LL GIVE YOU A CALL SOMETIME!
SCHULZ

BROTHERS AND SISTERS

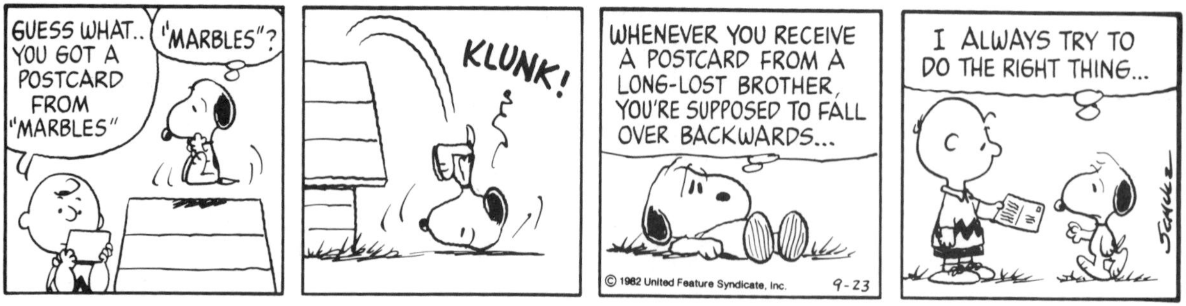

GUESS WHAT.. YOU GOT A POSTCARD FROM "MARBLES"
"MARBLES"?
KLUNK!
WHENEVER YOU RECEIVE A POSTCARD FROM A LONG-LOST BROTHER, YOU'RE SUPPOSED TO FALL OVER BACKWARDS...
© 1982 United Feature Syndicate, Inc.
9-23
I ALWAYS TRY TO DO THE RIGHT THING...
SCHULZ

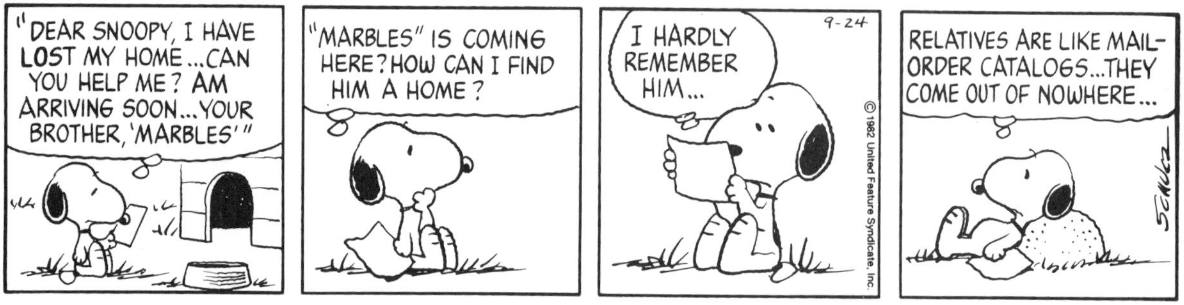

"DEAR SNOOPY, I HAVE LOST MY HOME...CAN YOU HELP ME? AM ARRIVING SOON...YOUR BROTHER, 'MARBLES'"
"MARBLES" IS COMING HERE? HOW CAN I FIND HIM A HOME?
9-24
I HARDLY REMEMBER HIM...
© 1982 United Feature Syndicate, Inc.
RELATIVES ARE LIKE MAIL-ORDER CATALOGS...THEY COME OUT OF NOWHERE...
SCHULZ

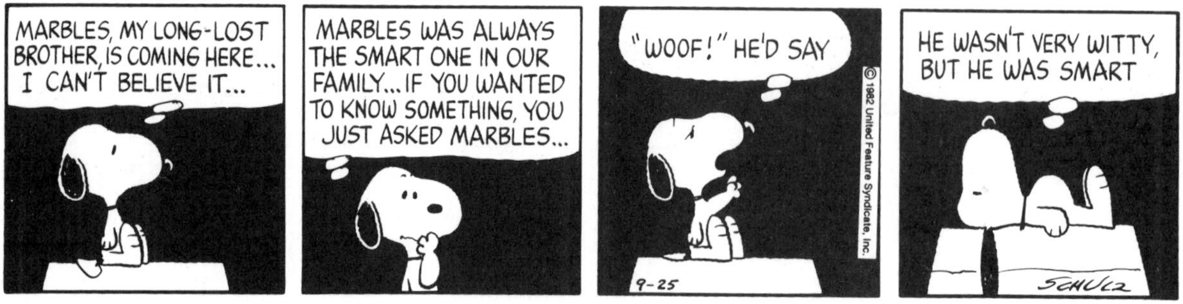

MARBLES, MY LONG-LOST BROTHER, IS COMING HERE... I CAN'T BELIEVE IT...
MARBLES WAS ALWAYS THE SMART ONE IN OUR FAMILY...IF YOU WANTED TO KNOW SOMETHING, YOU JUST ASKED MARBLES...
"WOOF!" HE'D SAY
© 1982 United Feature Syndicate, Inc.
9-25
HE WASN'T VERY WITTY, BUT HE WAS SMART
SCHULZ

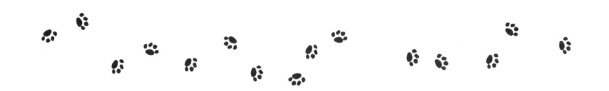

IT'S ALL RELATIVE

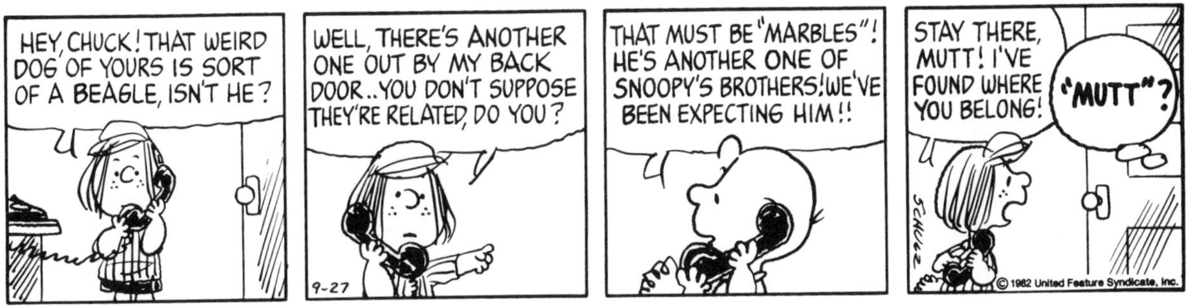

HEY, CHUCK! THAT WEIRD DOG OF YOURS IS SORT OF A BEAGLE, ISN'T HE?
WELL, THERE'S ANOTHER ONE OUT BY MY BACK DOOR..YOU DON'T SUPPOSE THEY'RE RELATED, DO YOU?
9-27
THAT MUST BE "MARBLES"! HE'S ANOTHER ONE OF SNOOPY'S BROTHERS! WE'VE BEEN EXPECTING HIM!!
STAY THERE, MUTT! I'VE FOUND WHERE YOU BELONG!
"MUTT"?
SCHULZ
© 1982 United Feature Syndicate, Inc.

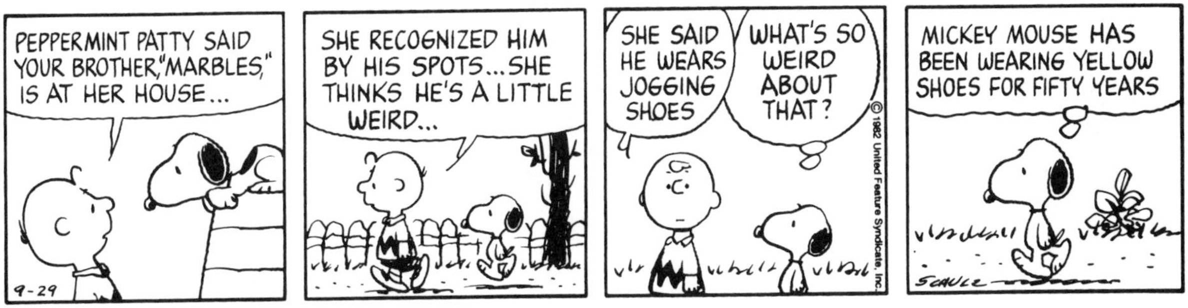

PEPPERMINT PATTY SAID YOUR BROTHER, "MARBLES," IS AT HER HOUSE...
9-29
SHE RECOGNIZED HIM BY HIS SPOTS...SHE THINKS HE'S A LITTLE WEIRD...
SHE SAID HE WEARS JOGGING SHOES
WHAT'S SO WEIRD ABOUT THAT?
© 1982 United Feature Syndicate, Inc.
MICKEY MOUSE HAS BEEN WEARING YELLOW SHOES FOR FIFTY YEARS
SCHULZ

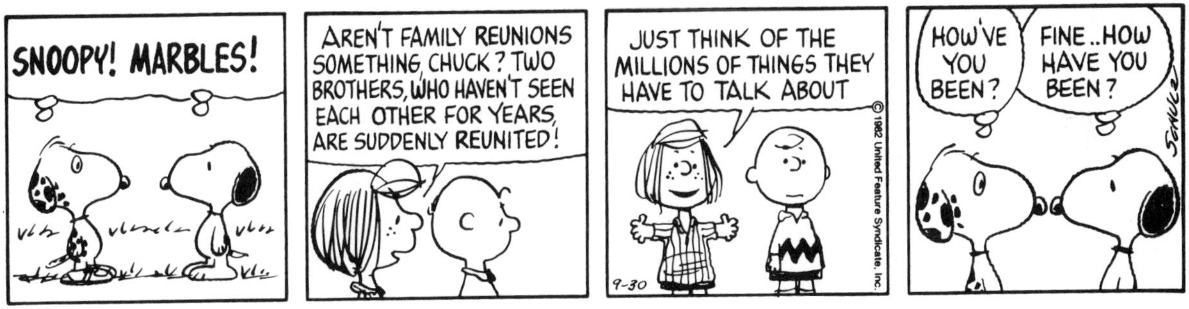

SNOOPY! MARBLES!
AREN'T FAMILY REUNIONS SOMETHING, CHUCK? TWO BROTHERS, WHO HAVEN'T SEEN EACH OTHER FOR YEARS, ARE SUDDENLY REUNITED!
JUST THINK OF THE MILLIONS OF THINGS THEY HAVE TO TALK ABOUT
9-30
© 1982 United Feature Syndicate, Inc.
HOW'VE YOU BEEN?
FINE..HOW HAVE YOU BEEN?
SCHULZ

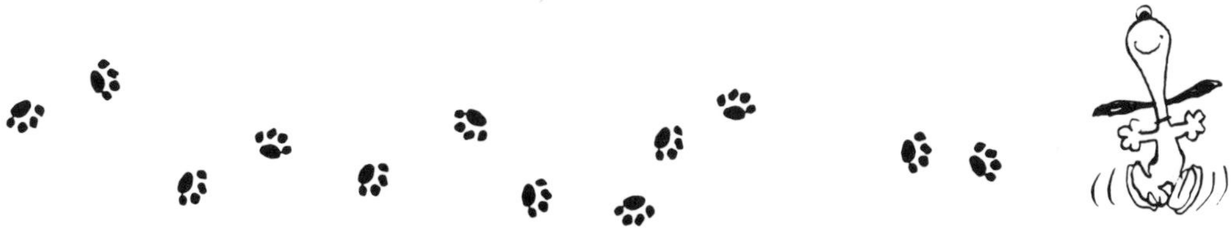

BROTHERS AND SISTERS

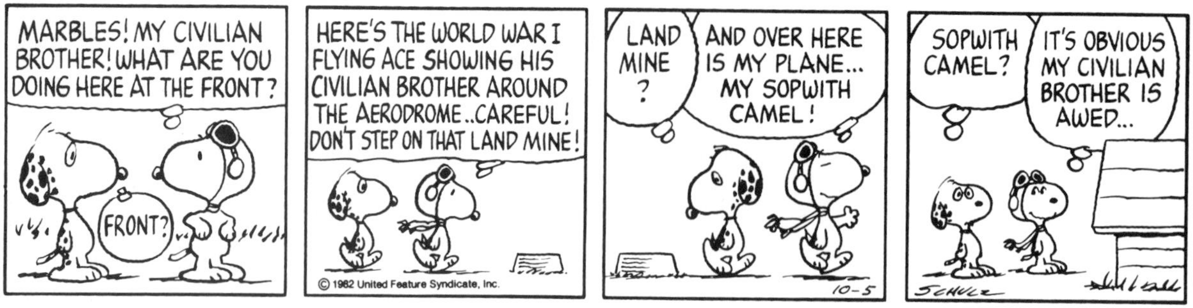

MARBLES! MY CIVILIAN BROTHER! WHAT ARE YOU DOING HERE AT THE FRONT?
FRONT?
HERE'S THE WORLD WAR I FLYING ACE SHOWING HIS CIVILIAN BROTHER AROUND THE AERODROME..CAREFUL! DON'T STEP ON THAT LAND MINE!
© 1982 United Feature Syndicate, Inc.
LAND MINE ?
AND OVER HERE IS MY PLANE... MY SOPWITH CAMEL!
10-5
SOPWITH CAMEL?
IT'S OBVIOUS MY CIVILIAN BROTHER IS AWED...
SCHULZ

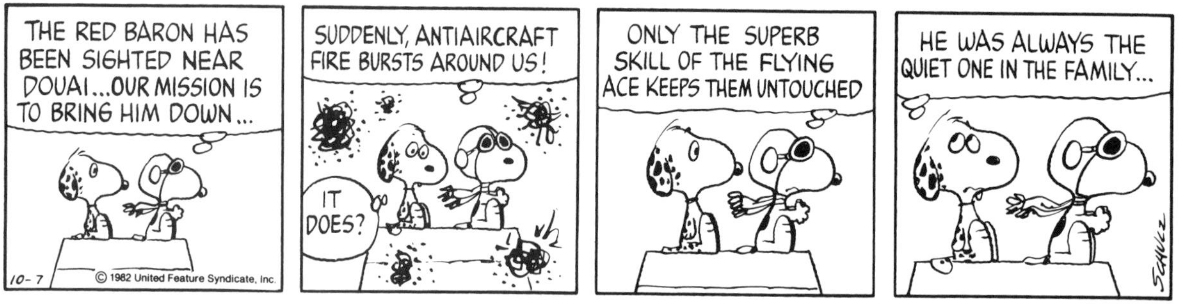

THE RED BARON HAS BEEN SIGHTED NEAR DOUAI...OUR MISSION IS TO BRING HIM DOWN...
10-7
© 1982 United Feature Syndicate, Inc.
SUDDENLY, ANTIAIRCRAFT FIRE BURSTS AROUND US!
IT DOES?
ONLY THE SUPERB SKILL OF THE FLYING ACE KEEPS THEM UNTOUCHED
HE WAS ALWAYS THE QUIET ONE IN THE FAMILY...
SCHULZ

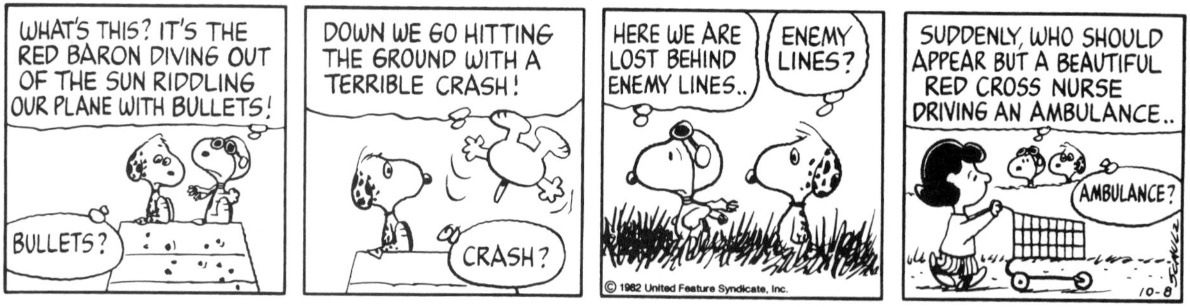

WHAT'S THIS? IT'S THE RED BARON DIVING OUT OF THE SUN RIDDLING OUR PLANE WITH BULLETS!
BULLETS?
DOWN WE GO HITTING THE GROUND WITH A TERRIBLE CRASH!
CRASH?
HERE WE ARE LOST BEHIND ENEMY LINES..
ENEMY LINES?
© 1982 United Feature Syndicate, Inc.
SUDDENLY, WHO SHOULD APPEAR BUT A BEAUTIFUL RED CROSS NURSE DRIVING AN AMBULANCE..
AMBULANCE?
SCHULZ
10-8

IT'S ALL RELATIVE

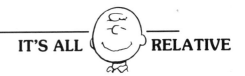

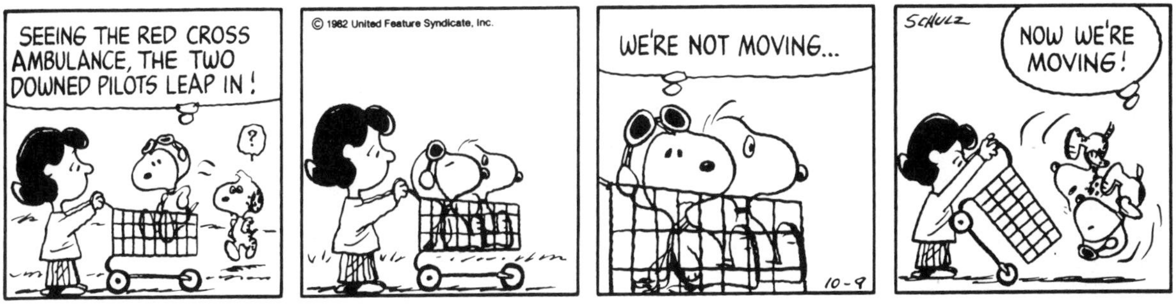
SEEING THE RED CROSS AMBULANCE, THE TWO DOWNED PILOTS LEAP IN!
?
© 1982 United Feature Syndicate, Inc.
WE'RE NOT MOVING...
10-9
SCHULZ
NOW WE'RE MOVING!

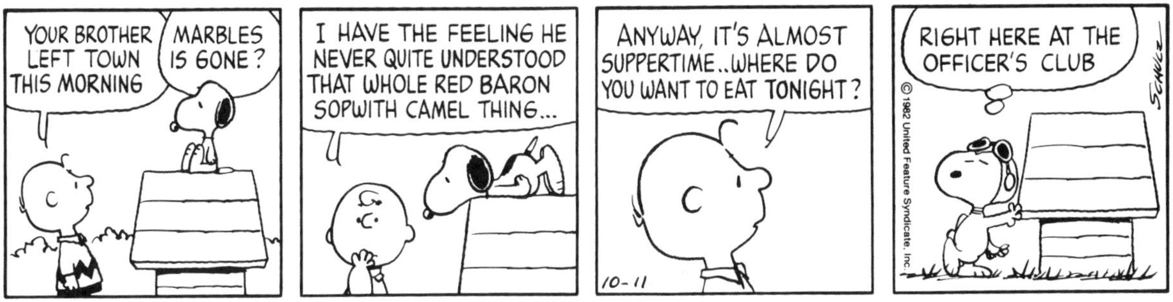
YOUR BROTHER LEFT TOWN THIS MORNING
MARBLES IS GONE?
I HAVE THE FEELING HE NEVER QUITE UNDERSTOOD THAT WHOLE RED BARON SOPWITH CAMEL THING...
ANYWAY, IT'S ALMOST SUPPERTIME..WHERE DO YOU WANT TO EAT TONIGHT?
10-11
RIGHT HERE AT THE OFFICER'S CLUB
© 1982 United Feature Syndicate, Inc.
SCHULZ

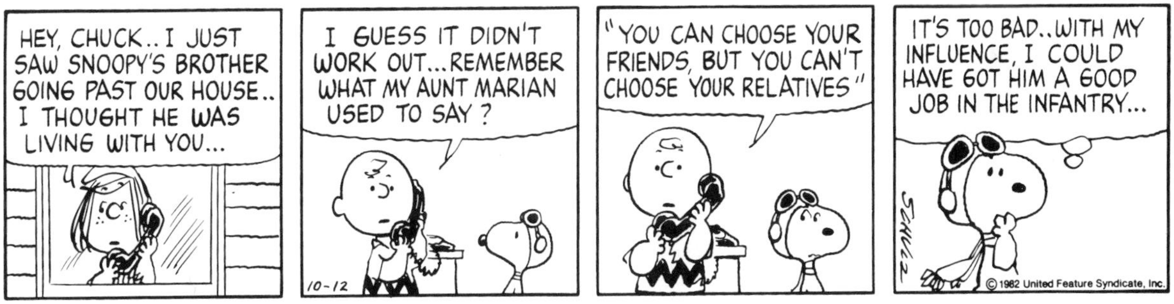
HEY, CHUCK..I JUST SAW SNOOPY'S BROTHER GOING PAST OUR HOUSE.. I THOUGHT HE WAS LIVING WITH YOU...
I GUESS IT DIDN'T WORK OUT...REMEMBER WHAT MY AUNT MARIAN USED TO SAY?
10-12
"YOU CAN CHOOSE YOUR FRIENDS, BUT YOU CAN'T CHOOSE YOUR RELATIVES"
IT'S TOO BAD..WITH MY INFLUENCE, I COULD HAVE GOT HIM A GOOD JOB IN THE INFANTRY...
SCHULZ
© 1982 United Feature Syndicate, Inc.

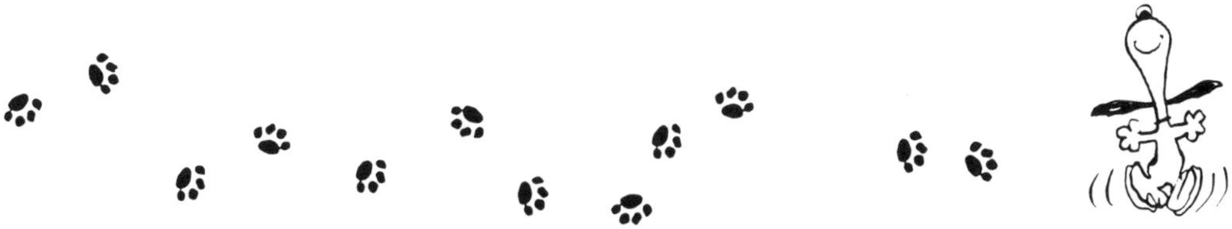

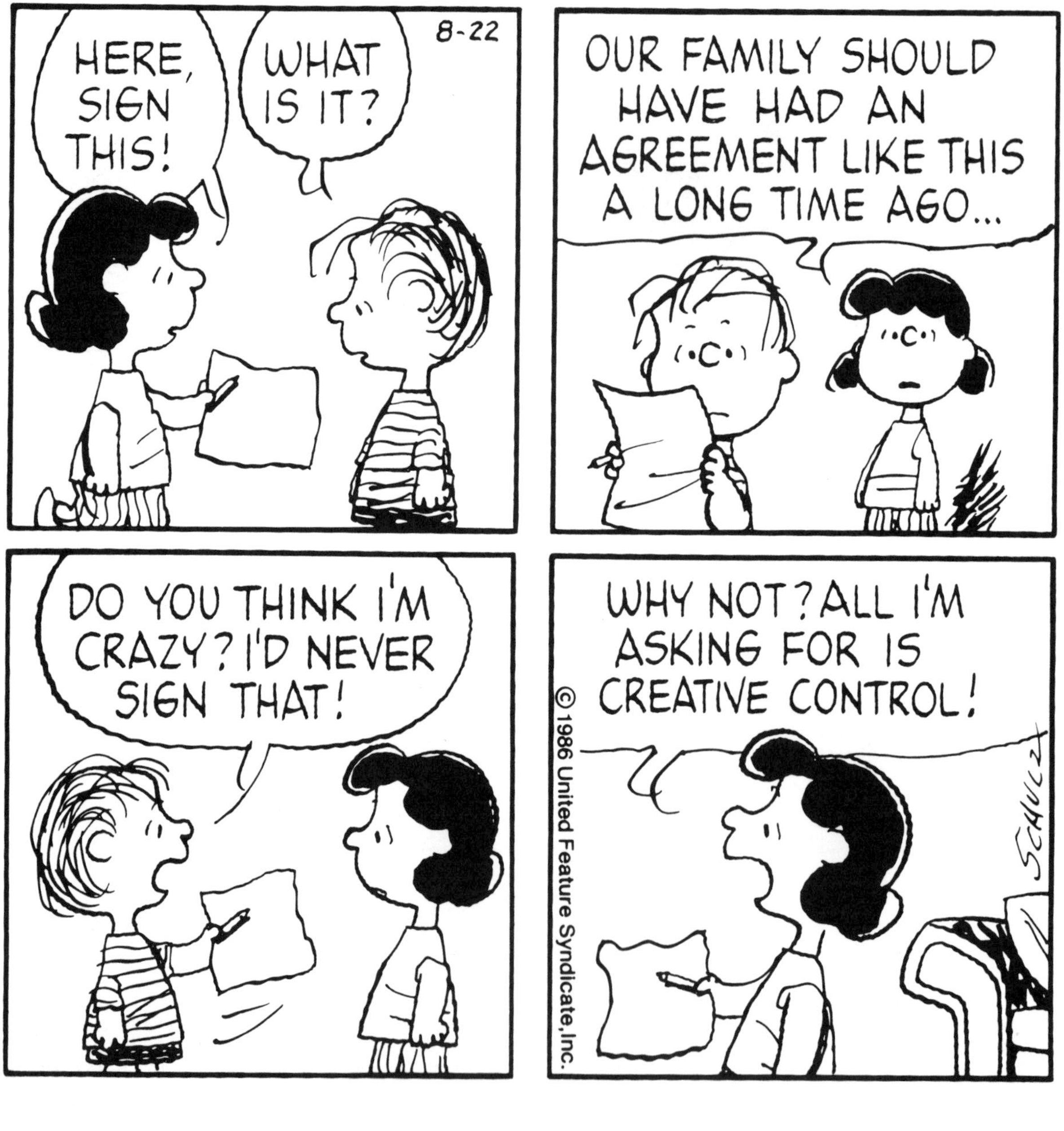
8-22
HERE, SIGN THIS!
WHAT IS IT?
OUR FAMILY SHOULD HAVE HAD AN AGREEMENT LIKE THIS A LONG TIME AGO...
DO YOU THINK I'M CRAZY? I'D NEVER SIGN THAT!
WHY NOT? ALL I'M ASKING FOR IS CREATIVE CONTROL!
© 1986 United Feature Syndicate, Inc.
SCHULZ

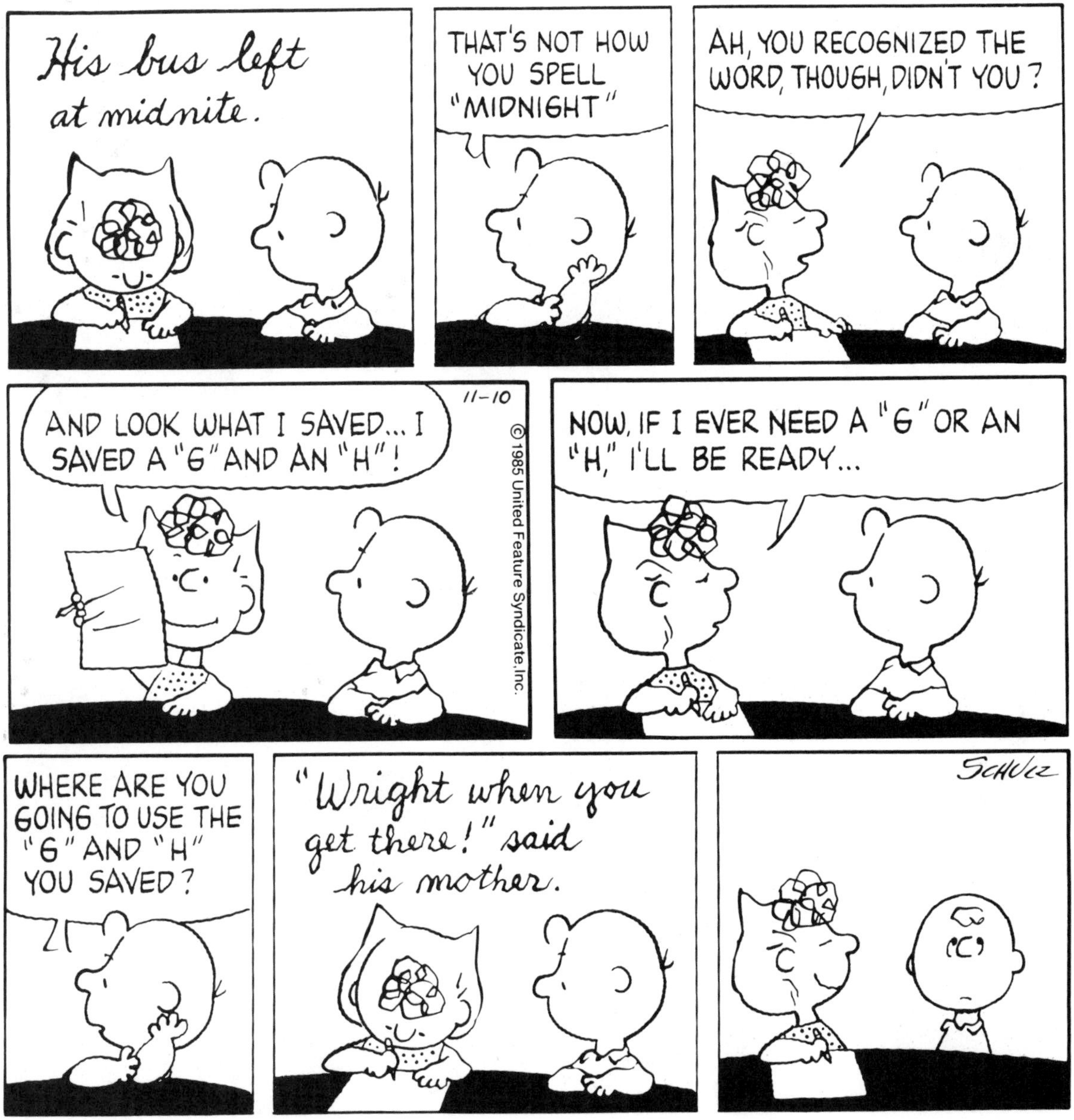
His bus left at midnite.
THAT'S NOT HOW YOU SPELL "MIDNIGHT"
AH, YOU RECOGNIZED THE WORD, THOUGH, DIDN'T YOU?
11-10
© 1985 United Feature Syndicate, Inc.
AND LOOK WHAT I SAVED... I SAVED A "G" AND AN "H"!
NOW, IF I EVER NEED A "G" OR AN "H," I'LL BE READY...
WHERE ARE YOU GOING TO USE THE "G" AND "H" YOU SAVED?
"Wright when you get there!" said his mother.
SCHULZ

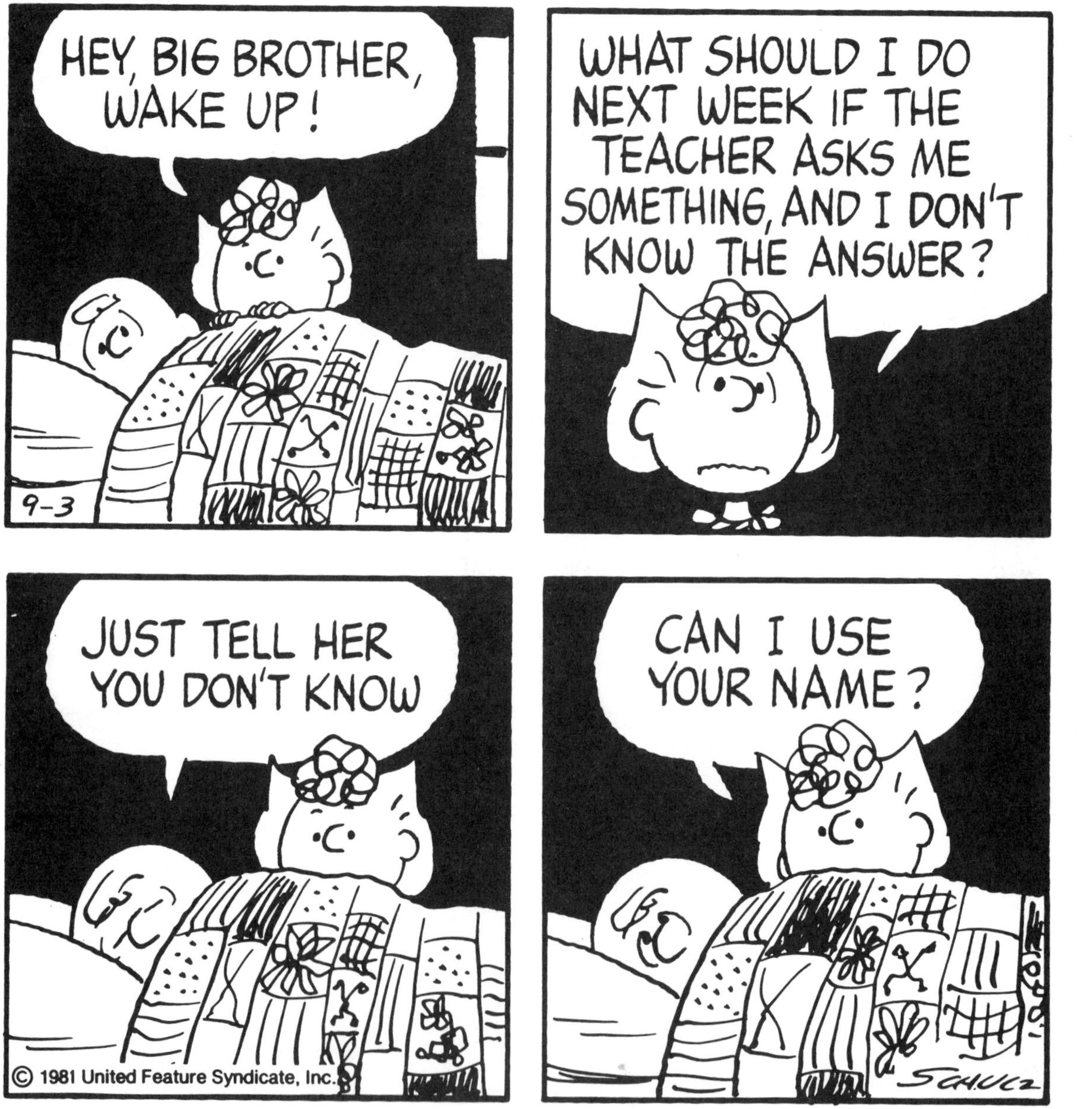
HEY, BIG BROTHER, WAKE UP!
9-3
WHAT SHOULD I DO NEXT WEEK IF THE TEACHER ASKS ME SOMETHING, AND I DON'T KNOW THE ANSWER?
JUST TELL HER YOU DON'T KNOW
© 1981 United Feature Syndicate, Inc.
CAN I USE YOUR NAME?
SCHULZ

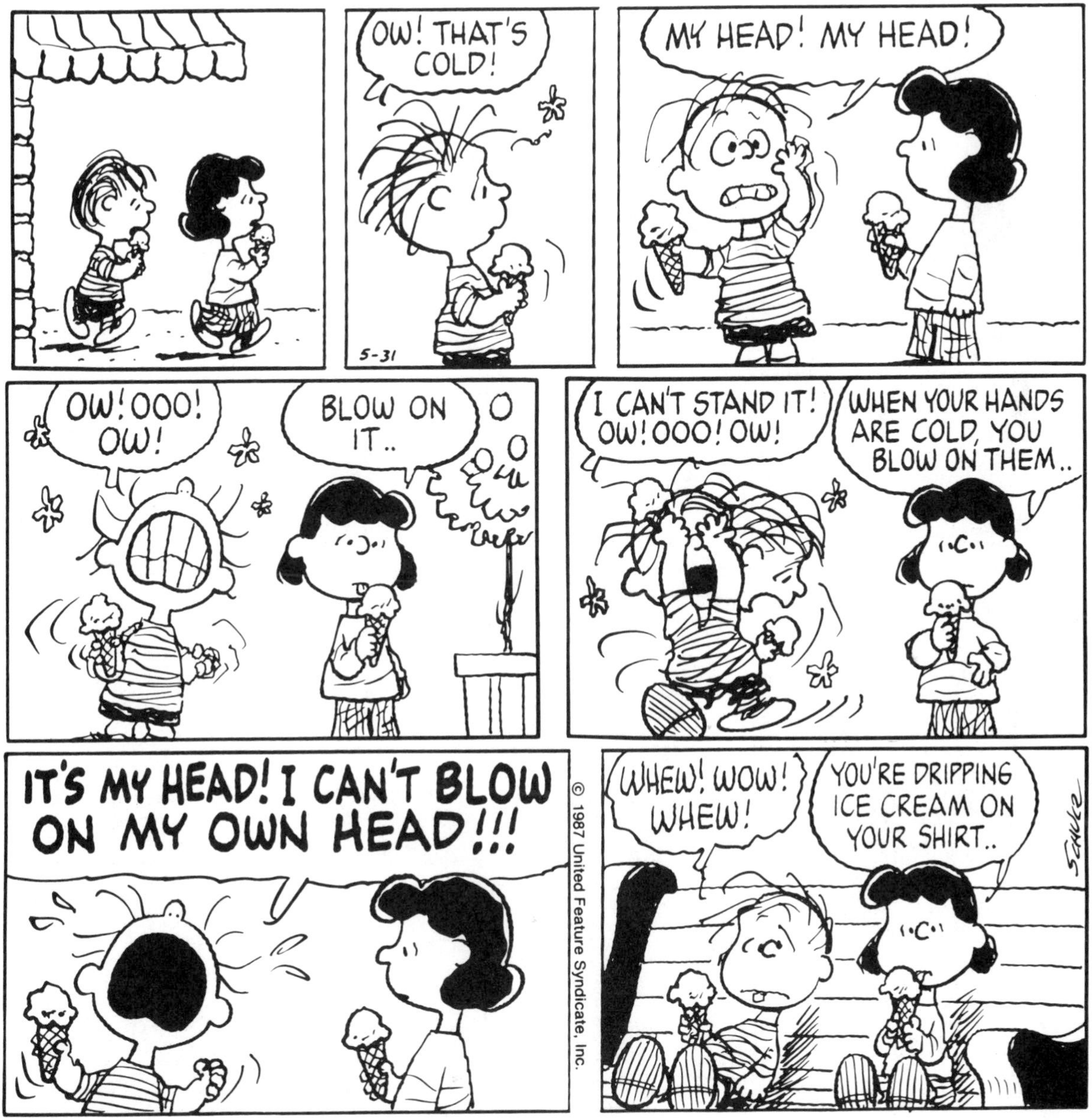
OW! THAT'S COLD!
5-31
MY HEAD! MY HEAD!
OW! OOO! OW!
BLOW ON IT..
I CAN'T STAND IT! OW! OOO! OW!
WHEN YOUR HANDS ARE COLD, YOU BLOW ON THEM..
IT'S MY HEAD! I CAN'T BLOW ON MY OWN HEAD!!!
WHEW! WOW! WHEW!
YOU'RE DRIPPING ICE CREAM ON YOUR SHIRT..
SCHULZ

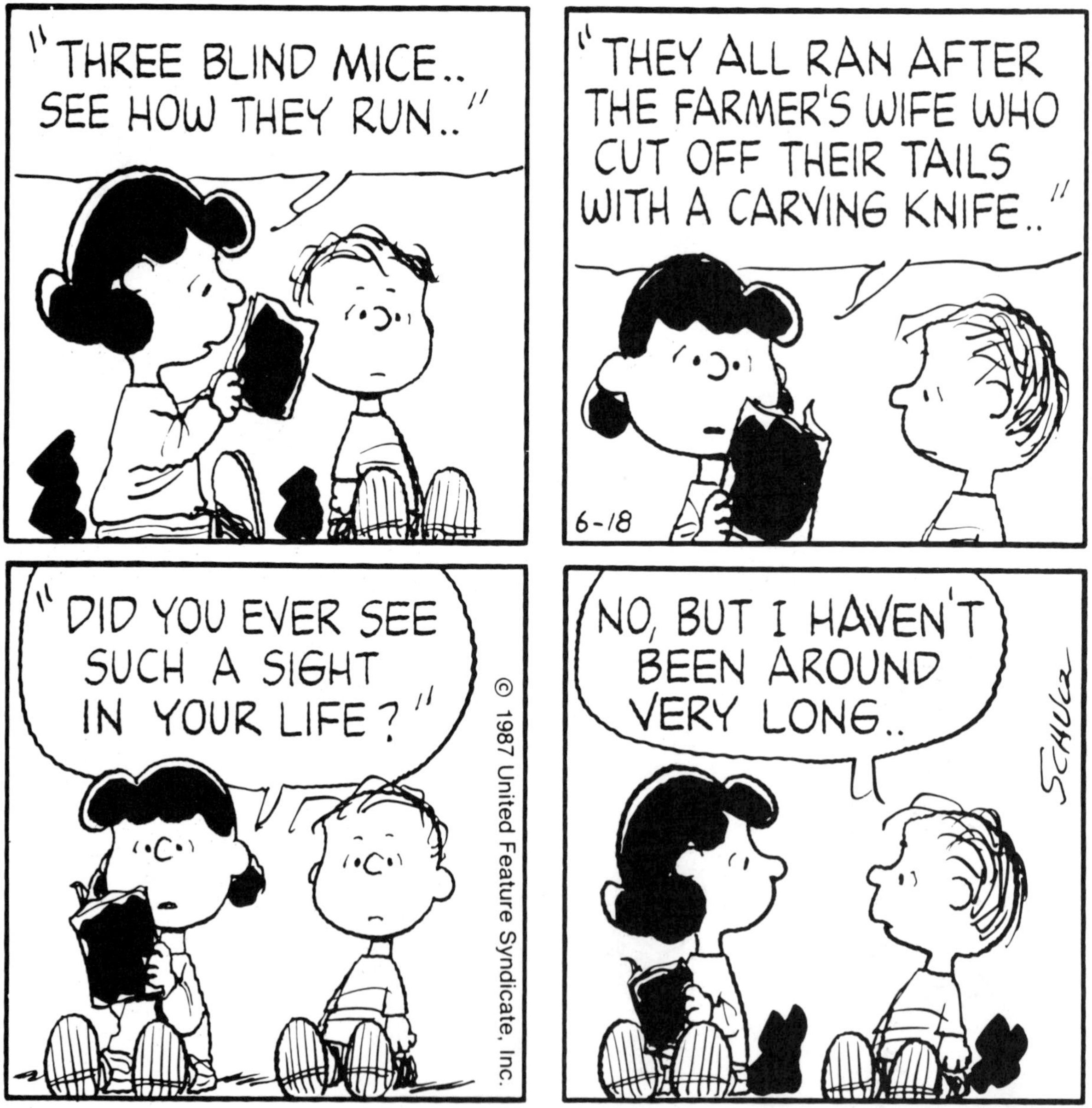
"THREE BLIND MICE.. SEE HOW THEY RUN.."
"THEY ALL RAN AFTER THE FARMER'S WIFE WHO CUT OFF THEIR TAILS WITH A CARVING KNIFE.."
6-18
"DID YOU EVER SEE SUCH A SIGHT IN YOUR LIFE?"
© 1987 United Feature Syndicate, Inc.
NO, BUT I HAVEN'T BEEN AROUND VERY LONG..
SCHULZ

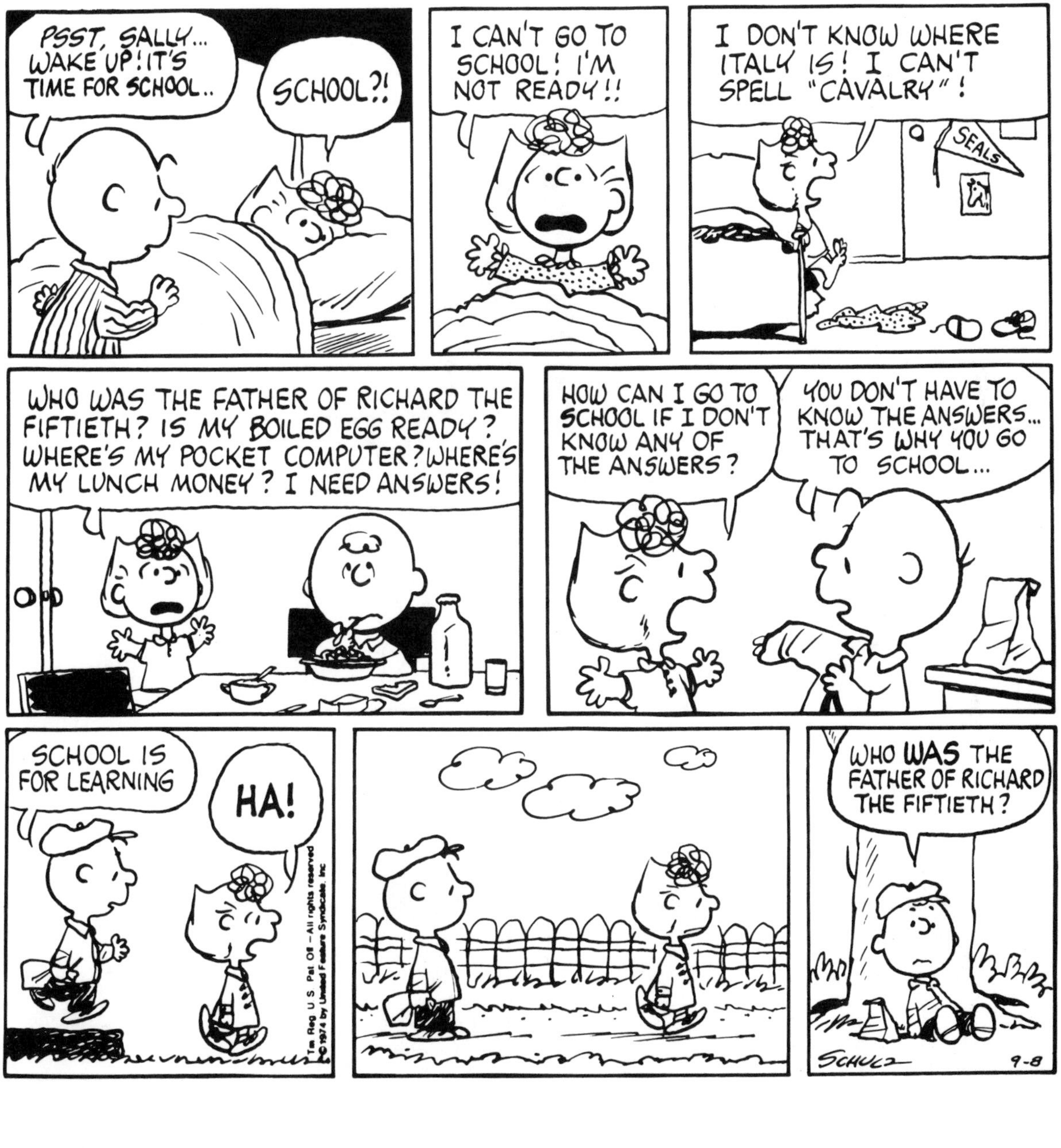
PSST, SALLY... WAKE UP! IT'S TIME FOR SCHOOL..
SCHOOL?!
I CAN'T GO TO SCHOOL! I'M NOT READY!!
I DON'T KNOW WHERE ITALY IS! I CAN'T SPELL "CAVALRY"!
SEALS
WHO WAS THE FATHER OF RICHARD THE FIFTIETH? IS MY BOILED EGG READY? WHERE'S MY POCKET COMPUTER? WHERE'S MY LUNCH MONEY? I NEED ANSWERS!
HOW CAN I GO TO SCHOOL IF I DON'T KNOW ANY OF THE ANSWERS?
YOU DON'T HAVE TO KNOW THE ANSWERS... THAT'S WHY YOU GO TO SCHOOL...
SCHOOL IS FOR LEARNING
HA!
Tm. Reg. U.S. Pat. Off.—All rights reserved
© 1974 by United Feature Syndicate, Inc
WHO WAS THE FATHER OF RICHARD THE FIFTIETH?
SCHULZ
9-8

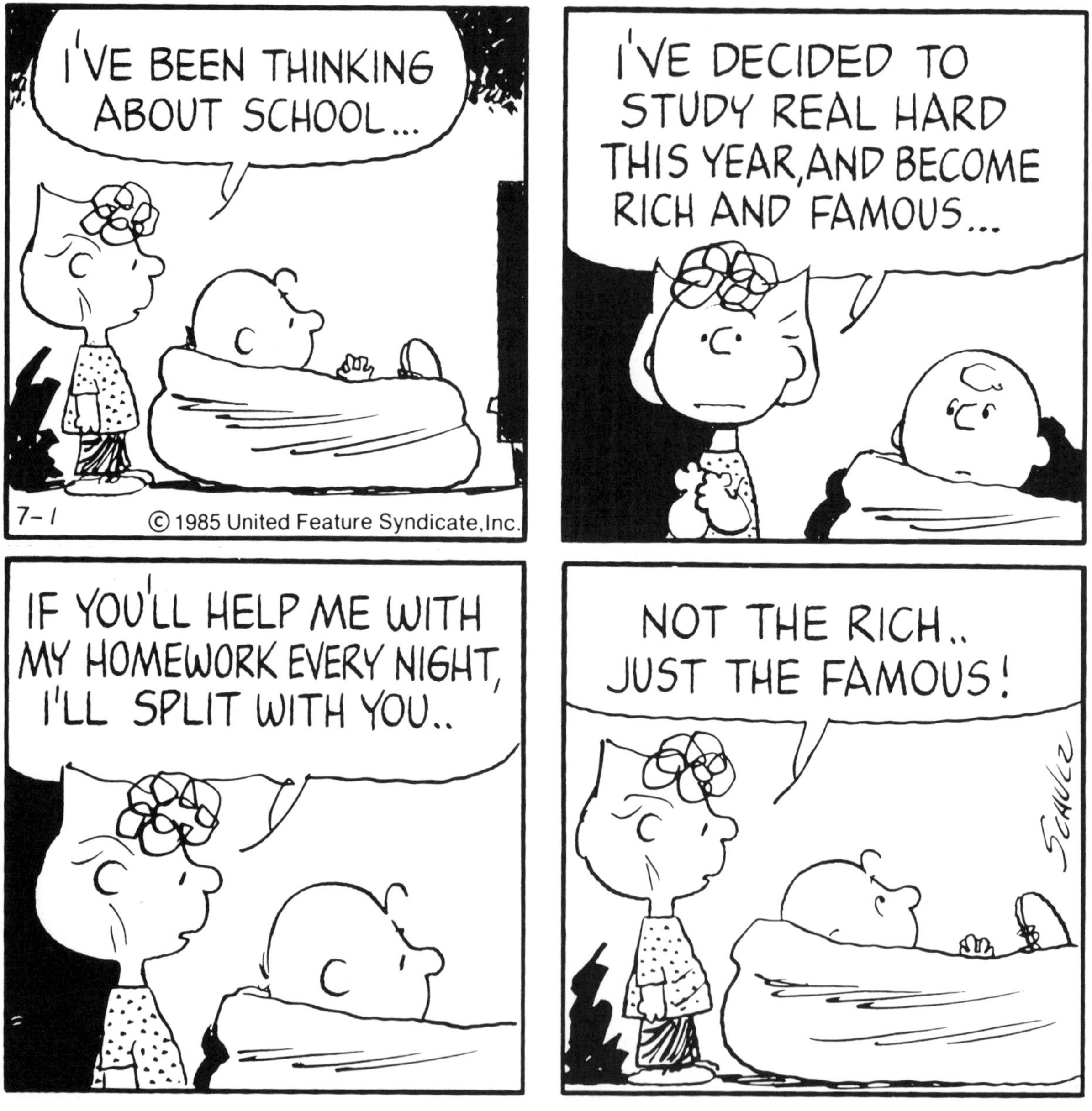
I'VE BEEN THINKING ABOUT SCHOOL...
7-1
© 1985 United Feature Syndicate, Inc.
I'VE DECIDED TO STUDY REAL HARD THIS YEAR, AND BECOME RICH AND FAMOUS...
IF YOU'LL HELP ME WITH MY HOMEWORK EVERY NIGHT, I'LL SPLIT WITH YOU..
NOT THE RICH.. JUST THE FAMOUS!
SCHULZ

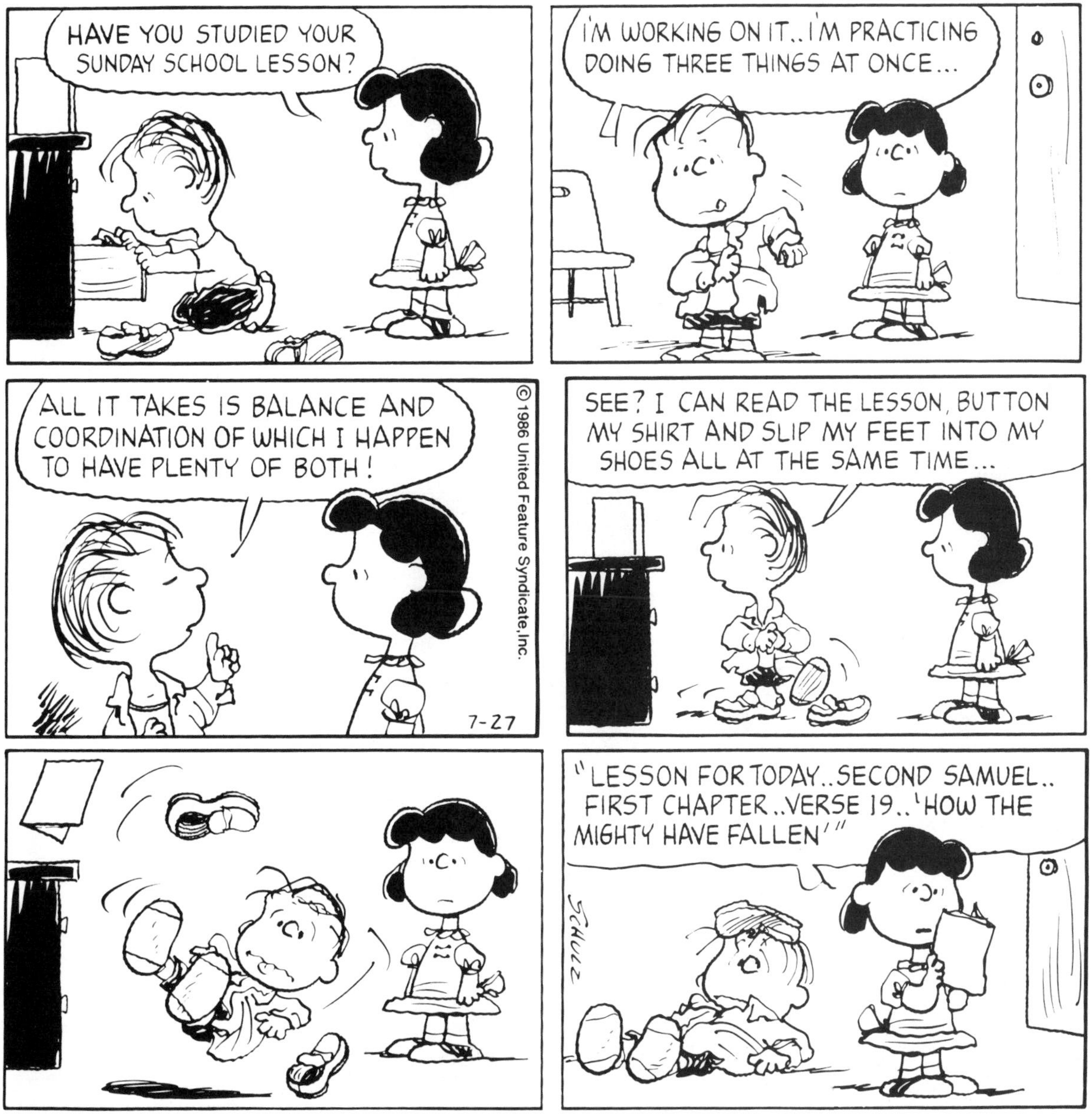
HAVE YOU STUDIED YOUR SUNDAY SCHOOL LESSON?
I'M WORKING ON IT.. I'M PRACTICING DOING THREE THINGS AT ONCE...
ALL IT TAKES IS BALANCE AND COORDINATION OF WHICH I HAPPEN TO HAVE PLENTY OF BOTH!
© 1986 United Feature Syndicate, Inc.
7-27
SEE? I CAN READ THE LESSON, BUTTON MY SHIRT AND SLIP MY FEET INTO MY SHOES ALL AT THE SAME TIME...
"LESSON FOR TODAY.. SECOND SAMUEL.. FIRST CHAPTER..VERSE 19..'HOW THE MIGHTY HAVE FALLEN'"
SCHULZ

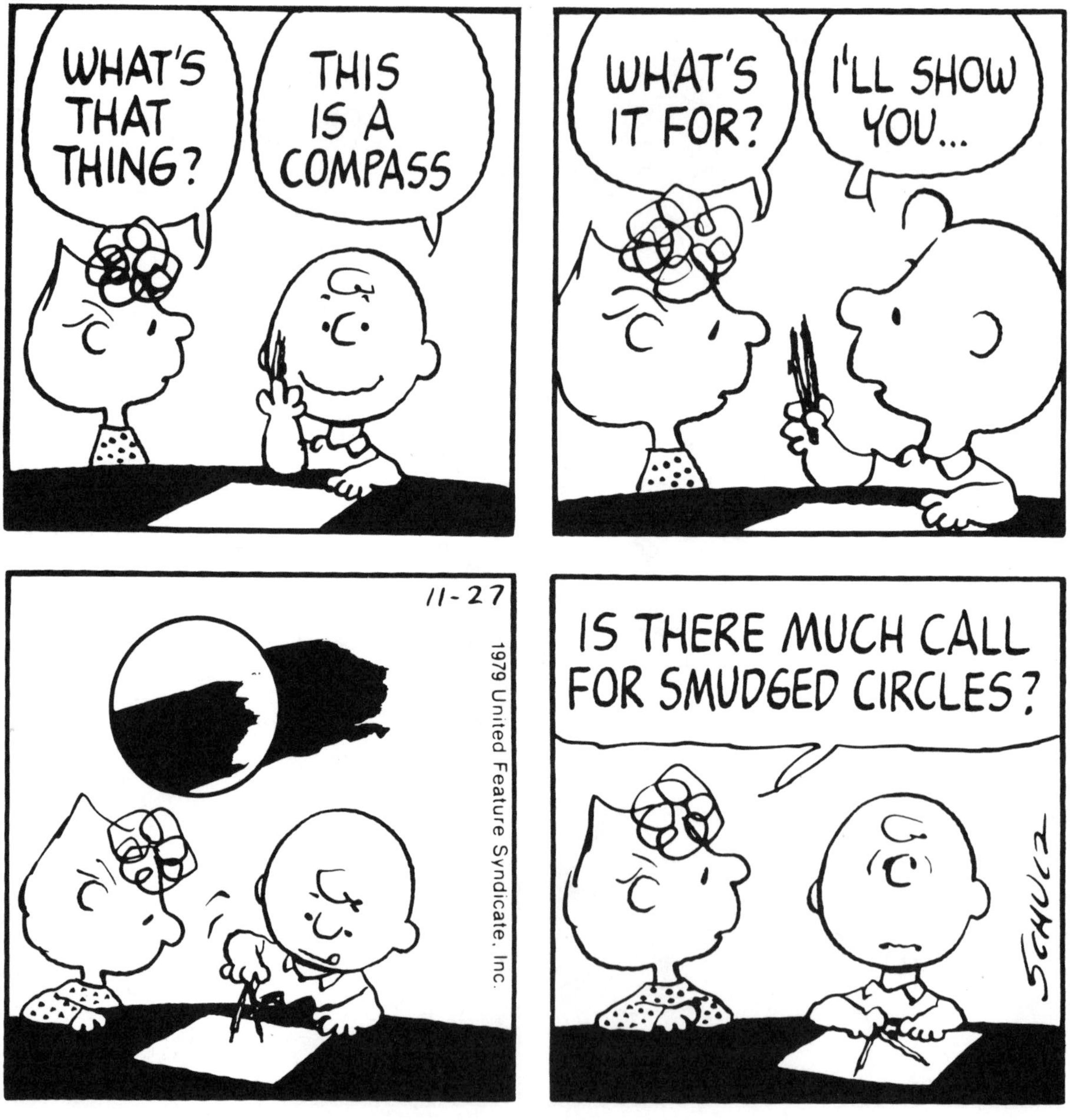
WHAT'S THAT THING?
THIS IS A COMPASS
WHAT'S IT FOR?
I'LL SHOW YOU...
11-27
1979 United Feature Syndicate, Inc.
IS THERE MUCH CALL FOR SMUDGED CIRCLES?
SCHULZ

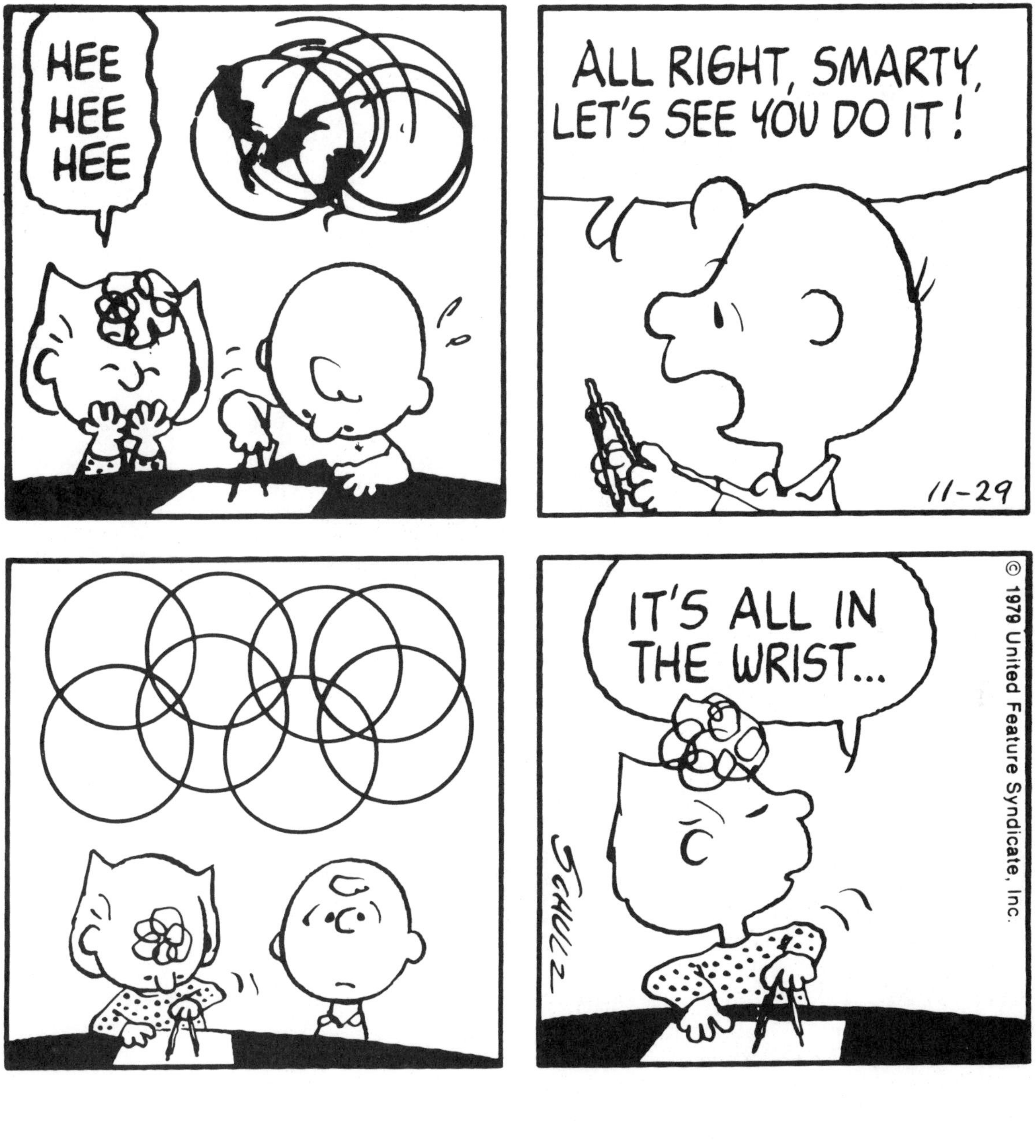
HEE HEE HEE
ALL RIGHT, SMARTY, LET'S SEE YOU DO IT!
11-29
IT'S ALL IN THE WRIST...
SCHULZ
© 1979 United Feature Syndicate, Inc.

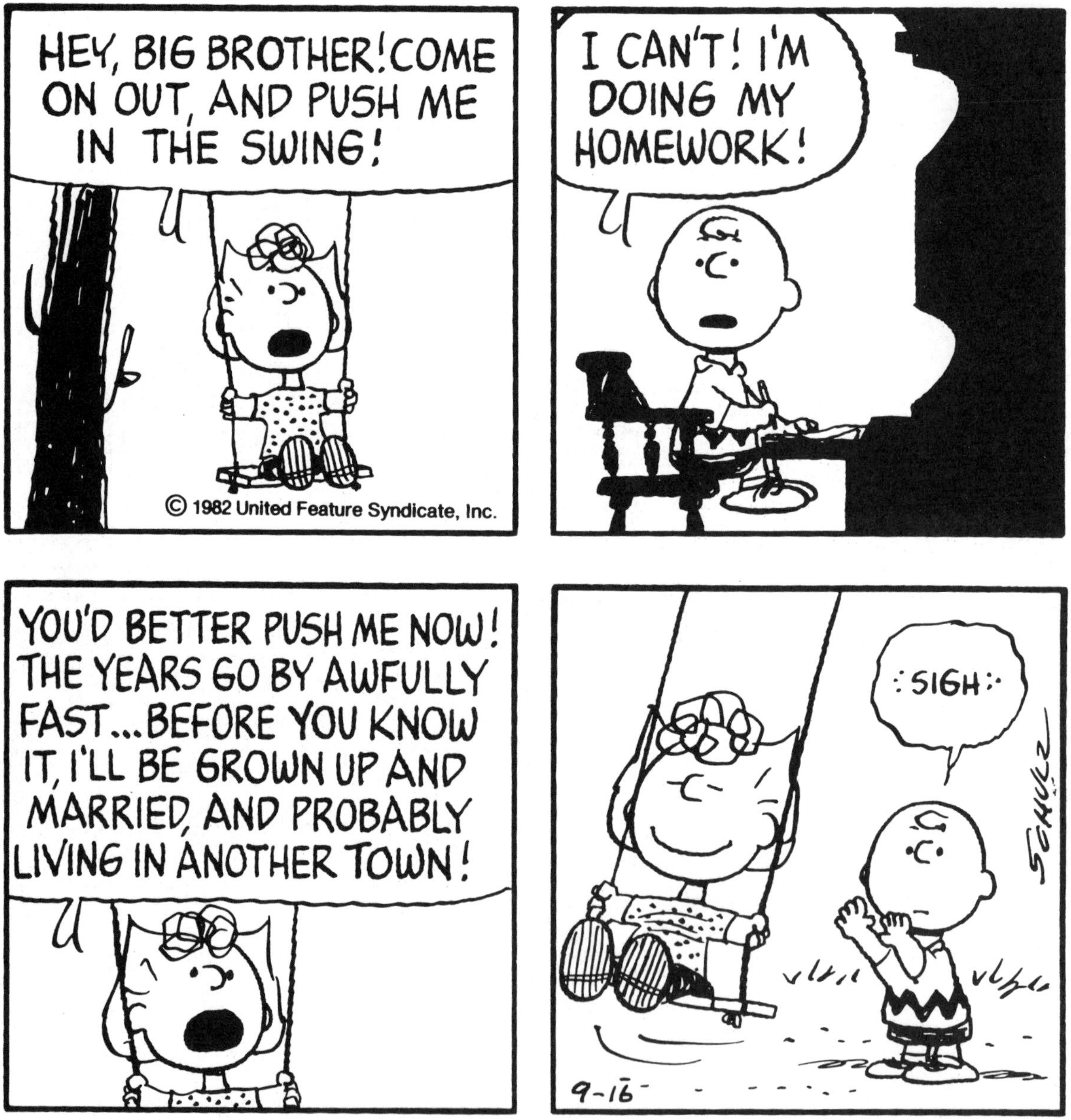
HEY, BIG BROTHER! COME ON OUT, AND PUSH ME IN THE SWING!
© 1982 United Feature Syndicate, Inc.
I CAN'T! I'M DOING MY HOMEWORK!
YOU'D BETTER PUSH ME NOW! THE YEARS GO BY AWFULLY FAST...BEFORE YOU KNOW IT, I'LL BE GROWN UP AND MARRIED, AND PROBABLY LIVING IN ANOTHER TOWN!
SIGH
SCHULZ
9-16

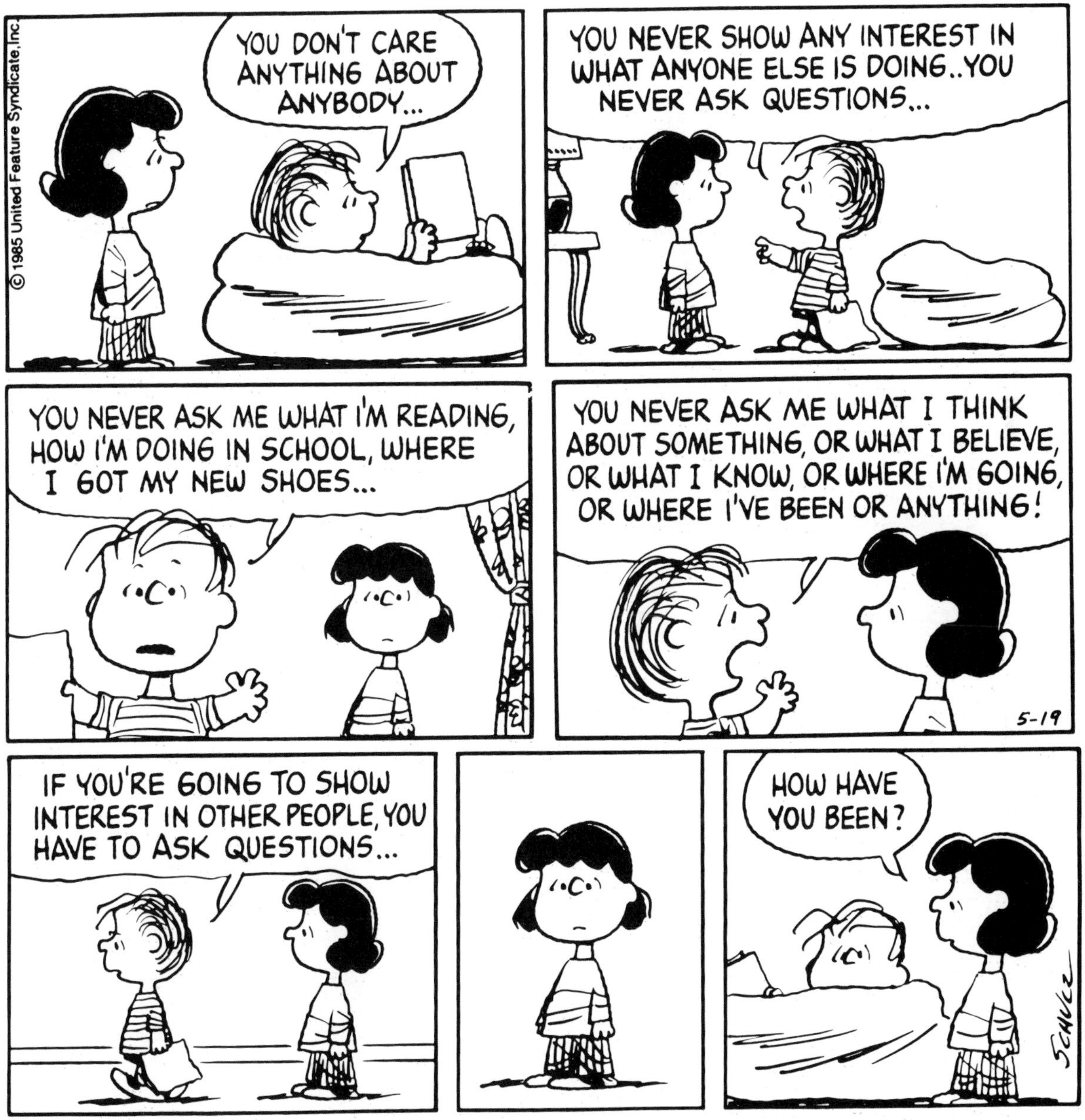
© 1985 United Feature Syndicate, Inc.
YOU DON'T CARE ANYTHING ABOUT ANYBODY...
YOU NEVER SHOW ANY INTEREST IN WHAT ANYONE ELSE IS DOING..YOU NEVER ASK QUESTIONS...
YOU NEVER ASK ME WHAT I'M READING, HOW I'M DOING IN SCHOOL, WHERE I GOT MY NEW SHOES...
YOU NEVER ASK ME WHAT I THINK ABOUT SOMETHING, OR WHAT I BELIEVE, OR WHAT I KNOW, OR WHERE I'M GOING, OR WHERE I'VE BEEN OR ANYTHING!
5-19
IF YOU'RE GOING TO SHOW INTEREST IN OTHER PEOPLE, YOU HAVE TO ASK QUESTIONS...
HOW HAVE YOU BEEN?
SCHULZ

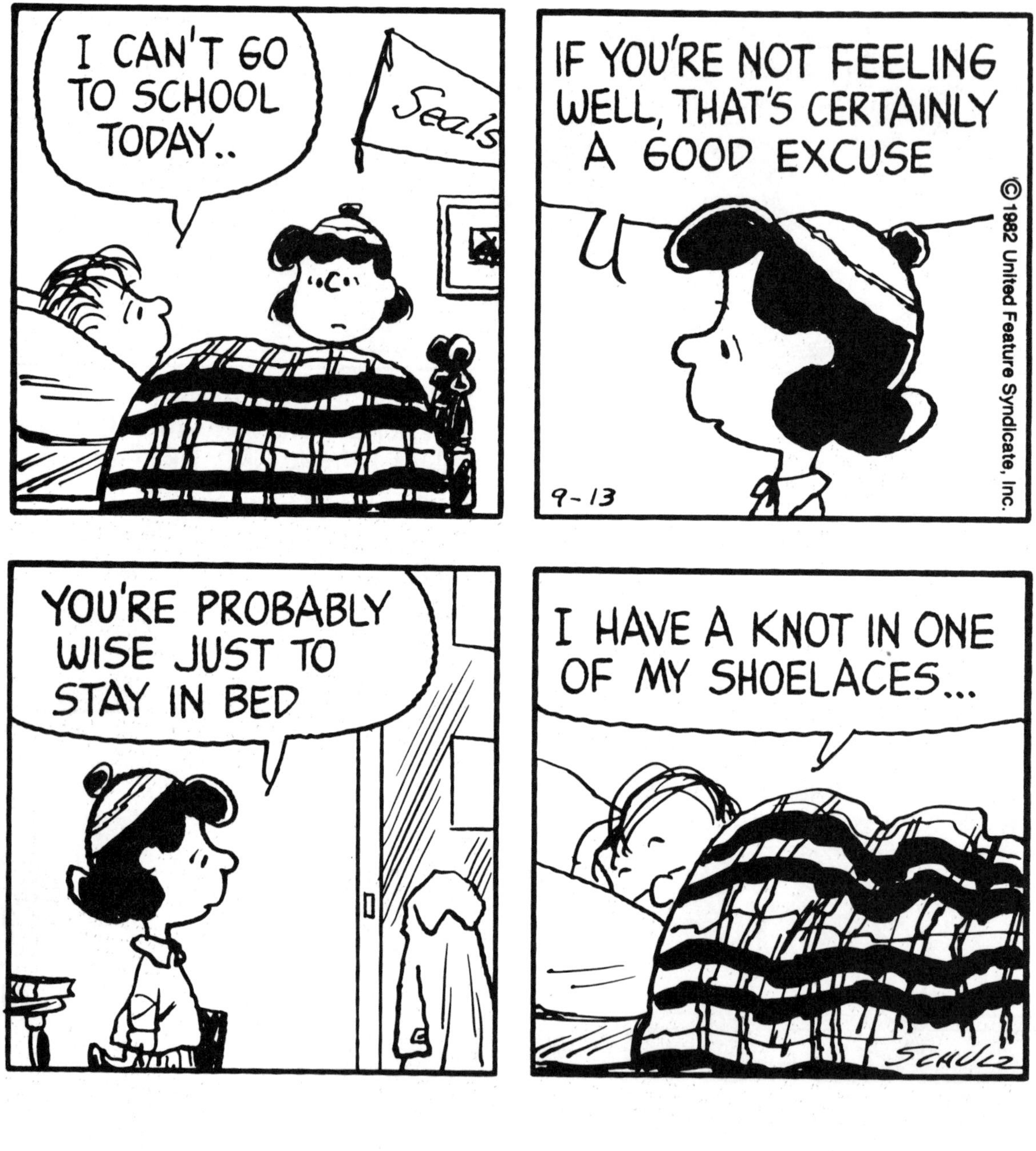
I CAN'T GO TO SCHOOL TODAY..
Seals
IF YOU'RE NOT FEELING WELL, THAT'S CERTAINLY A GOOD EXCUSE
9-13
© 1982 United Feature Syndicate, Inc.
YOU'RE PROBABLY WISE JUST TO STAY IN BED
I HAVE A KNOT IN ONE OF MY SHOELACES...
SCHULZ

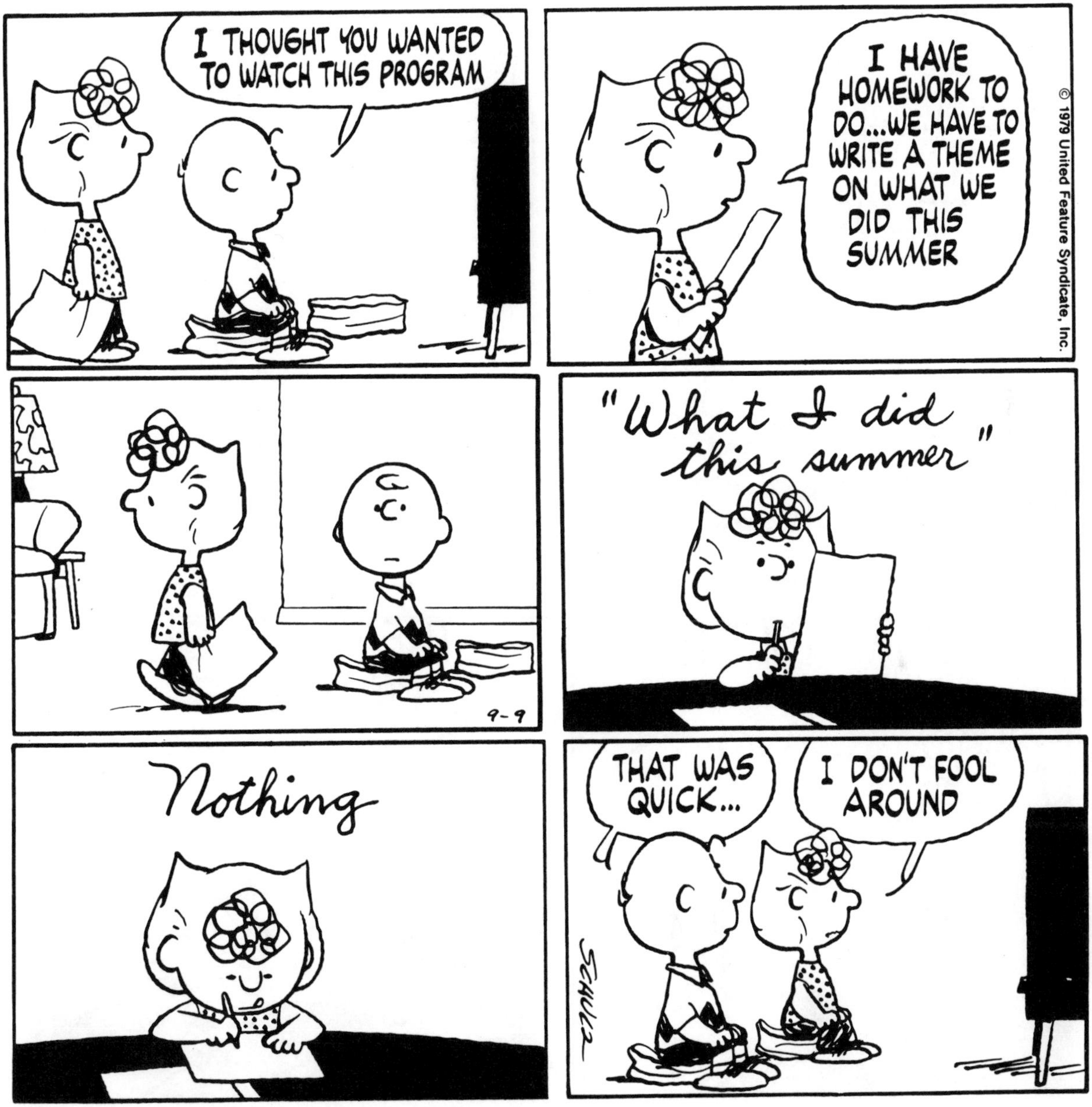
I THOUGHT YOU WANTED TO WATCH THIS PROGRAM
I HAVE HOMEWORK TO DO...WE HAVE TO WRITE A THEME ON WHAT WE DID THIS SUMMER
© 1979 United Feature Syndicate, Inc.
9-9
"What I did this summer"
Nothing
THAT WAS QUICK...
I DON'T FOOL AROUND
SCHULZ

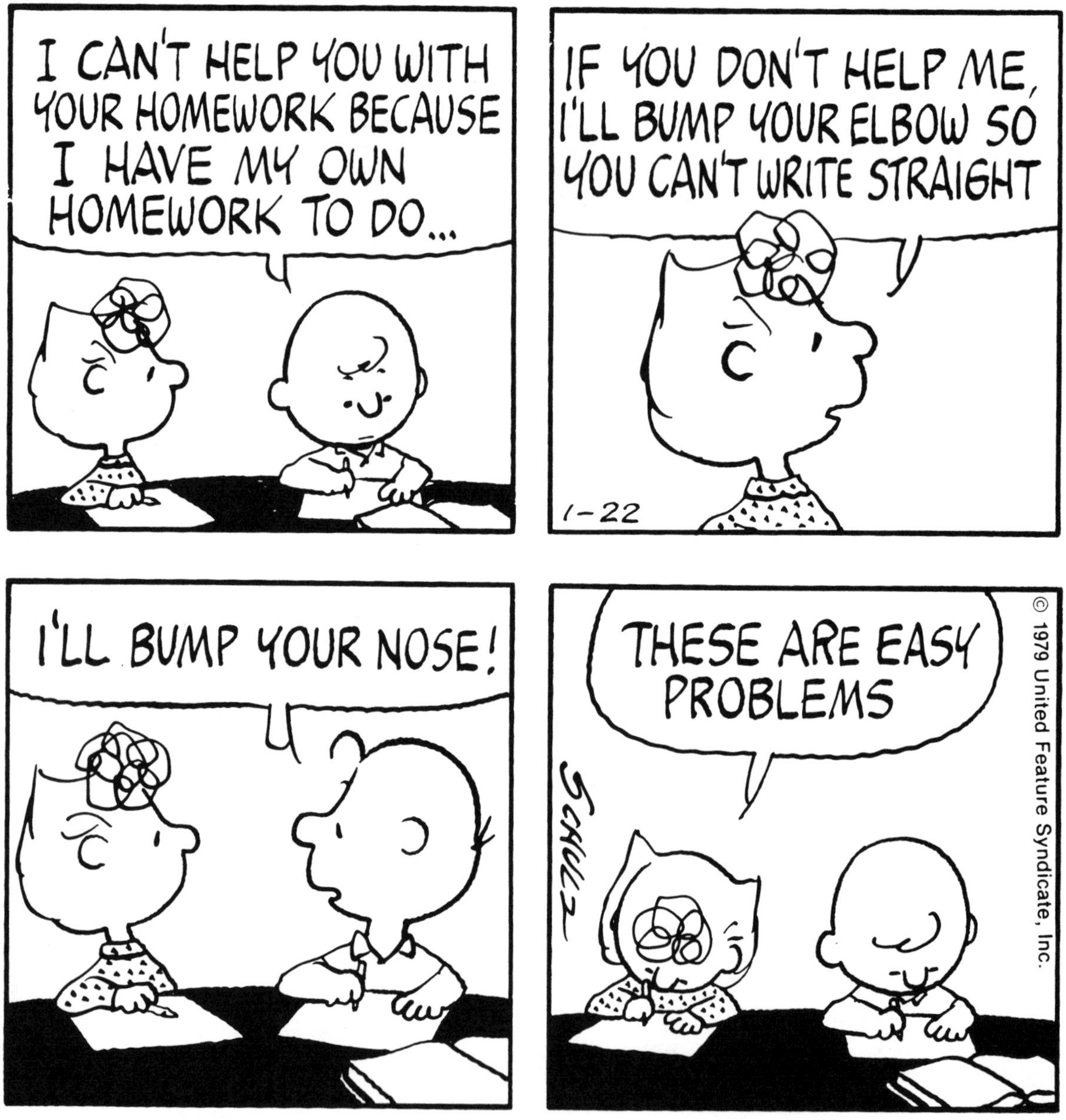
I CAN'T HELP YOU WITH YOUR HOMEWORK BECAUSE I HAVE MY OWN HOMEWORK TO DO...
IF YOU DON'T HELP ME, I'LL BUMP YOUR ELBOW SO YOU CAN'T WRITE STRAIGHT
1-22
I'LL BUMP YOUR NOSE!
THESE ARE EASY PROBLEMS
SCHULZ
© 1979 United Feature Syndicate, Inc.

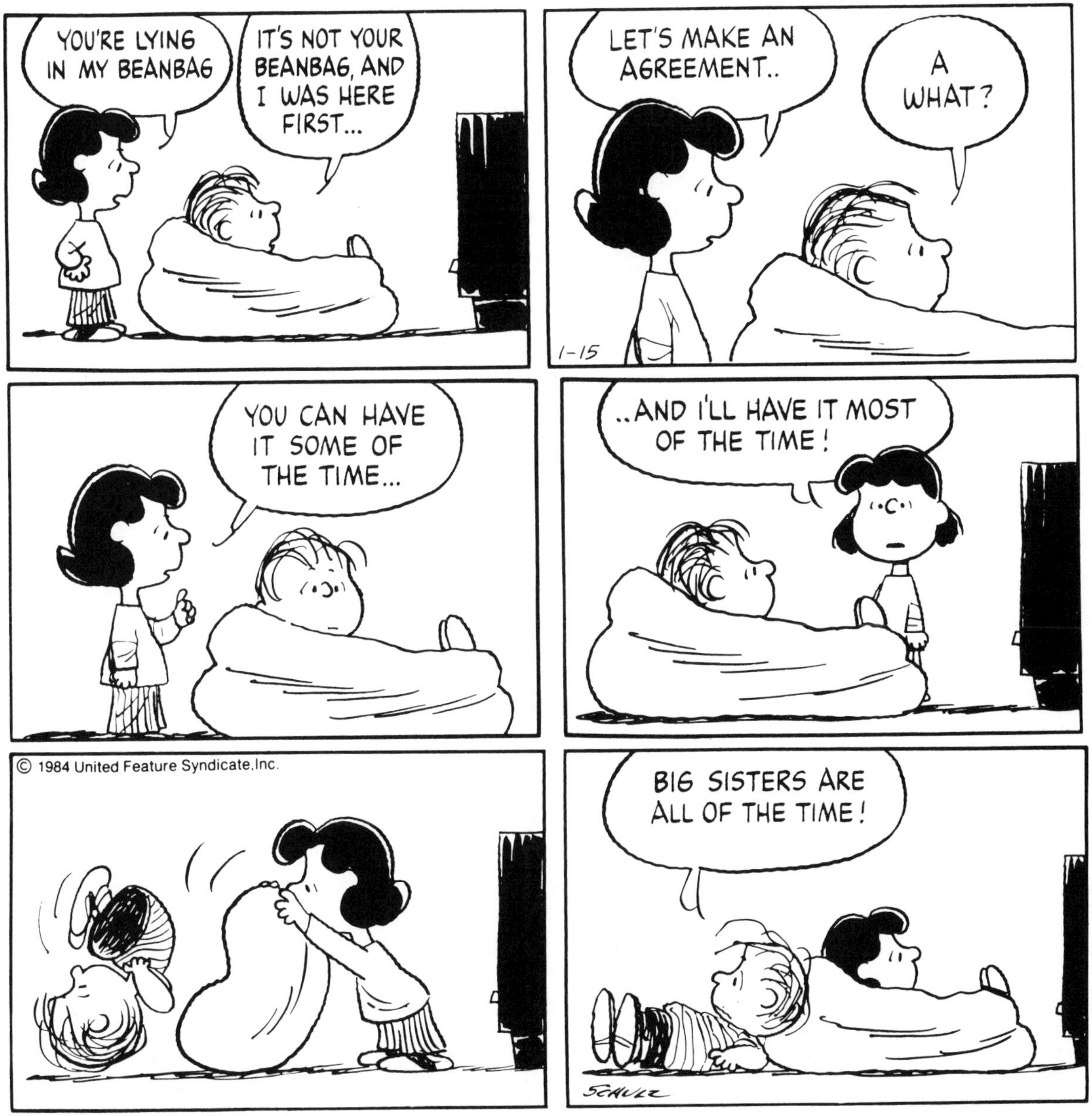
YOU'RE LYING IN MY BEANBAG
IT'S NOT YOUR BEANBAG, AND I WAS HERE FIRST...
LET'S MAKE AN AGREEMENT..
A WHAT?
1-15
YOU CAN HAVE IT SOME OF THE TIME...
..AND I'LL HAVE IT MOST OF THE TIME!
© 1984 United Feature Syndicate, Inc.
BIG SISTERS ARE ALL OF THE TIME!
SCHULZ

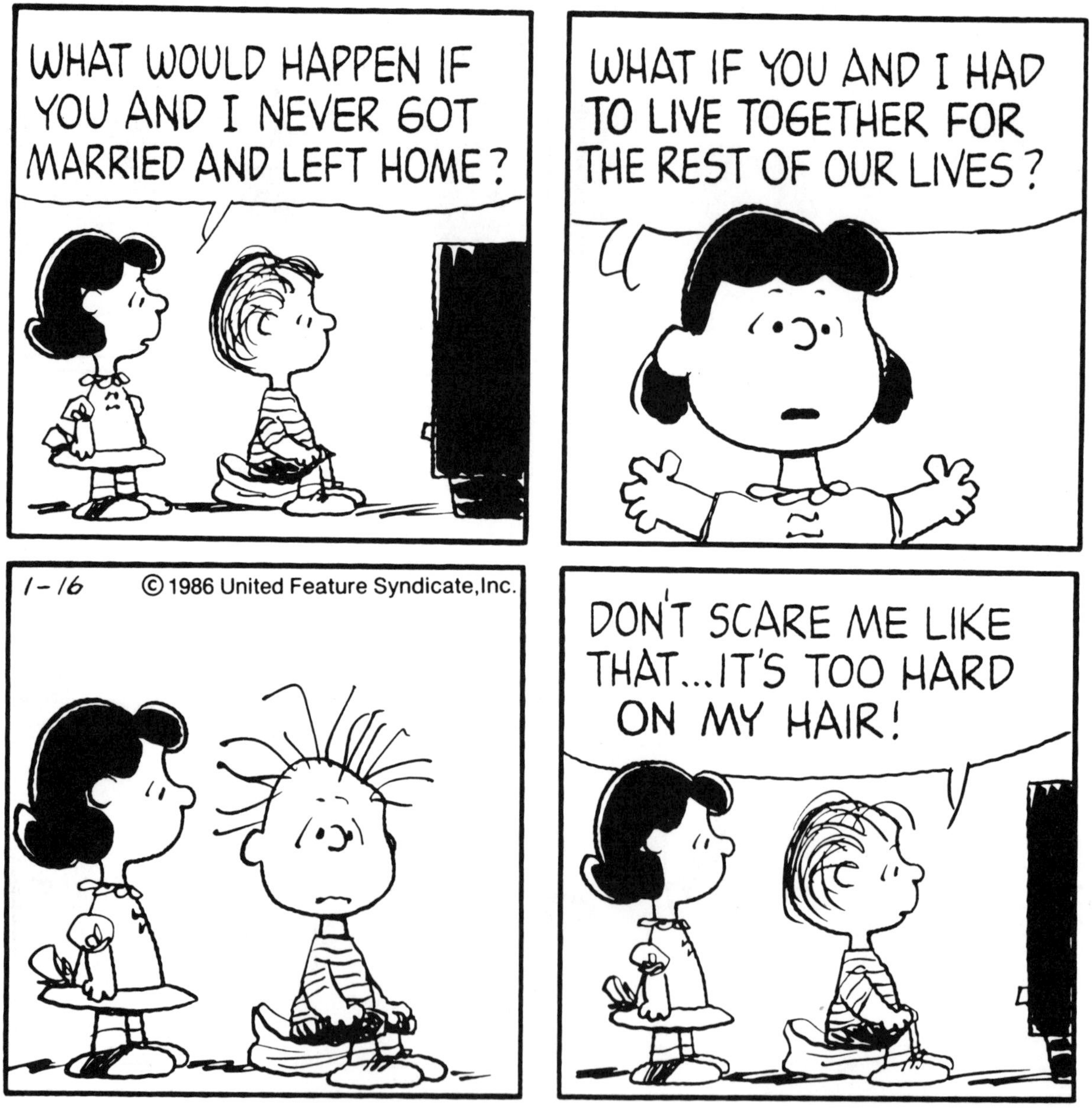
WHAT WOULD HAPPEN IF YOU AND I NEVER GOT MARRIED AND LEFT HOME?
WHAT IF YOU AND I HAD TO LIVE TOGETHER FOR THE REST OF OUR LIVES?
1-16
© 1986 United Feature Syndicate, Inc.
DON'T SCARE ME LIKE THAT...IT'S TOO HARD ON MY HAIR!

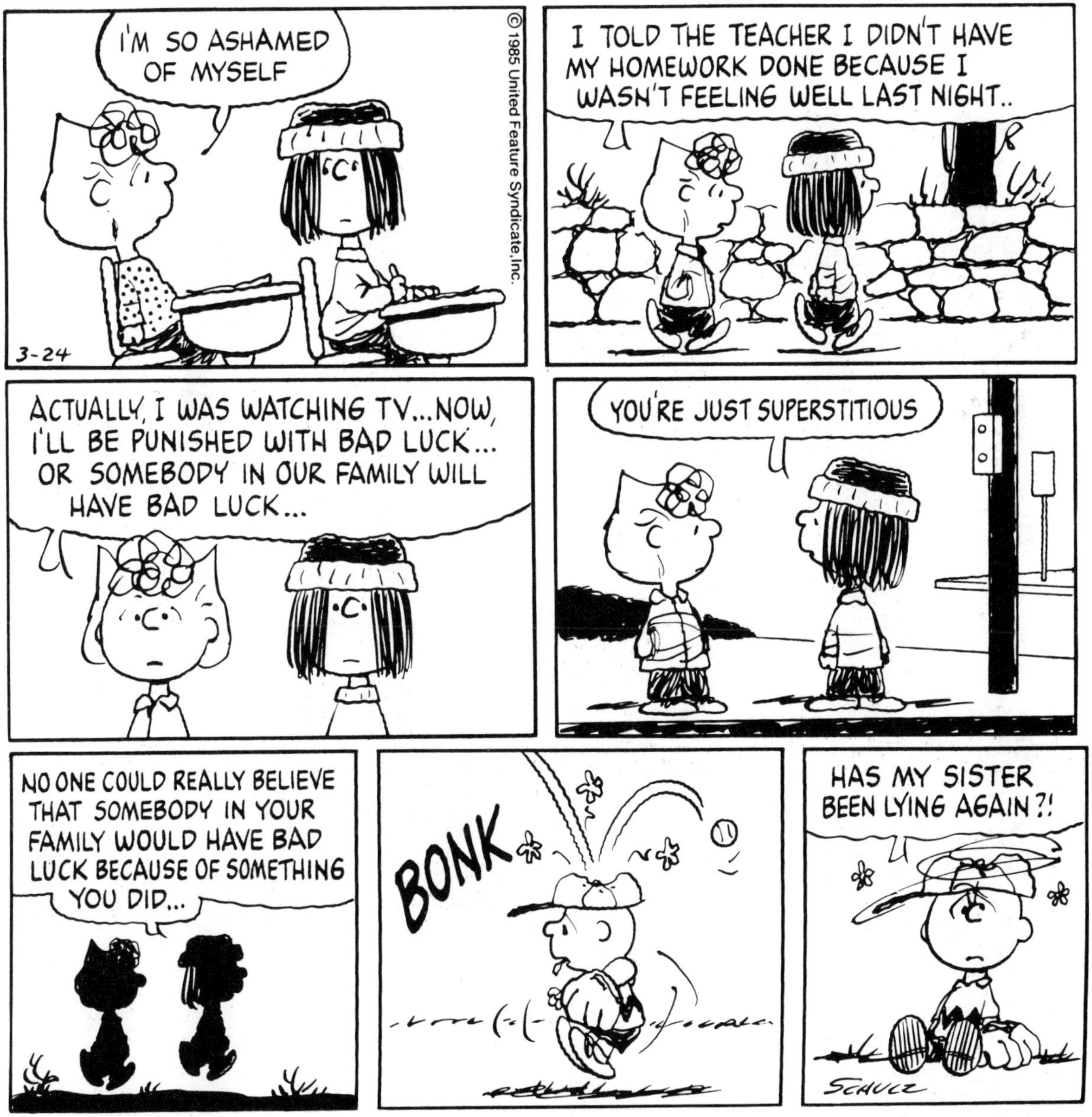
I'M SO ASHAMED OF MYSELF
© 1985 United Feature Syndicate, Inc.
3-24
I TOLD THE TEACHER I DIDN'T HAVE MY HOMEWORK DONE BECAUSE I WASN'T FEELING WELL LAST NIGHT..
ACTUALLY, I WAS WATCHING TV...NOW, I'LL BE PUNISHED WITH BAD LUCK... OR SOMEBODY IN OUR FAMILY WILL HAVE BAD LUCK...
YOU'RE JUST SUPERSTITIOUS
NO ONE COULD REALLY BELIEVE THAT SOMEBODY IN YOUR FAMILY WOULD HAVE BAD LUCK BECAUSE OF SOMETHING YOU DID...
BONK
HAS MY SISTER BEEN LYING AGAIN?!
SCHULZ

© 1978 United Feature Syndicate, Inc.
WILL YOU WALK HOME FROM SCHOOL WITH ME, LINUS?
I THINK THE POWERS OF DARKNESS ARE OUT TO GET ME...
1-18
I DOUBT IF I COULD EVER PROTECT YOU FROM THE POWERS OF DARKNESS
HOW ABOUT A THIRD-GRADER WHO CLAIMS I BROKE HIS RULER?
SCHULZ

IT'S FOR YOU...SOME KID FROM SCHOOL...
HE SAYS YOU BORROWED HIS RULER, AND THEN YOU BROKE IT...IS THAT TRUE?
© 1978 United Feature Syndicate, Inc.
IT WASN'T MY FAULT
1-19
I WAS MEASURING THE STREET, AND A TRUCK RAN OVER IT!
SCHULZ

NOW IF SOME KID COMES UP, AND STARTS ASKING ABOUT A RULER, YOU HOLD HIM OFF...
HOLD HIM OFF?
YES, YOU HOLD HIM OFF WHILE I RUN FOR IT!
1-20
WHAT IF HE TRIES TO HIT ME?
REASON WITH HIM
© 1978 United Feature Syndicate, Inc.
TELL HIM HIS STUPID RULER WOULDN'T HAVE BEEN ANY GOOD AFTER WE SWITCHED TO METRICS, ANYWAY!
SCHULZ

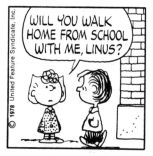

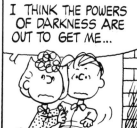

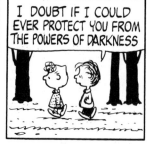

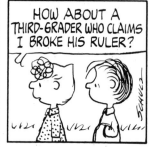

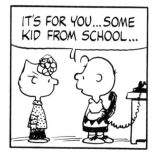

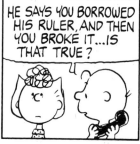

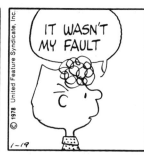

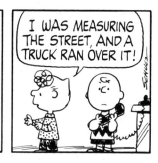

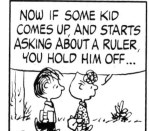

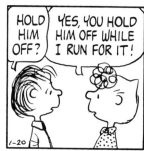

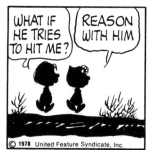

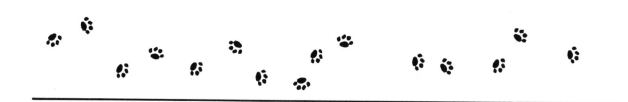

IT'S ALL RELATIVE

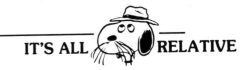

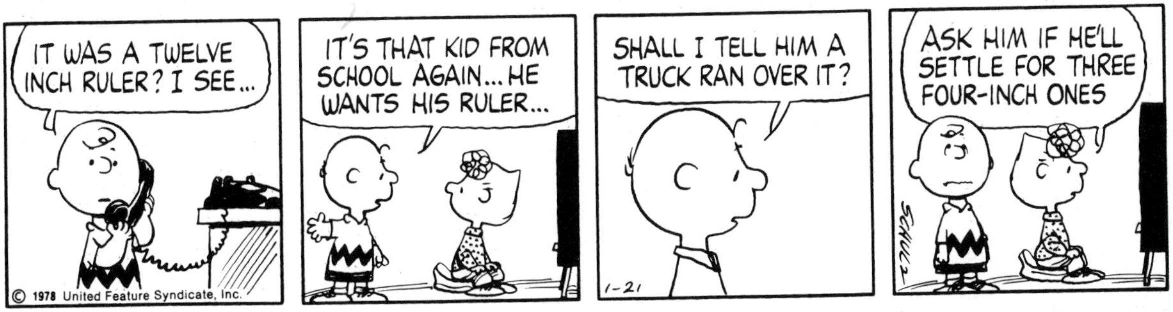
IT WAS A TWELVE INCH RULER? I SEE...
© 1978 United Feature Syndicate, Inc.
IT'S THAT KID FROM SCHOOL AGAIN... HE WANTS HIS RULER...
SHALL I TELL HIM A TRUCK RAN OVER IT?
1-21
ASK HIM IF HE'LL SETTLE FOR THREE FOUR-INCH ONES
SCHULZ

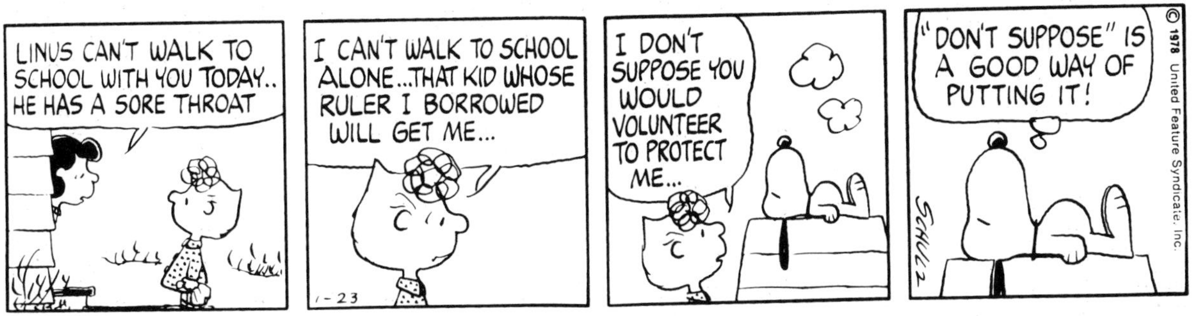
LINUS CAN'T WALK TO SCHOOL WITH YOU TODAY.. HE HAS A SORE THROAT
I CAN'T WALK TO SCHOOL ALONE...THAT KID WHOSE RULER I BORROWED WILL GET ME...
1-23
I DON'T SUPPOSE YOU WOULD VOLUNTEER TO PROTECT ME...
"DON'T SUPPOSE" IS A GOOD WAY OF PUTTING IT!
SCHULZ
© 1978 United Feature Syndicate, Inc.

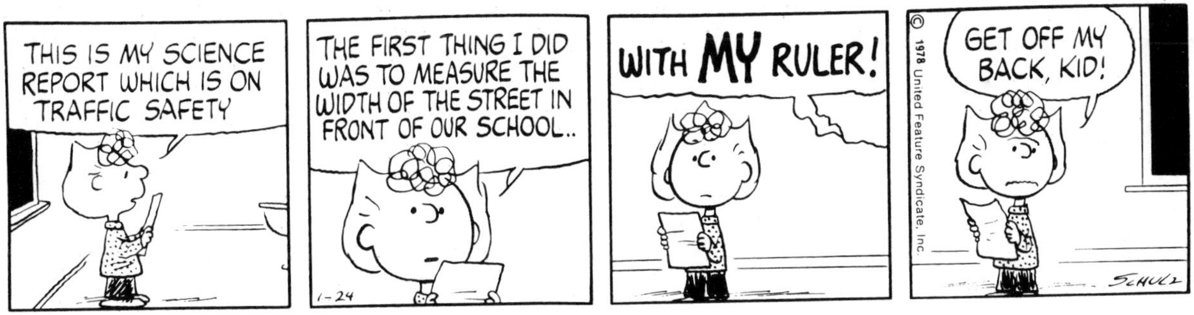
THIS IS MY SCIENCE REPORT WHICH IS ON TRAFFIC SAFETY
THE FIRST THING I DID WAS TO MEASURE THE WIDTH OF THE STREET IN FRONT OF OUR SCHOOL..
1-24
WITH MY RULER!
© 1978 United Feature Syndicate, Inc.
GET OFF MY BACK, KID!
SCHULZ

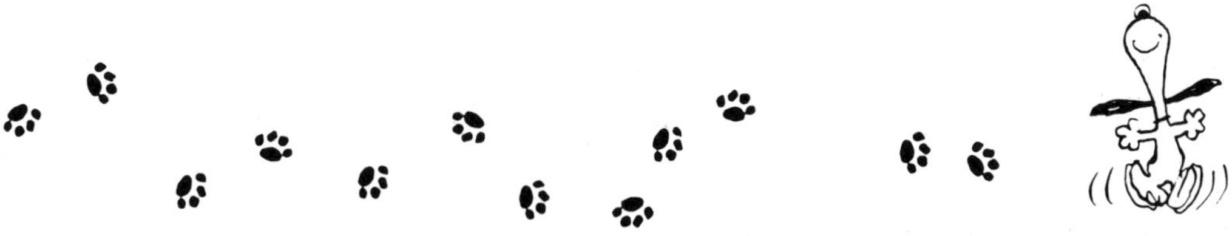

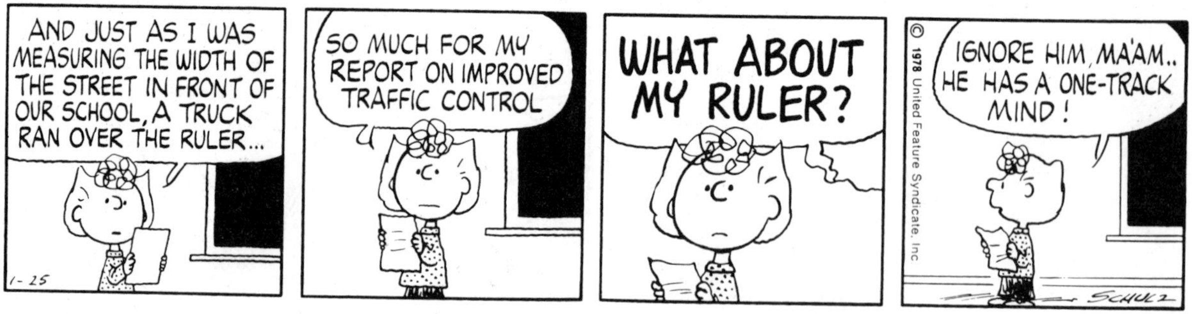
AND JUST AS I WAS MEASURING THE WIDTH OF THE STREET IN FRONT OF OUR SCHOOL, A TRUCK RAN OVER THE RULER...
1-25
SO MUCH FOR MY REPORT ON IMPROVED TRAFFIC CONTROL
WHAT ABOUT MY RULER?
© 1978 United Feature Syndicate, Inc.
IGNORE HIM, MA'AM.. HE HAS A ONE-TRACK MIND!
SCHULZ

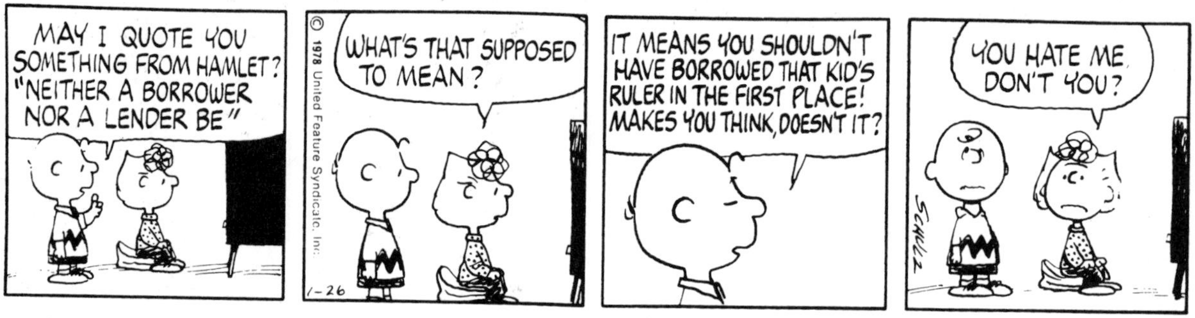
MAY I QUOTE YOU SOMETHING FROM HAMLET? "NEITHER A BORROWER NOR A LENDER BE"
© 1978 United Feature Syndicate, Inc.
WHAT'S THAT SUPPOSED TO MEAN?
1-26
IT MEANS YOU SHOULDN'T HAVE BORROWED THAT KID'S RULER IN THE FIRST PLACE! MAKES YOU THINK, DOESN'T IT?
YOU HATE ME, DON'T YOU?
SCHULZ

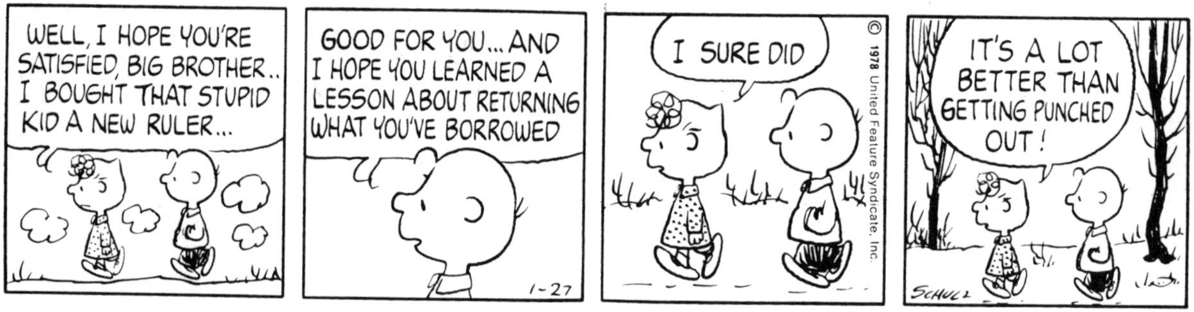
WELL, I HOPE YOU'RE SATISFIED, BIG BROTHER.. I BOUGHT THAT STUPID KID A NEW RULER...
GOOD FOR YOU... AND I HOPE YOU LEARNED A LESSON ABOUT RETURNING WHAT YOU'VE BORROWED
1-27
I SURE DID
© 1978 United Feature Syndicate, Inc.
IT'S A LOT BETTER THAN GETTING PUNCHED OUT!
SCHULZ

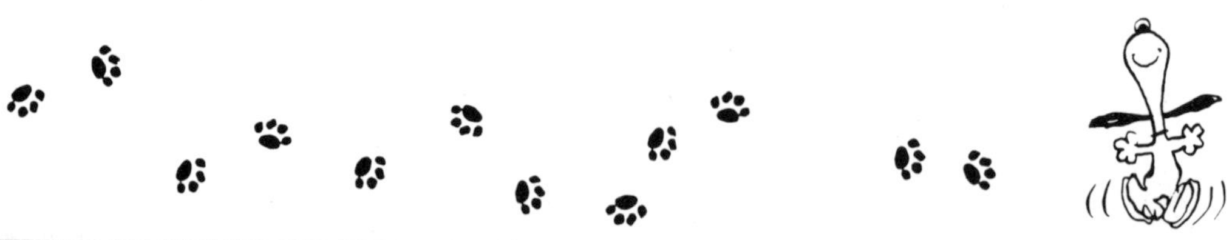

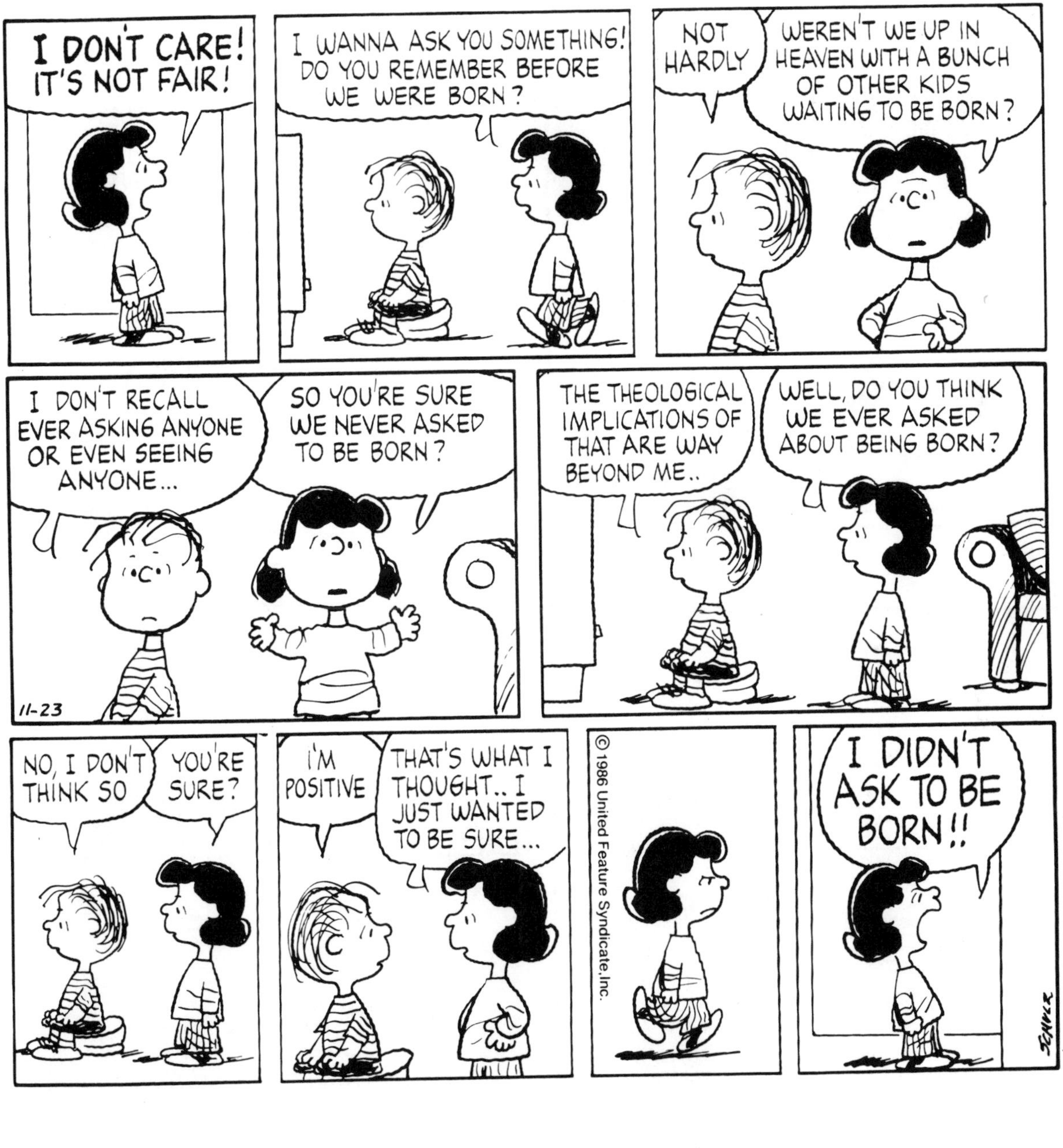
I DON'T CARE! IT'S NOT FAIR!
I WANNA ASK YOU SOMETHING! DO YOU REMEMBER BEFORE WE WERE BORN?
NOT HARDLY
WEREN'T WE UP IN HEAVEN WITH A BUNCH OF OTHER KIDS WAITING TO BE BORN?
I DON'T RECALL EVER ASKING ANYONE OR EVEN SEEING ANYONE...
SO YOU'RE SURE WE NEVER ASKED TO BE BORN?
11-23
THE THEOLOGICAL IMPLICATIONS OF THAT ARE WAY BEYOND ME..
WELL, DO YOU THINK WE EVER ASKED ABOUT BEING BORN?
NO, I DON'T THINK SO
YOU'RE SURE?
I'M POSITIVE
THAT'S WHAT I THOUGHT.. I JUST WANTED TO BE SURE...
© 1986 United Feature Syndicate, Inc.
I DIDN'T ASK TO BE BORN!!
SCHULZ

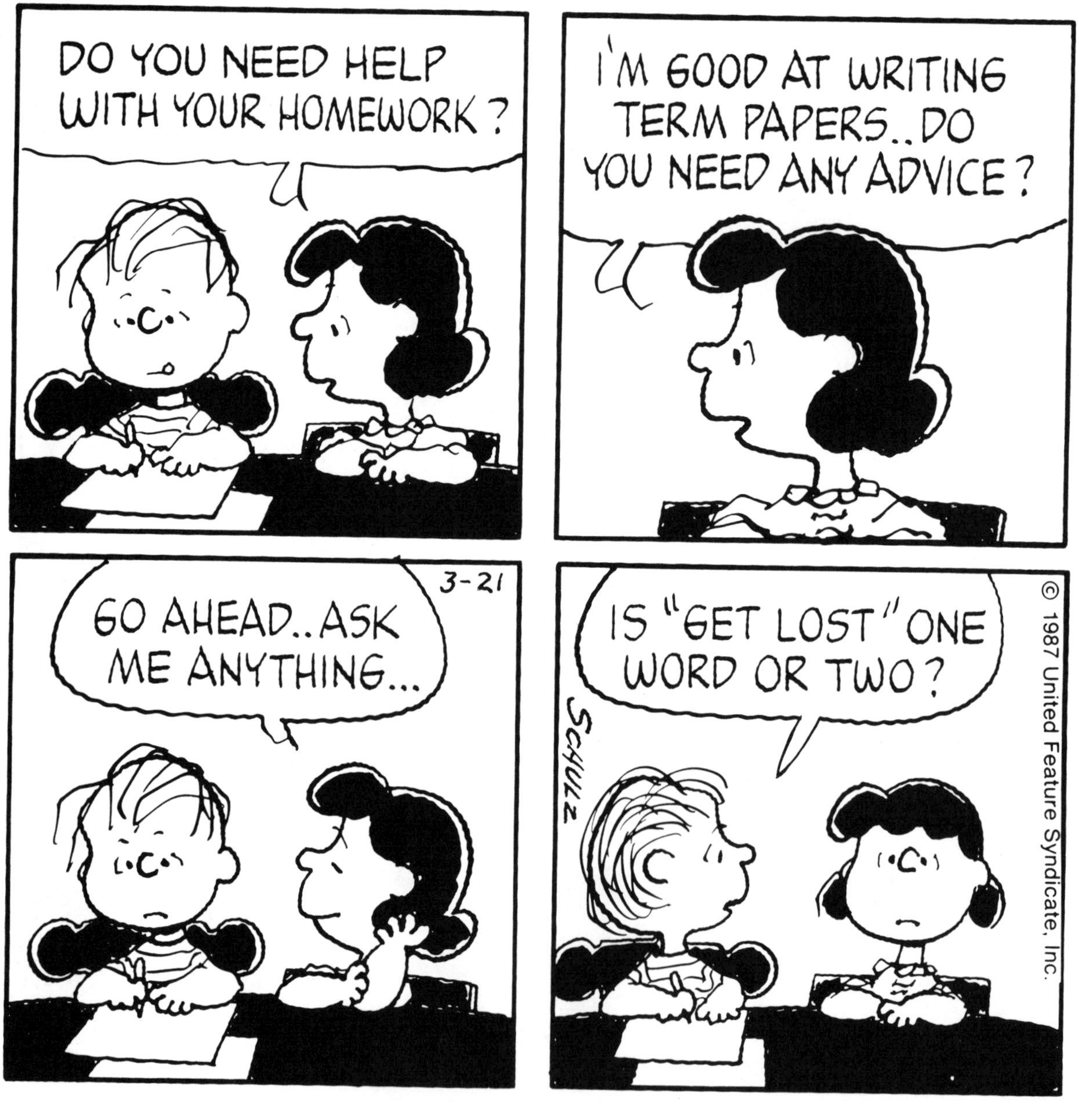
DO YOU NEED HELP WITH YOUR HOMEWORK?
I'M GOOD AT WRITING TERM PAPERS..DO YOU NEED ANY ADVICE?
3-21
GO AHEAD..ASK ME ANYTHING...
SCHULZ
IS "GET LOST" ONE WORD OR TWO?
© 1987 United Feature Syndicate, Inc.

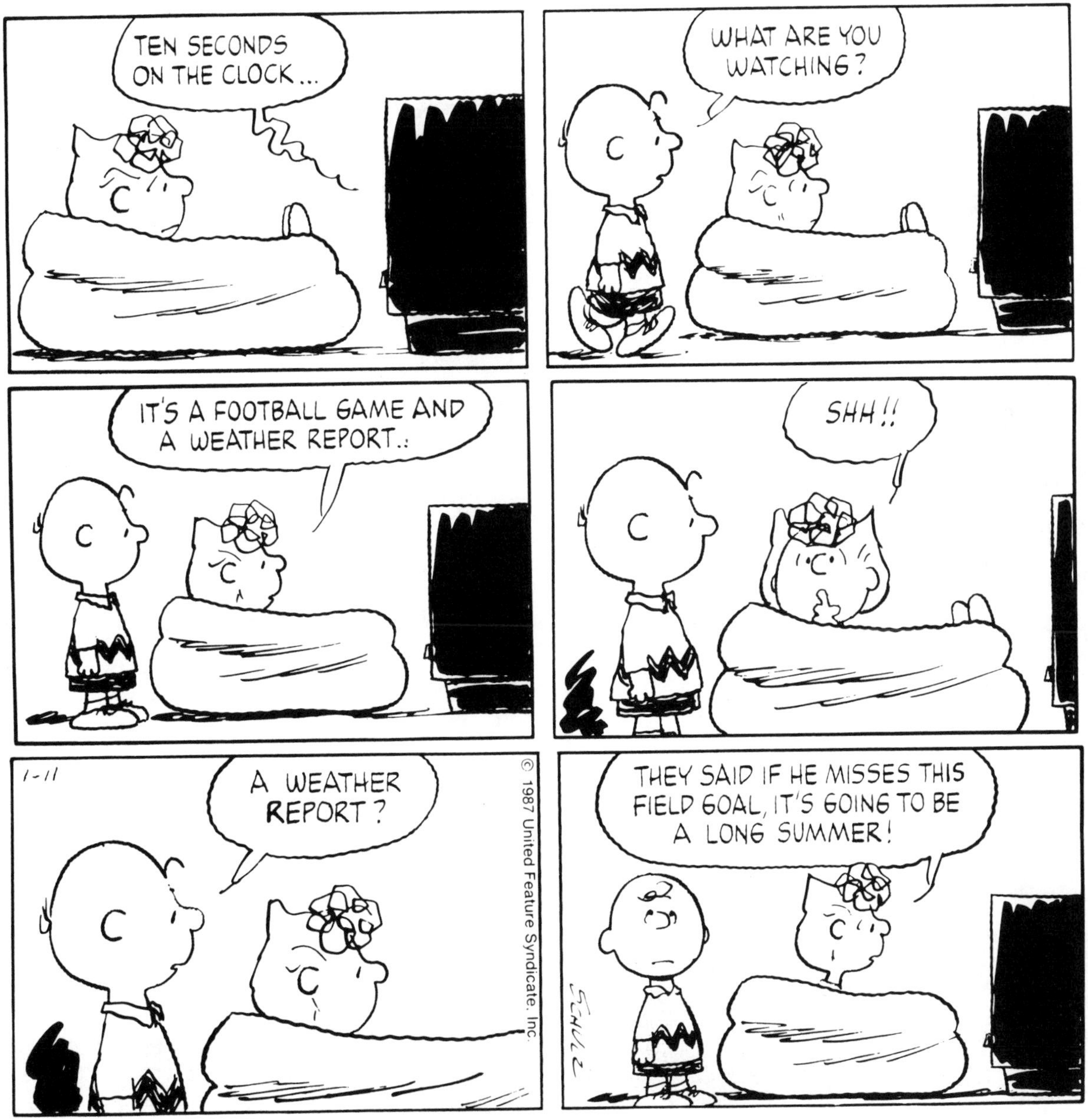
TEN SECONDS ON THE CLOCK...
WHAT ARE YOU WATCHING?
IT'S A FOOTBALL GAME AND A WEATHER REPORT..
SHH!!
1-11
A WEATHER REPORT?
© 1987 United Feature Syndicate, Inc.
THEY SAID IF HE MISSES THIS FIELD GOAL, IT'S GOING TO BE A LONG SUMMER!
SCHULZ

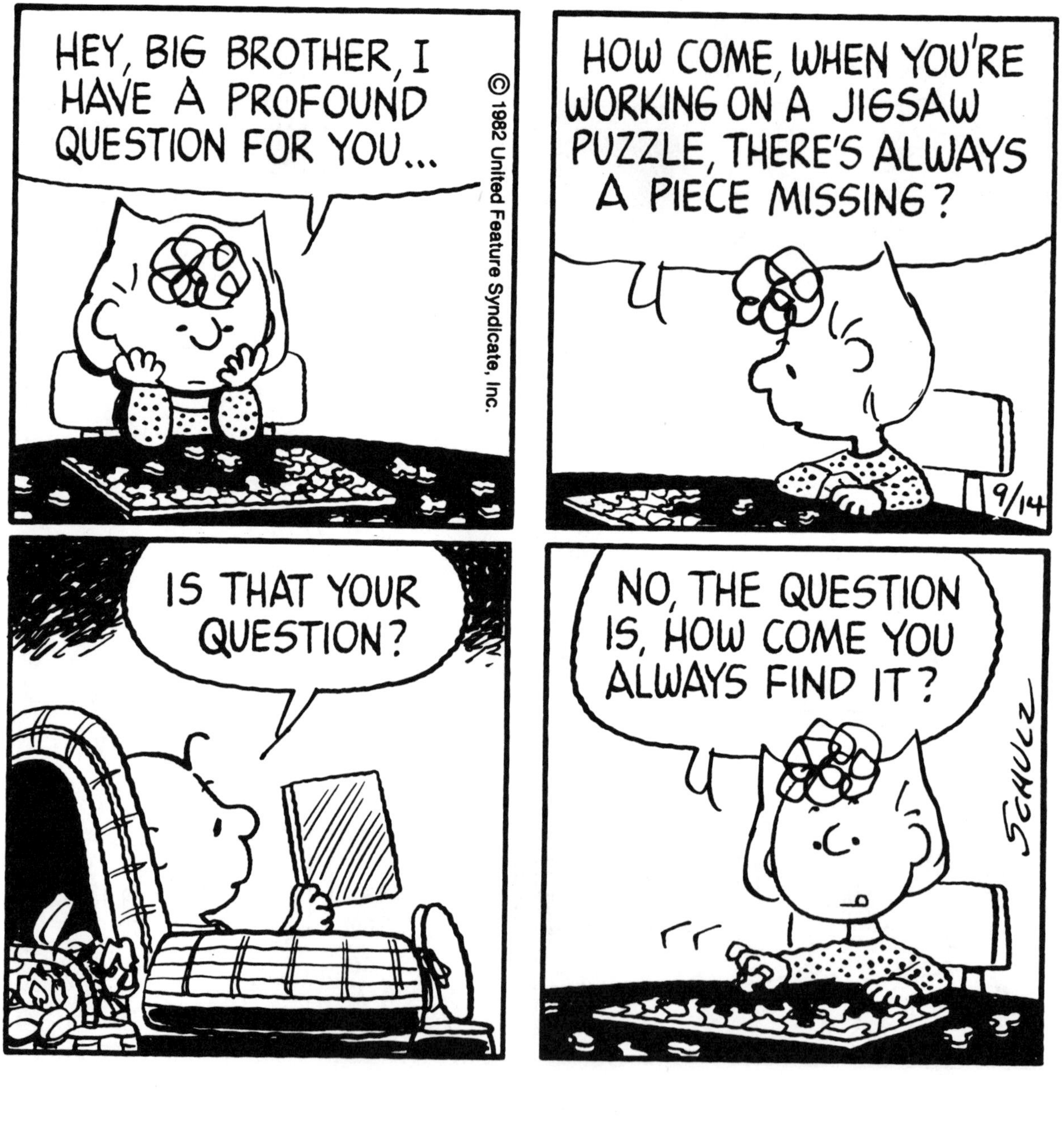
HEY, BIG BROTHER, I HAVE A PROFOUND QUESTION FOR YOU...
© 1982 United Feature Syndicate, Inc.
HOW COME, WHEN YOU'RE WORKING ON A JIGSAW PUZZLE, THERE'S ALWAYS A PIECE MISSING?
9/14
IS THAT YOUR QUESTION?
NO, THE QUESTION IS, HOW COME YOU ALWAYS FIND IT?
SCHULZ

LINUS, YOU REMEMBER EUDORA, DON'T YOU?

SURE... HOW ARE YOU?

HALLOWEEN IS COMING!

ON HALLOWEEN NIGHT THE GREAT PUMPKIN RISES OUT OF THE PUMPKIN PATCH AND BRINGS TOYS TO ALL THE CHILDREN IN THE WORLD

BUT FIRST HE LOOKS OVER ALL THE PUMPKIN PATCHES TO SEE WHICH ONE IS THE MOST SINCERE.. IF HE CHOOSES THIS PUMPKIN PATCH, I'LL GET TO MEET HIM!

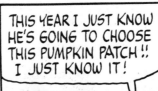

THIS YEAR I JUST KNOW HE'S GOING TO CHOOSE THIS PUMPKIN PATCH!! I JUST KNOW IT!

OH, WHAT A GLORIOUS MOMENT THAT WILL BE!!!

SEE?

© 1980 United Feature Syndicate, Inc.

10-26

HOW SHARPER THAN A SERPENT'S TOOTH IS A SISTER'S "SEE?"

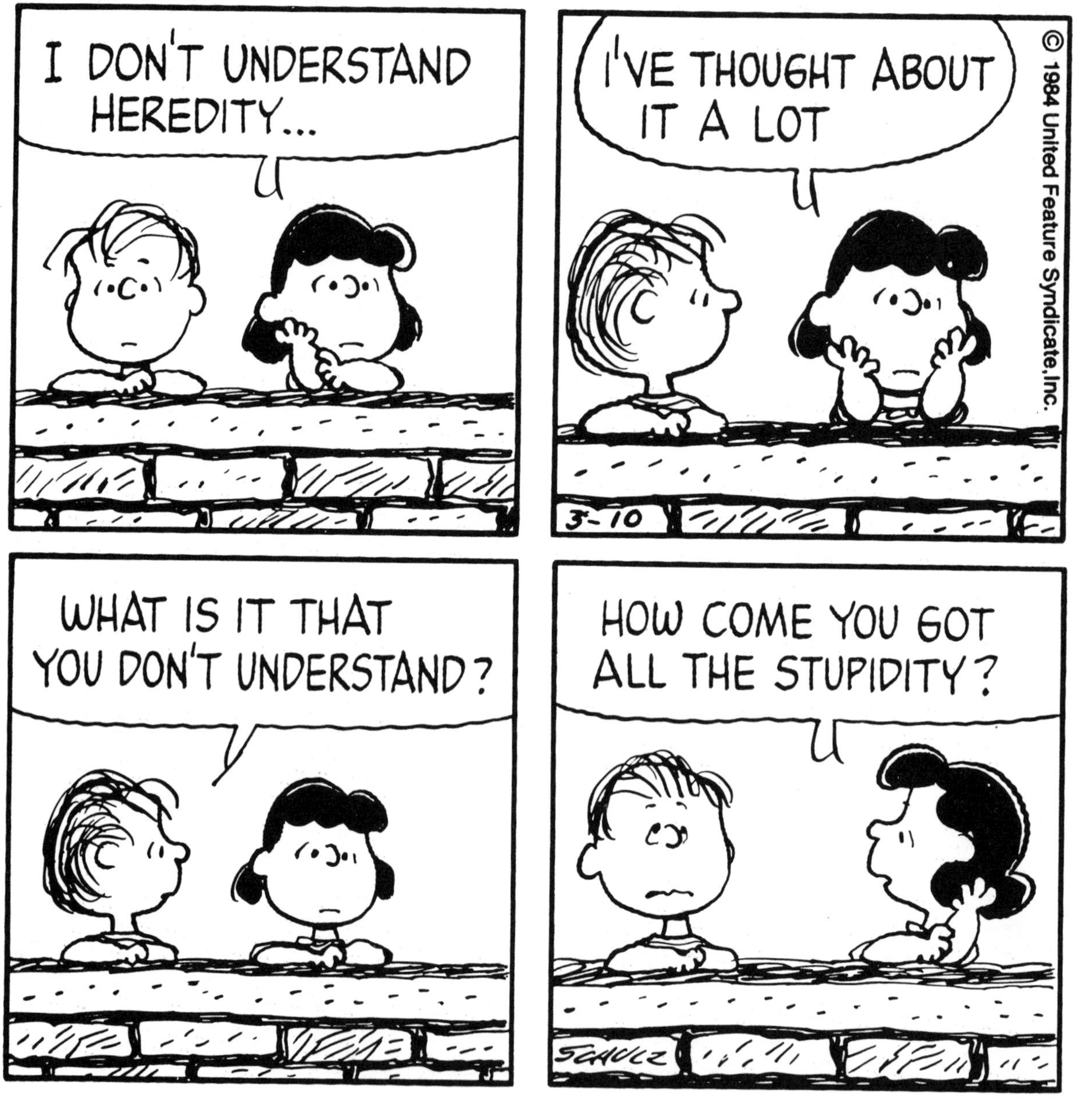
I DON'T UNDERSTAND HEREDITY...
I'VE THOUGHT ABOUT IT A LOT
© 1984 United Feature Syndicate, Inc.
3-10
WHAT IS IT THAT YOU DON'T UNDERSTAND?
HOW COME YOU GOT ALL THE STUPIDITY?
SCHULZ

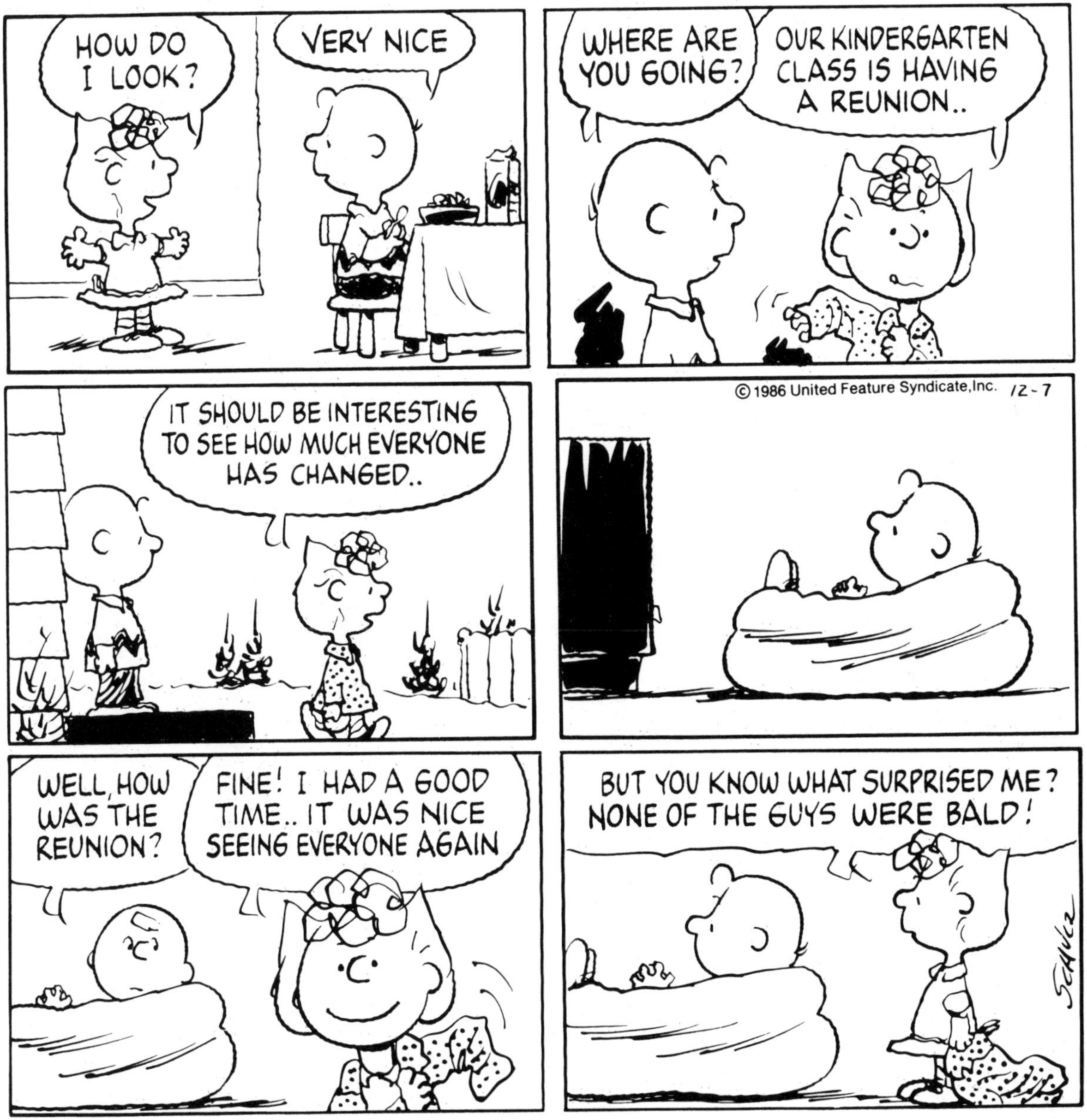
HOW DO I LOOK?
VERY NICE
WHERE ARE YOU GOING?
OUR KINDERGARTEN CLASS IS HAVING A REUNION..
IT SHOULD BE INTERESTING TO SEE HOW MUCH EVERYONE HAS CHANGED..
© 1986 United Feature Syndicate, Inc. 12-7
WELL, HOW WAS THE REUNION?
FINE! I HAD A GOOD TIME.. IT WAS NICE SEEING EVERYONE AGAIN
BUT YOU KNOW WHAT SURPRISED ME? NONE OF THE GUYS WERE BALD!
SCHULZ

BROTHERS AND SISTERS

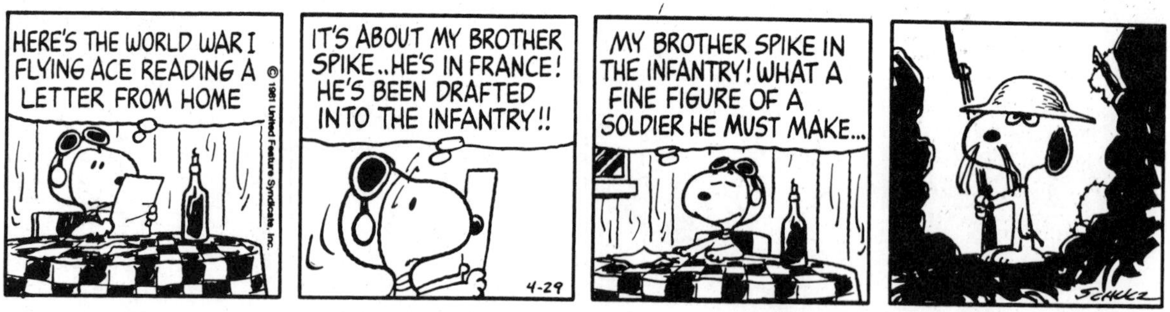
HERE'S THE WORLD WAR I FLYING ACE READING A LETTER FROM HOME
© 1981 United Feature Syndicate, Inc.
IT'S ABOUT MY BROTHER SPIKE..HE'S IN FRANCE! HE'S BEEN DRAFTED INTO THE INFANTRY!!
4-29
MY BROTHER SPIKE IN THE INFANTRY! WHAT A FINE FIGURE OF A SOLDIER HE MUST MAKE...
SCHULZ

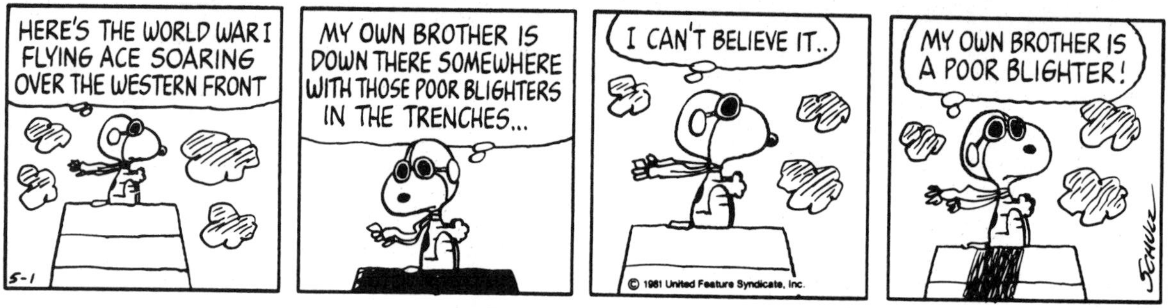
HERE'S THE WORLD WAR I FLYING ACE SOARING OVER THE WESTERN FRONT
5-1
MY OWN BROTHER IS DOWN THERE SOMEWHERE WITH THOSE POOR BLIGHTERS IN THE TRENCHES...
I CAN'T BELIEVE IT..
© 1981 United Feature Syndicate, Inc.
MY OWN BROTHER IS A POOR BLIGHTER!
SCHULZ

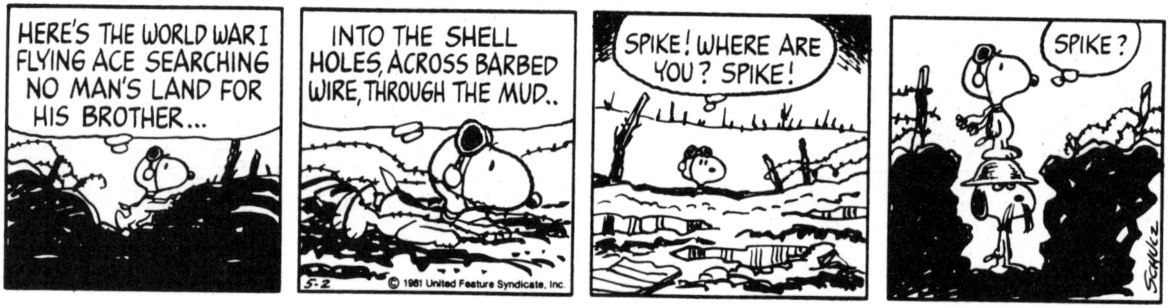
HERE'S THE WORLD WAR I FLYING ACE SEARCHING NO MAN'S LAND FOR HIS BROTHER...
INTO THE SHELL HOLES, ACROSS BARBED WIRE, THROUGH THE MUD..
5-2
© 1981 United Feature Syndicate, Inc.
SPIKE! WHERE ARE YOU? SPIKE!
SPIKE?
SCHULZ

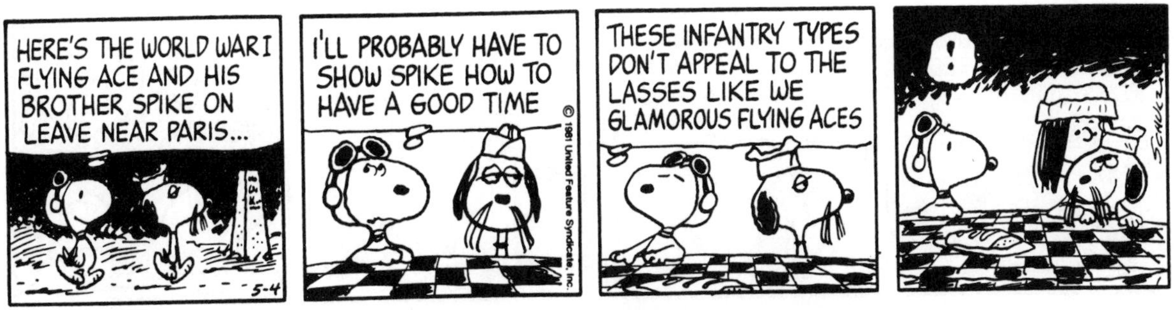
HERE'S THE WORLD WAR I FLYING ACE AND HIS BROTHER SPIKE ON LEAVE NEAR PARIS...
5-4
I'LL PROBABLY HAVE TO SHOW SPIKE HOW TO HAVE A GOOD TIME
© 1981 United Feature Syndicate, Inc.
THESE INFANTRY TYPES DON'T APPEAL TO THE LASSES LIKE WE GLAMOROUS FLYING ACES
!
SCHULZ

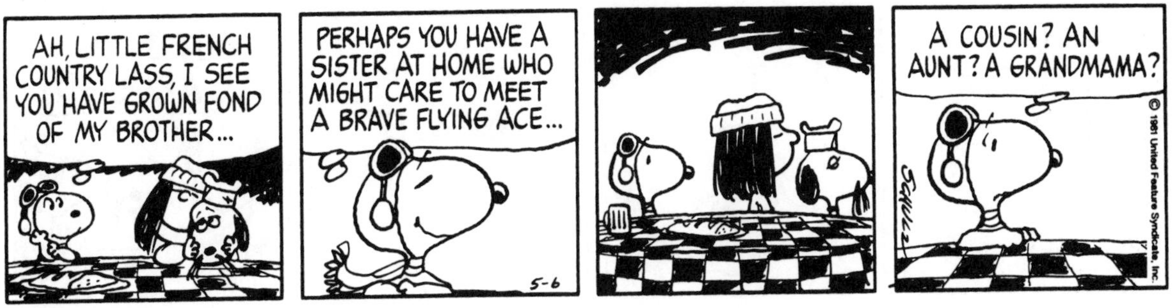
AH, LITTLE FRENCH COUNTRY LASS, I SEE YOU HAVE GROWN FOND OF MY BROTHER...
PERHAPS YOU HAVE A SISTER AT HOME WHO MIGHT CARE TO MEET A BRAVE FLYING ACE...
5-6
A COUSIN? AN AUNT? A GRANDMAMA?
SCHULZ
© 1981 United Feature Syndicate, Inc.

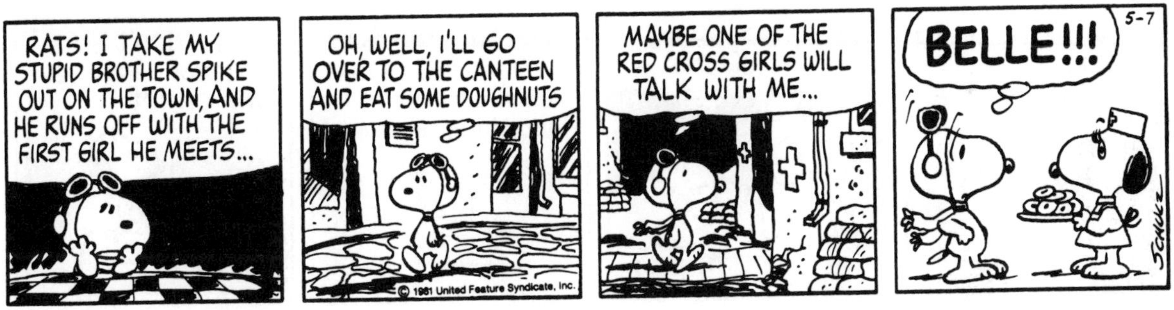
RATS! I TAKE MY STUPID BROTHER SPIKE OUT ON THE TOWN, AND HE RUNS OFF WITH THE FIRST GIRL HE MEETS...
OH, WELL, I'LL GO OVER TO THE CANTEEN AND EAT SOME DOUGHNUTS
© 1981 United Feature Syndicate, Inc.
MAYBE ONE OF THE RED CROSS GIRLS WILL TALK WITH ME...
BELLE!!!
5-7
SCHULZ

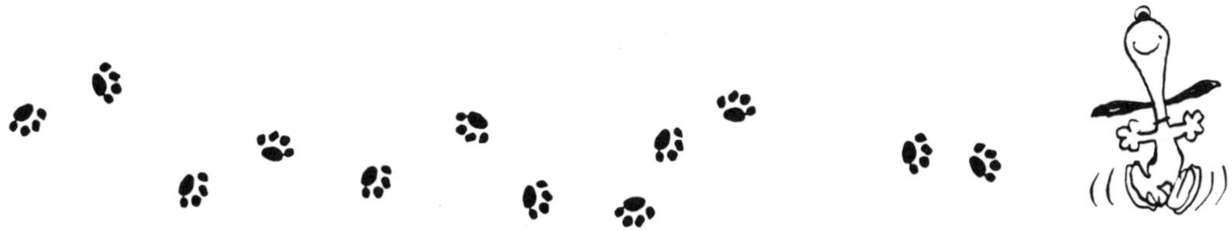

BROTHERS AND SISTERS

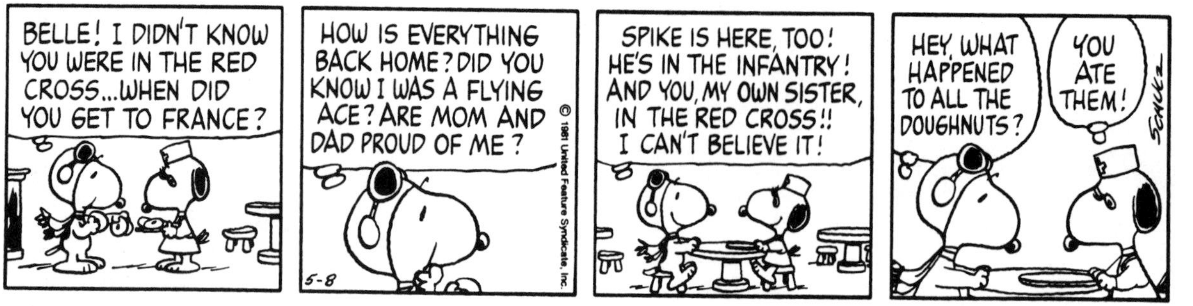
BELLE! I DIDN'T KNOW YOU WERE IN THE RED CROSS...WHEN DID YOU GET TO FRANCE?
HOW IS EVERYTHING BACK HOME? DID YOU KNOW I WAS A FLYING ACE? ARE MOM AND DAD PROUD OF ME?
5-8
© 1981 United Feature Syndicate, Inc.
SPIKE IS HERE, TOO! HE'S IN THE INFANTRY! AND YOU, MY OWN SISTER, IN THE RED CROSS!! I CAN'T BELIEVE IT!
HEY, WHAT HAPPENED TO ALL THE DOUGHNUTS?
YOU ATE THEM!
SCHULZ

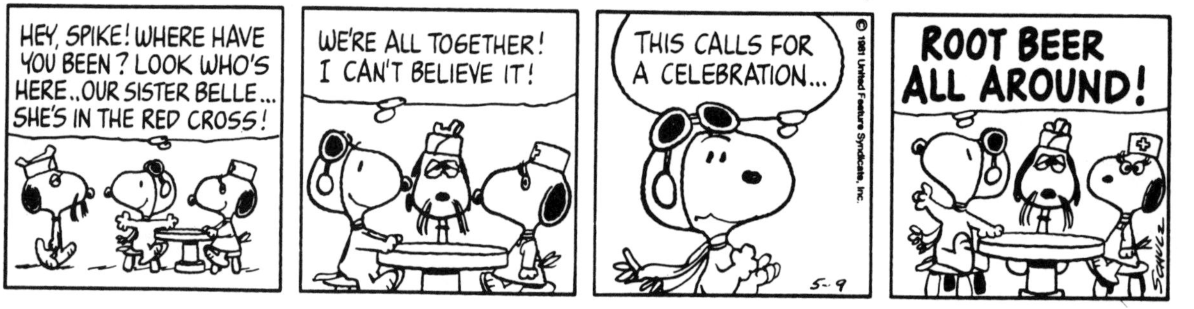
HEY, SPIKE! WHERE HAVE YOU BEEN? LOOK WHO'S HERE..OUR SISTER BELLE... SHE'S IN THE RED CROSS!
WE'RE ALL TOGETHER! I CAN'T BELIEVE IT!
THIS CALLS FOR A CELEBRATION...
© 1981 United Feature Syndicate, Inc.
5-9
ROOT BEER ALL AROUND!
SCHULZ

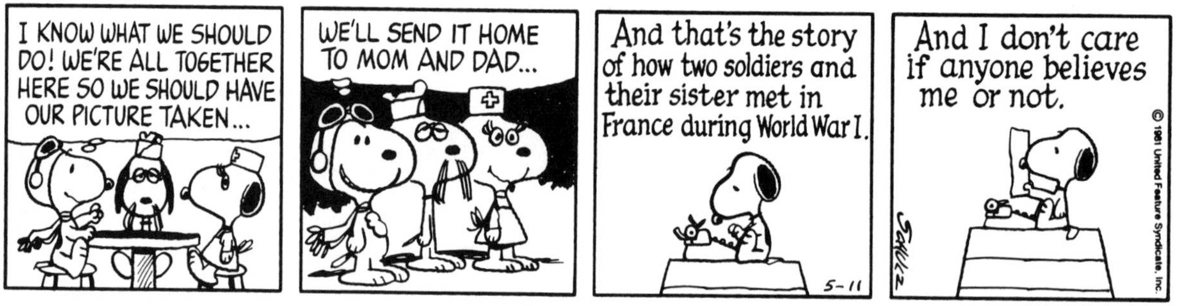
I KNOW WHAT WE SHOULD DO! WE'RE ALL TOGETHER HERE SO WE SHOULD HAVE OUR PICTURE TAKEN...
WE'LL SEND IT HOME TO MOM AND DAD...
And that's the story of how two soldiers and their sister met in France during World War I.
5-11
SCHULZ
And I don't care if anyone believes me or not.
© 1981 United Feature Syndicate, Inc.

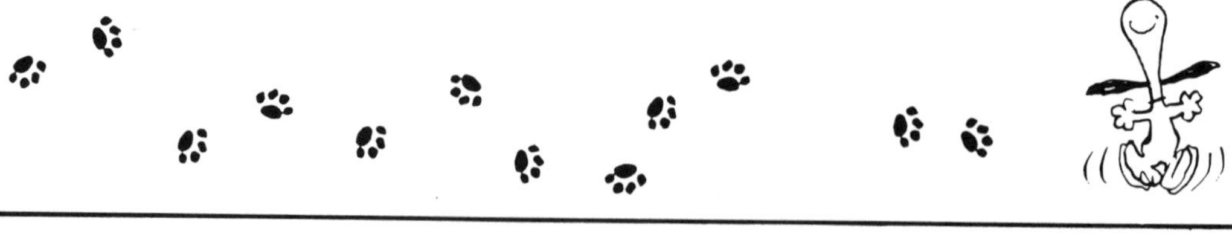

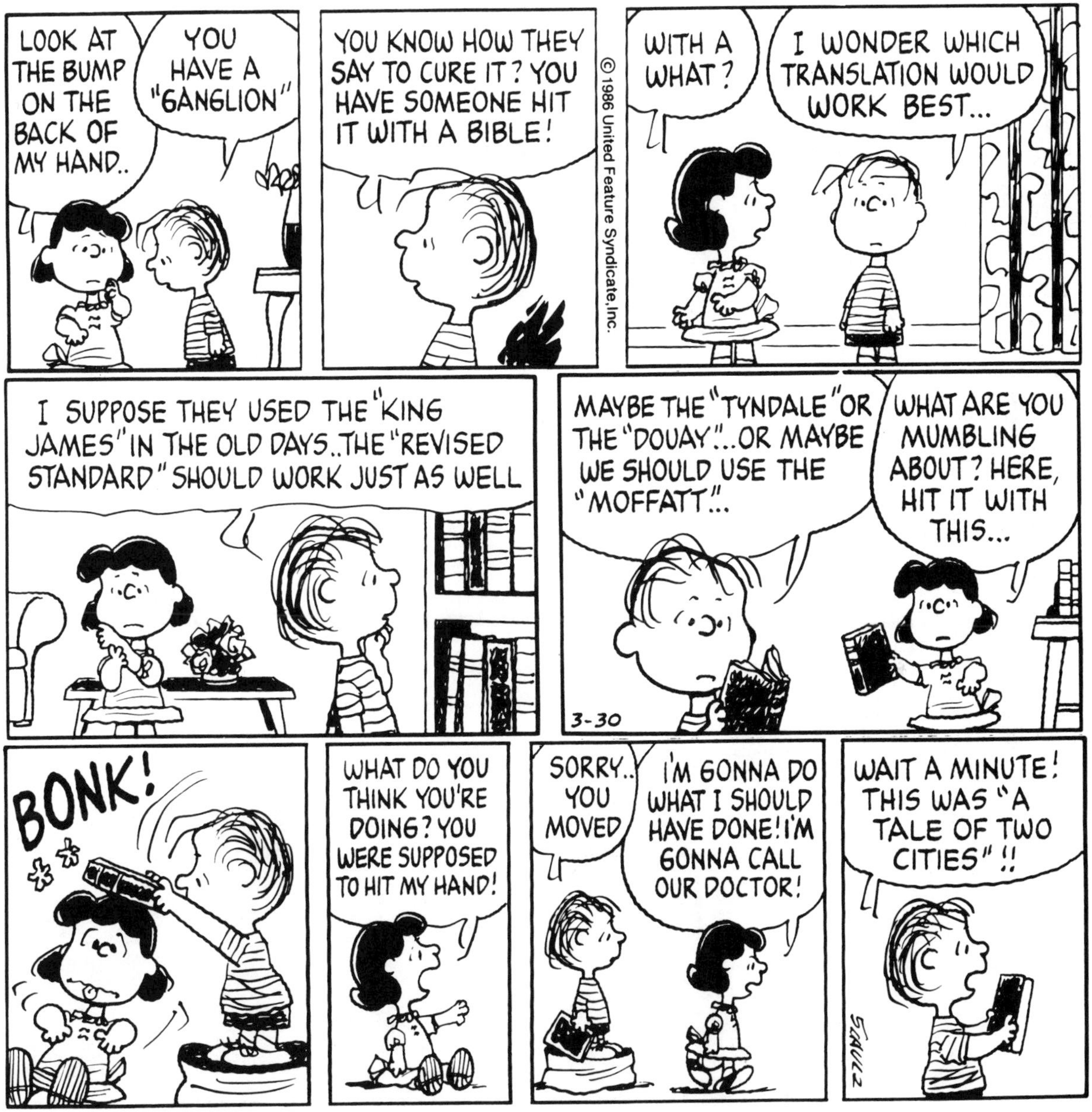
LOOK AT THE BUMP ON THE BACK OF MY HAND..
YOU HAVE A "GANGLION"
YOU KNOW HOW THEY SAY TO CURE IT? YOU HAVE SOMEONE HIT IT WITH A BIBLE!
© 1986 United Feature Syndicate, Inc.
WITH A WHAT?
I WONDER WHICH TRANSLATION WOULD WORK BEST...
I SUPPOSE THEY USED THE "KING JAMES" IN THE OLD DAYS..THE "REVISED STANDARD" SHOULD WORK JUST AS WELL
MAYBE THE "TYNDALE" OR THE "DOUAY"...OR MAYBE WE SHOULD USE THE "MOFFATT"...
WHAT ARE YOU MUMBLING ABOUT? HERE, HIT IT WITH THIS...
3-30
BONK!
WHAT DO YOU THINK YOU'RE DOING? YOU WERE SUPPOSED TO HIT MY HAND!
SORRY.. YOU MOVED
I'M GONNA DO WHAT I SHOULD HAVE DONE! I'M GONNA CALL OUR DOCTOR!
WAIT A MINUTE! THIS WAS "A TALE OF TWO CITIES"!!
SCHULZ

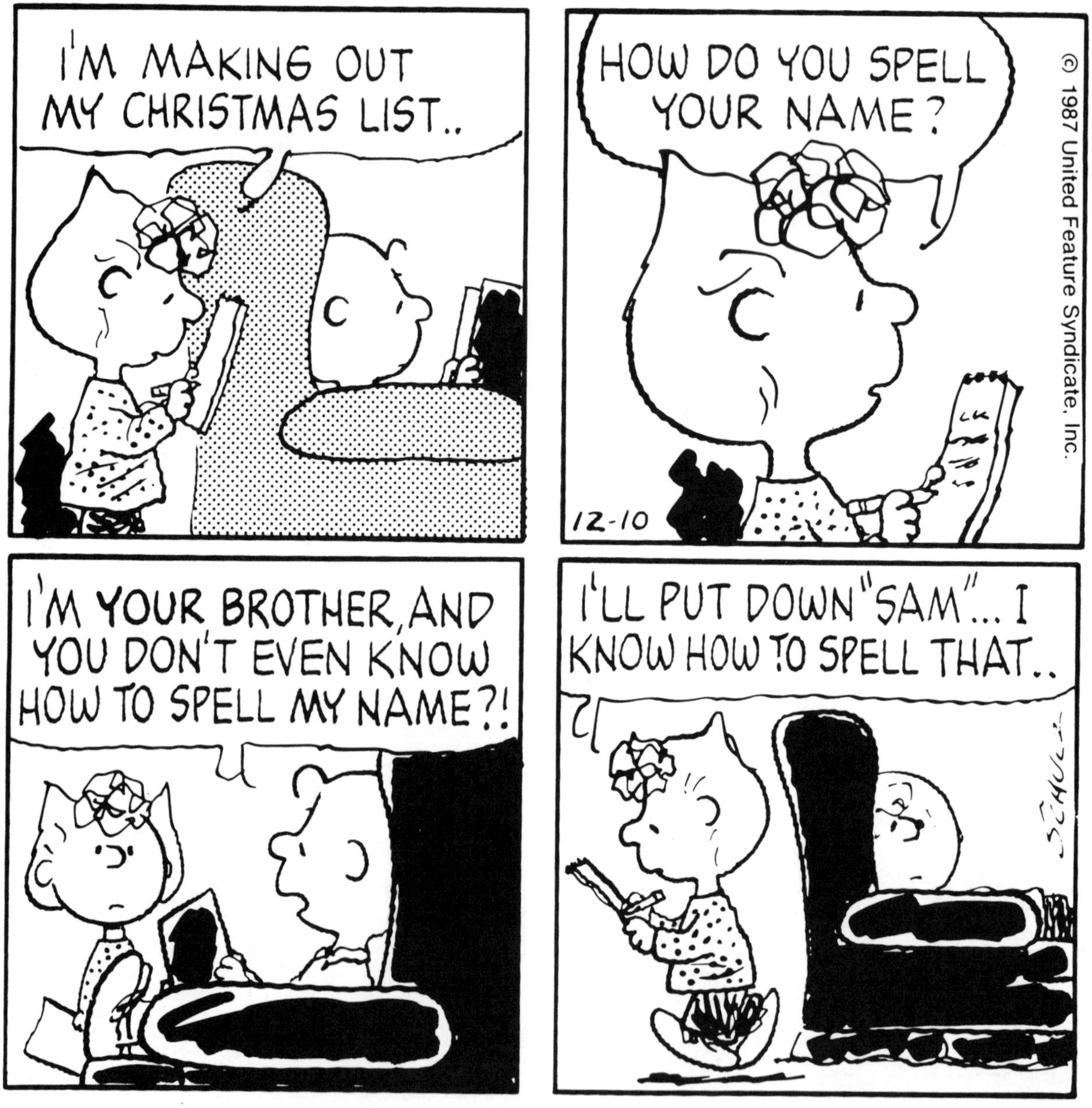
I'M MAKING OUT MY CHRISTMAS LIST..
HOW DO YOU SPELL YOUR NAME?
12-10
I'M YOUR BROTHER, AND YOU DON'T EVEN KNOW HOW TO SPELL MY NAME?!
I'LL PUT DOWN "SAM"... I KNOW HOW TO SPELL THAT..
SCHULZ
© 1987 United Feature Syndicate, Inc.

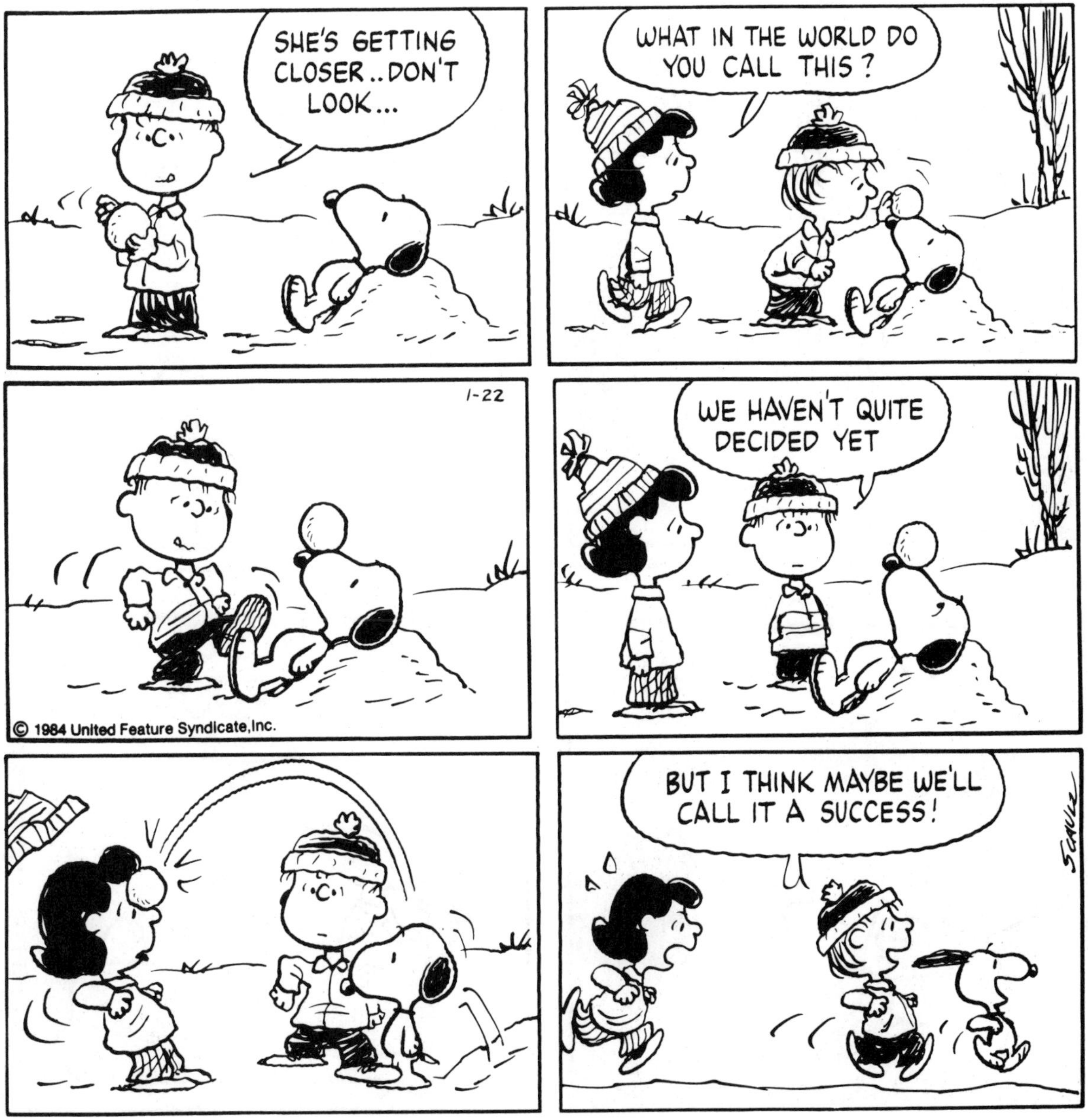
SHE'S GETTING CLOSER..DON'T LOOK...
WHAT IN THE WORLD DO YOU CALL THIS ?
1-22
WE HAVEN'T QUITE DECIDED YET
BUT I THINK MAYBE WE'LL CALL IT A SUCCESS!
SCHULZ
© 1984 United Feature Syndicate,Inc.

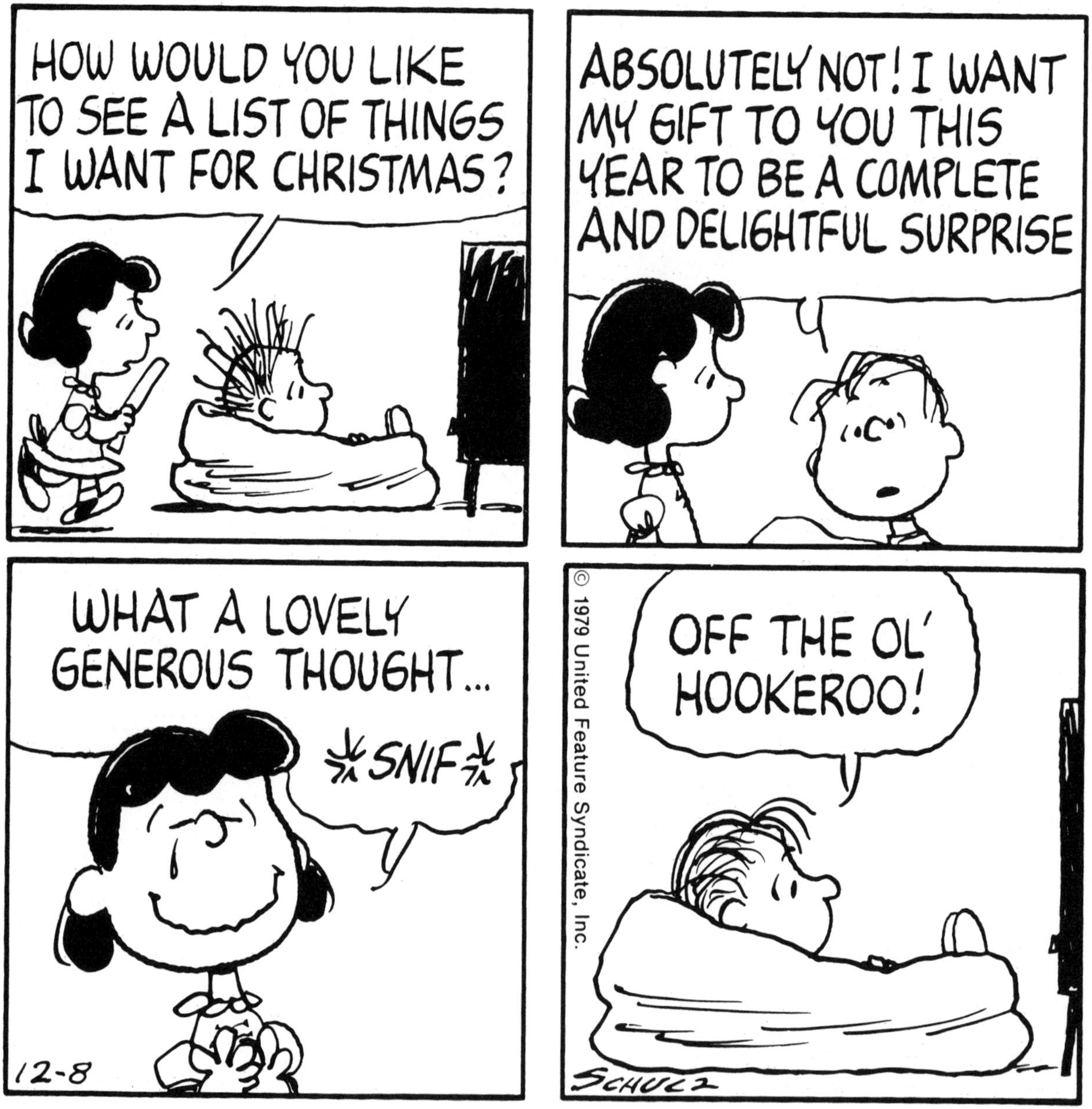
HOW WOULD YOU LIKE TO SEE A LIST OF THINGS I WANT FOR CHRISTMAS?
ABSOLUTELY NOT! I WANT MY GIFT TO YOU THIS YEAR TO BE A COMPLETE AND DELIGHTFUL SURPRISE
WHAT A LOVELY GENEROUS THOUGHT...
SNIF
12-8
© 1979 United Feature Syndicate, Inc.
OFF THE OL' HOOKEROO!
SCHULZ

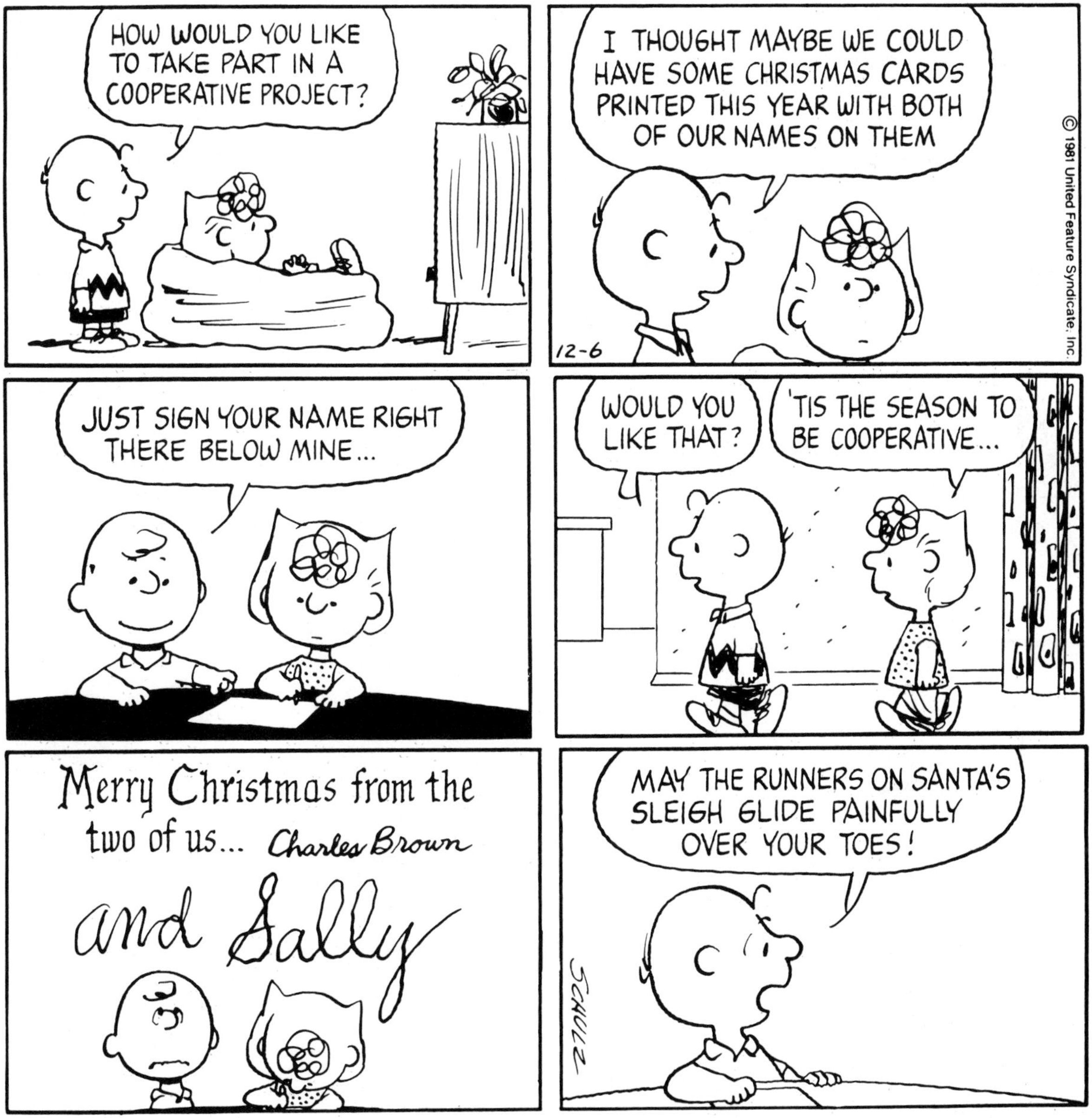
HOW WOULD YOU LIKE TO TAKE PART IN A COOPERATIVE PROJECT?
I THOUGHT MAYBE WE COULD HAVE SOME CHRISTMAS CARDS PRINTED THIS YEAR WITH BOTH OF OUR NAMES ON THEM
12-6
© 1981 United Feature Syndicate, Inc.
JUST SIGN YOUR NAME RIGHT THERE BELOW MINE...
WOULD YOU LIKE THAT?
'TIS THE SEASON TO BE COOPERATIVE...
Merry Christmas from the two of us... Charles Brown
and Sally
SCHULZ
MAY THE RUNNERS ON SANTA'S SLEIGH GLIDE PAINFULLY OVER YOUR TOES!

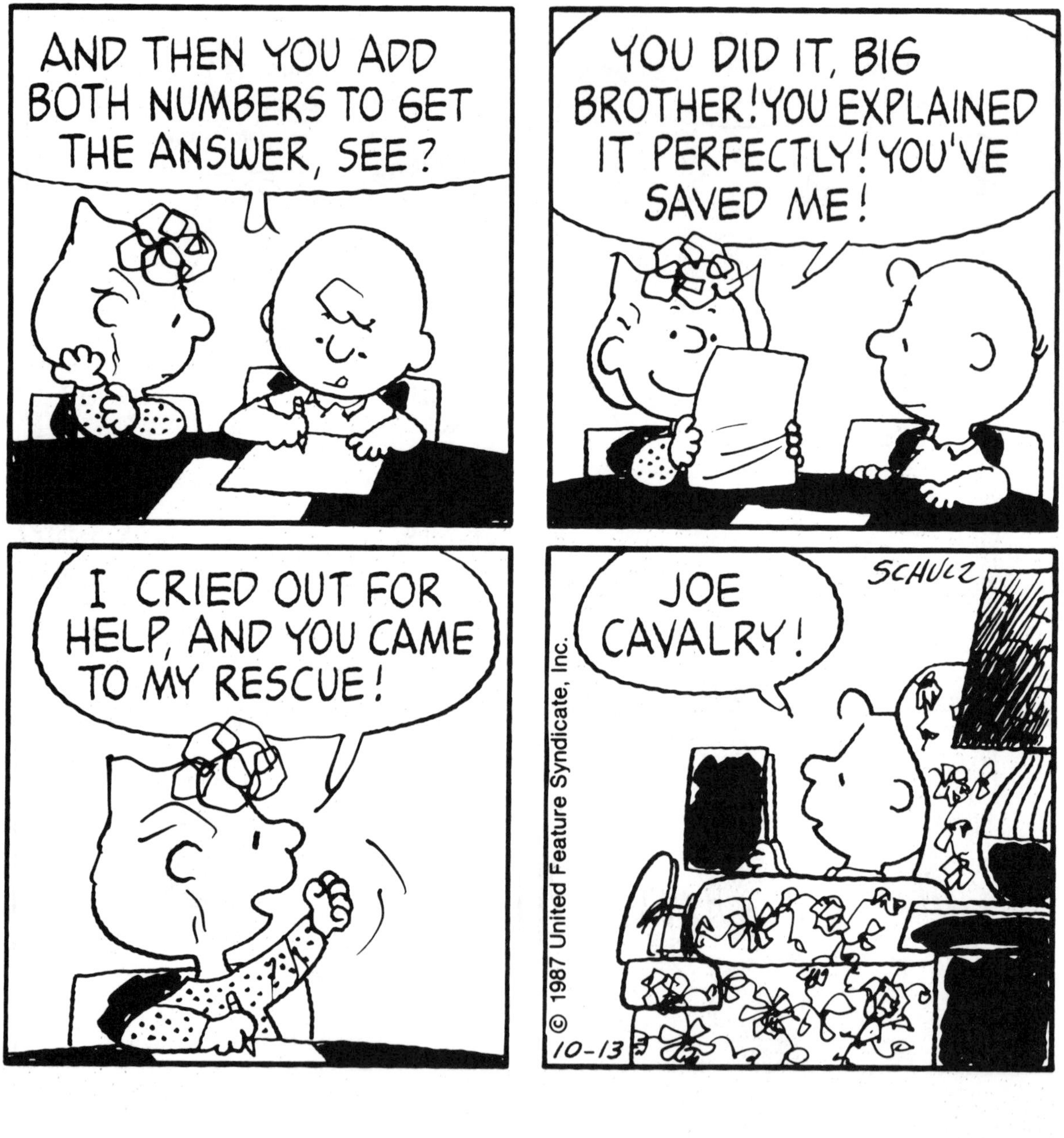
AND THEN YOU ADD BOTH NUMBERS TO GET THE ANSWER, SEE?
YOU DID IT, BIG BROTHER! YOU EXPLAINED IT PERFECTLY! YOU'VE SAVED ME!
I CRIED OUT FOR HELP, AND YOU CAME TO MY RESCUE!
JOE CAVALRY!
SCHULZ
© 1987 United Feature Syndicate, Inc.
10-13

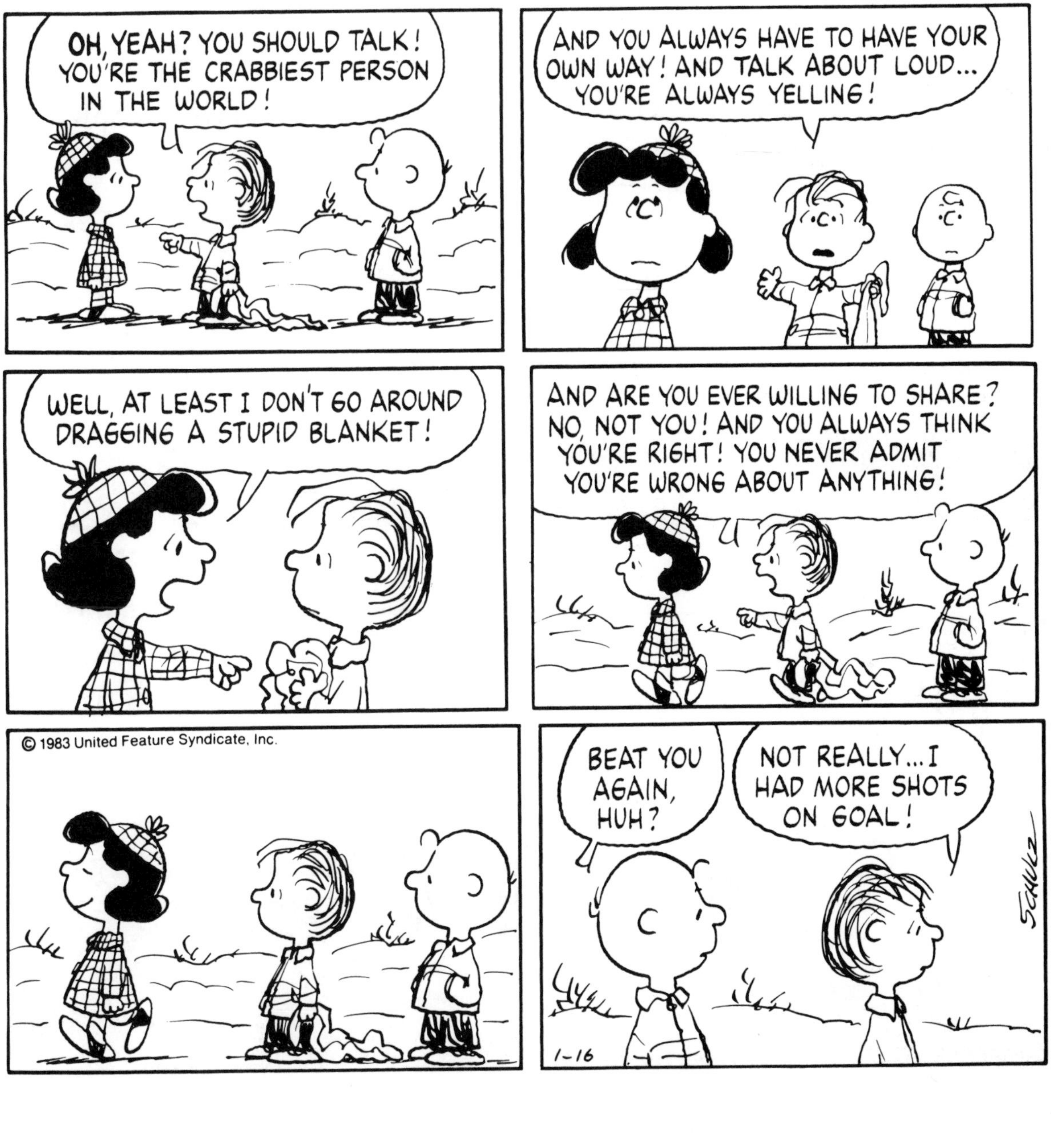
OH, YEAH? YOU SHOULD TALK! YOU'RE THE CRABBIEST PERSON IN THE WORLD!
AND YOU ALWAYS HAVE TO HAVE YOUR OWN WAY! AND TALK ABOUT LOUD... YOU'RE ALWAYS YELLING!
WELL, AT LEAST I DON'T GO AROUND DRAGGING A STUPID BLANKET!
AND ARE YOU EVER WILLING TO SHARE? NO, NOT YOU! AND YOU ALWAYS THINK YOU'RE RIGHT! YOU NEVER ADMIT YOU'RE WRONG ABOUT ANYTHING!
BEAT YOU AGAIN, HUH?
NOT REALLY... I HAD MORE SHOTS ON GOAL!
SCHULZ
1-16

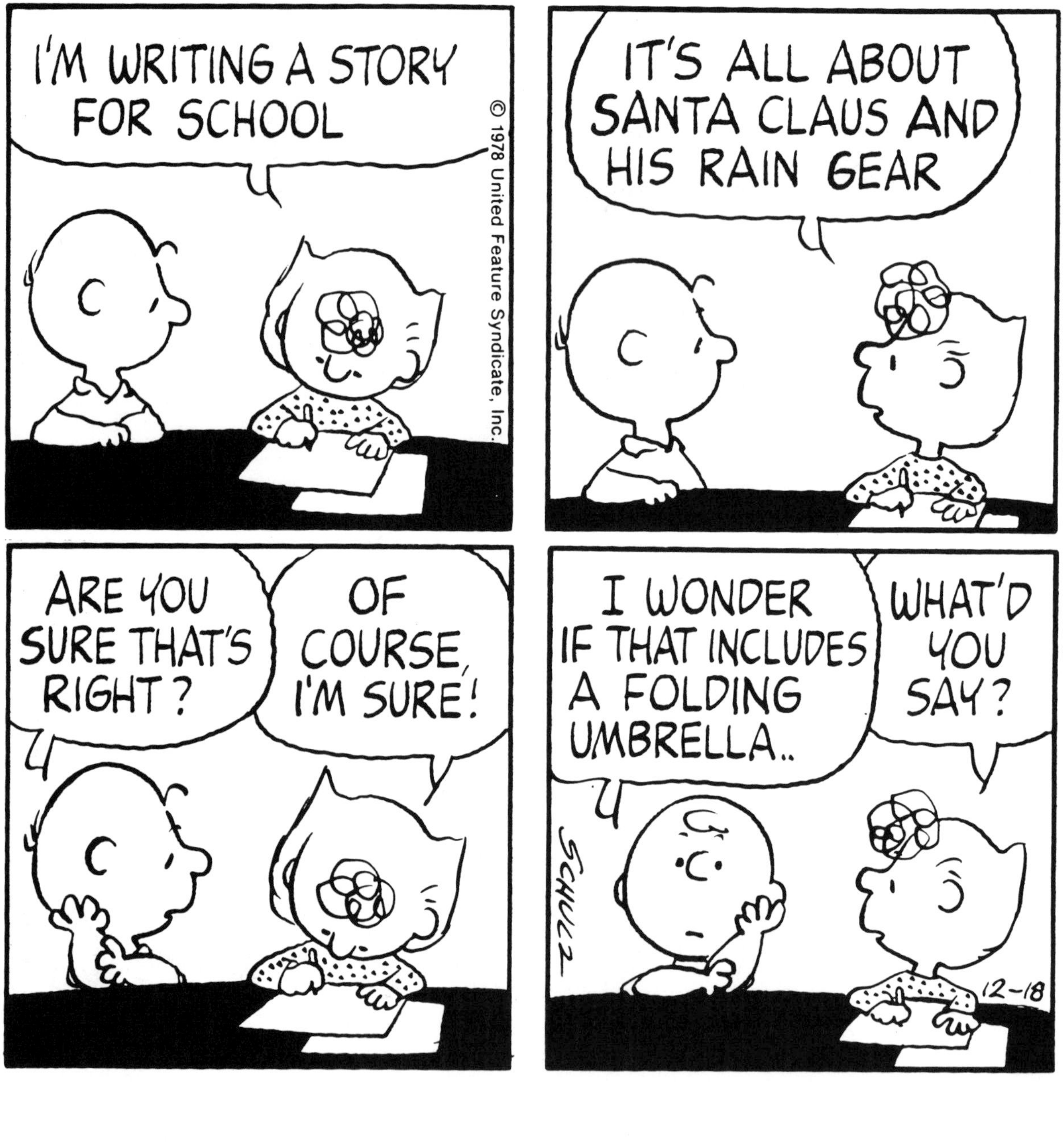
I'M WRITING A STORY FOR SCHOOL
IT'S ALL ABOUT SANTA CLAUS AND HIS RAIN GEAR
ARE YOU SURE THAT'S RIGHT?
OF COURSE, I'M SURE!
I WONDER IF THAT INCLUDES A FOLDING UMBRELLA..
WHAT'D YOU SAY?
SCHULZ
12-18

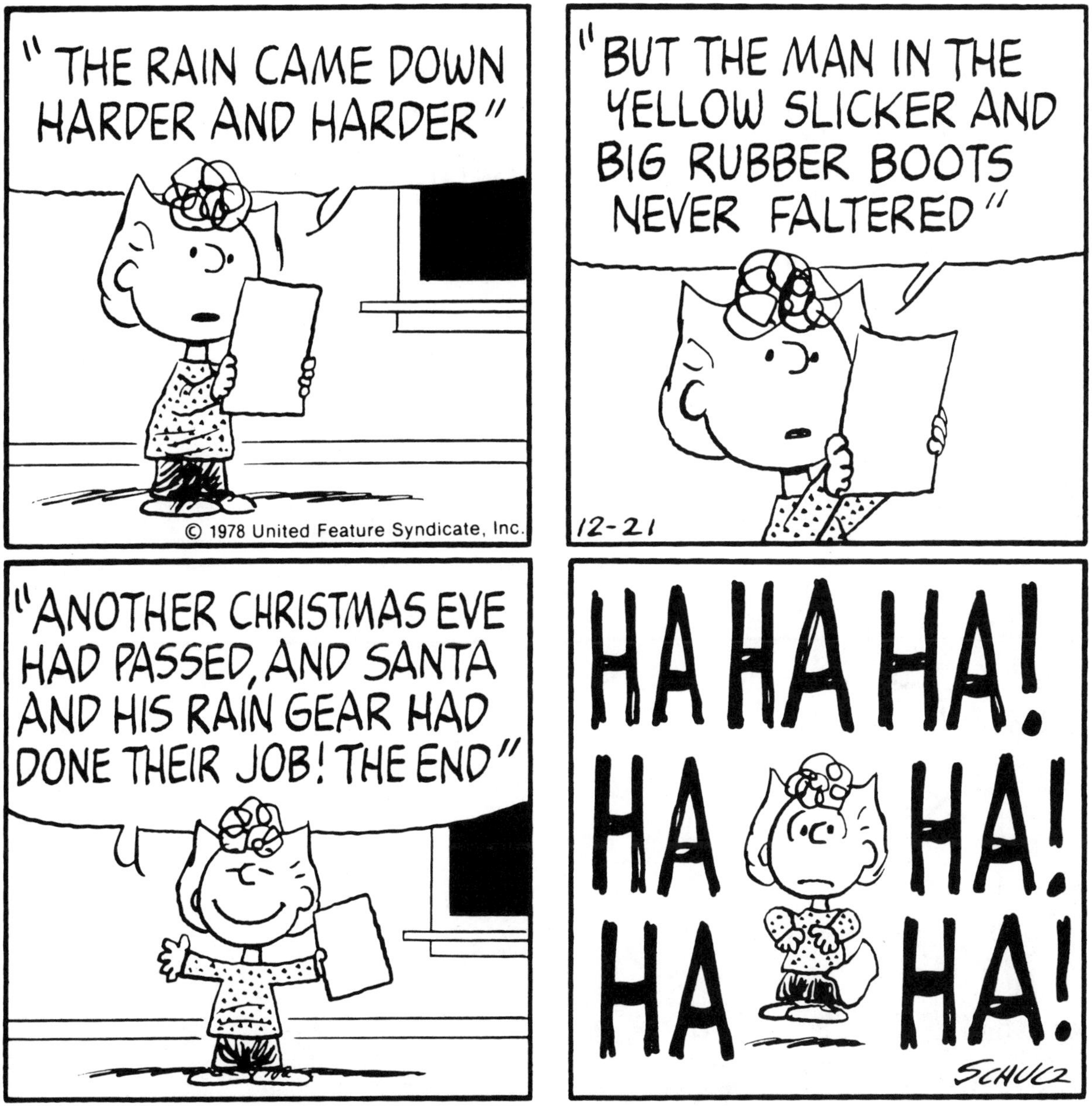
"THE RAIN CAME DOWN HARDER AND HARDER"
© 1978 United Feature Syndicate, Inc.
"BUT THE MAN IN THE YELLOW SLICKER AND BIG RUBBER BOOTS NEVER FALTERED"
12-21
"ANOTHER CHRISTMAS EVE HAD PASSED, AND SANTA AND HIS RAIN GEAR HAD DONE THEIR JOB! THE END"
HA HA HA HA! HA HA! HA HA!
SCHULZ

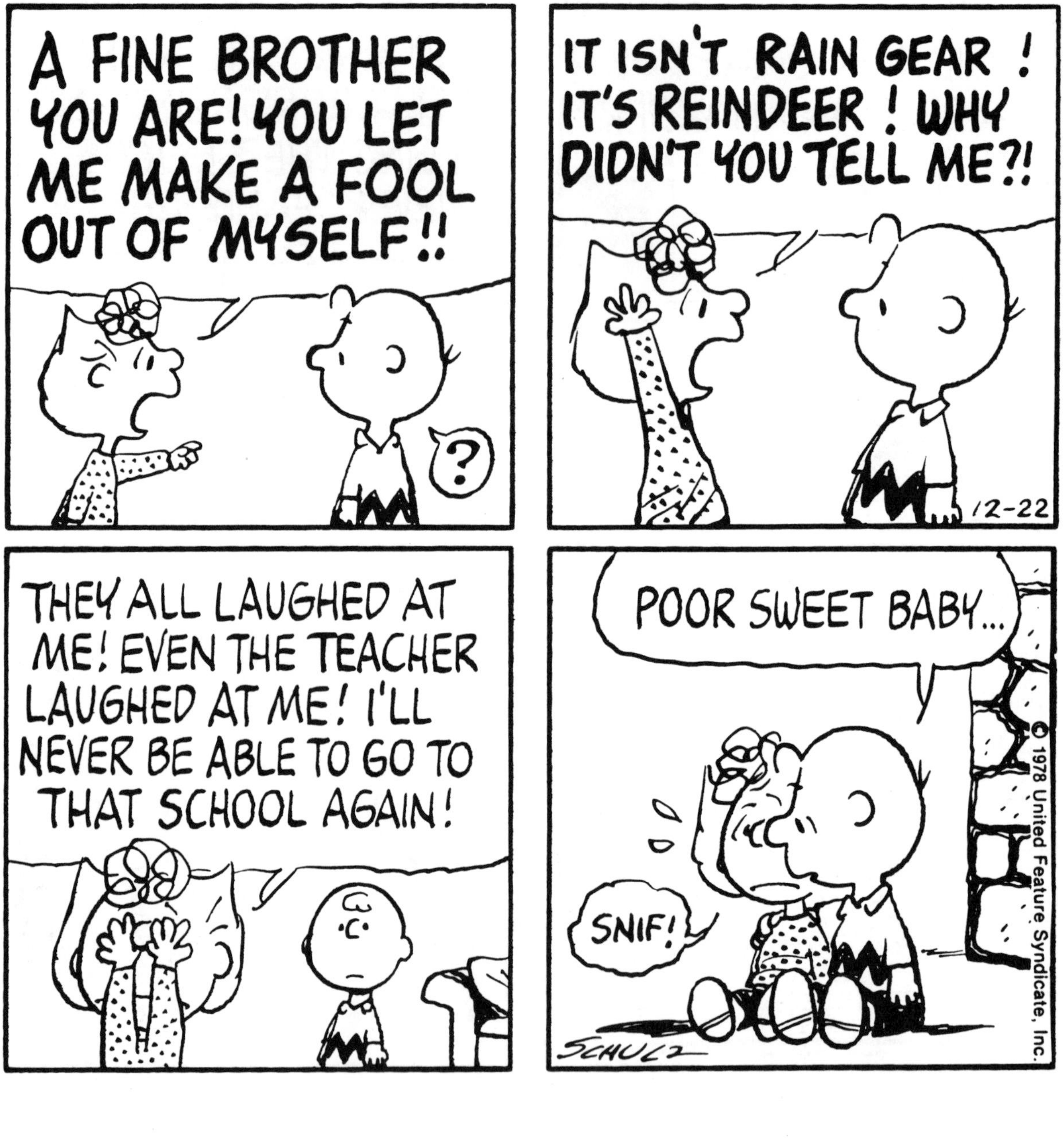
A FINE BROTHER YOU ARE! YOU LET ME MAKE A FOOL OUT OF MYSELF!!
?
IT ISN'T RAIN GEAR! IT'S REINDEER! WHY DIDN'T YOU TELL ME?!
12-22
THEY ALL LAUGHED AT ME! EVEN THE TEACHER LAUGHED AT ME! I'LL NEVER BE ABLE TO GO TO THAT SCHOOL AGAIN!
POOR SWEET BABY...
SNIF!
SCHULZ
© 1978 United Feature Syndicate, Inc.

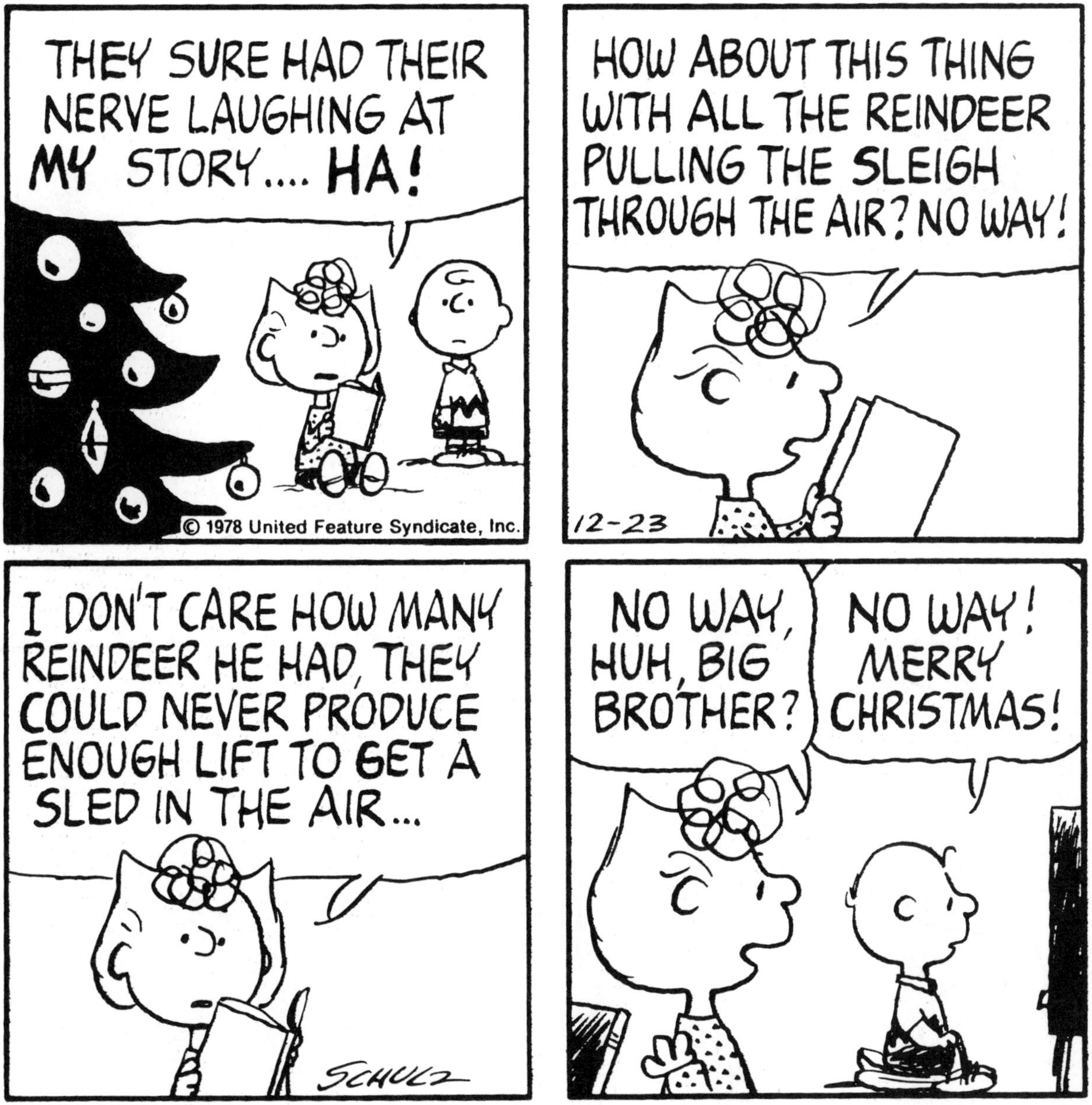
THEY SURE HAD THEIR NERVE LAUGHING AT MY STORY.... HA!
© 1978 United Feature Syndicate, Inc.
HOW ABOUT THIS THING WITH ALL THE REINDEER PULLING THE SLEIGH THROUGH THE AIR? NO WAY!
12-23
I DON'T CARE HOW MANY REINDEER HE HAD, THEY COULD NEVER PRODUCE ENOUGH LIFT TO GET A SLED IN THE AIR...
SCHULZ
NO WAY, HUH, BIG BROTHER?
NO WAY! MERRY CHRISTMAS!

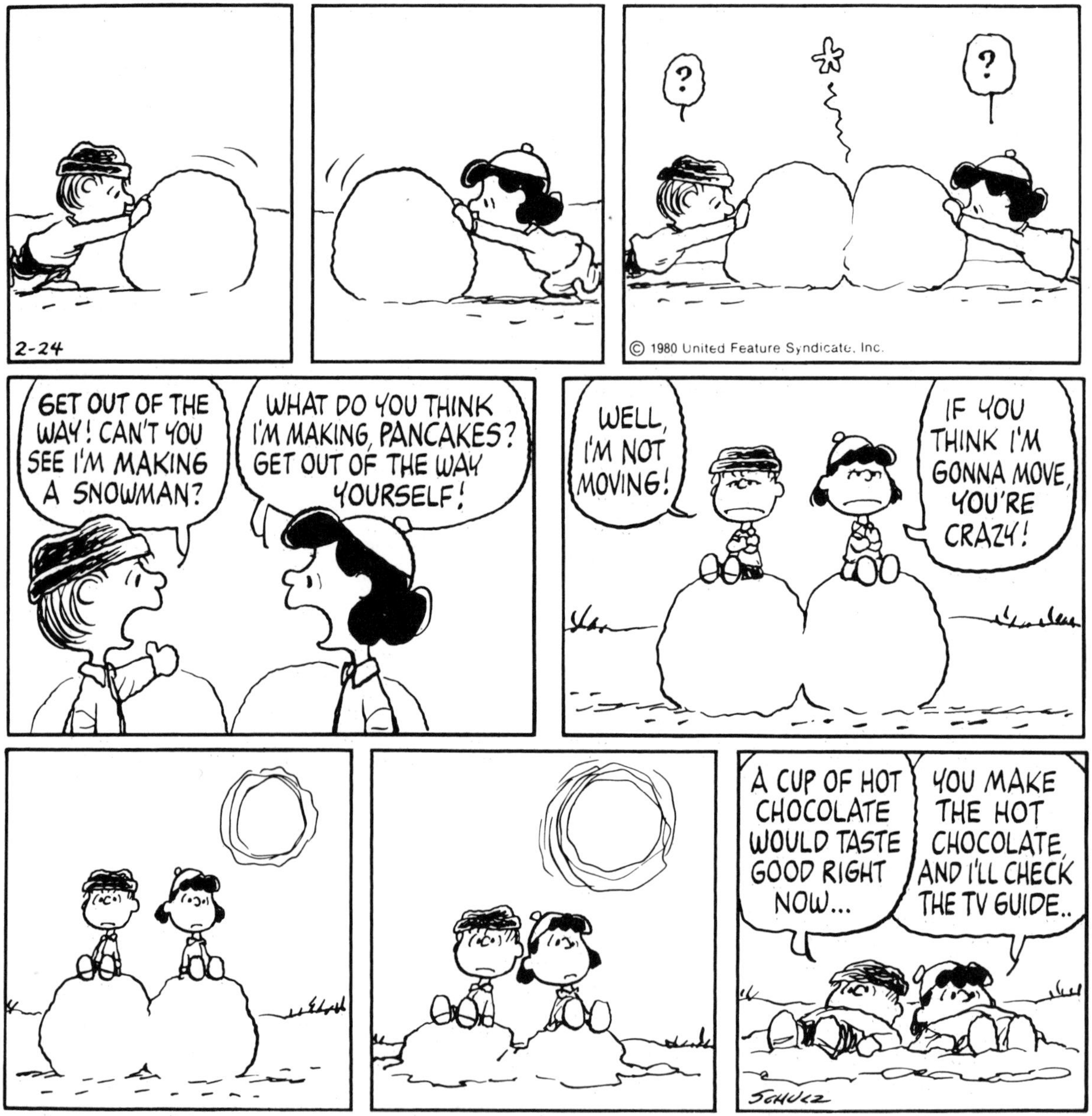
2-24
?
?
© 1980 United Feature Syndicate, Inc.
GET OUT OF THE WAY! CAN'T YOU SEE I'M MAKING A SNOWMAN?
WHAT DO YOU THINK I'M MAKING, PANCAKES? GET OUT OF THE WAY YOURSELF!
WELL, I'M NOT MOVING!
IF YOU THINK I'M GONNA MOVE, YOU'RE CRAZY!
A CUP OF HOT CHOCOLATE WOULD TASTE GOOD RIGHT NOW...
YOU MAKE THE HOT CHOCOLATE, AND I'LL CHECK THE TV GUIDE..
SCHULZ